SEMEIA 62

Textual Determinacy
Part One

Guest Editors:
Robert C. Culley
Robert B. Robinson

©1993
by the Society of Biblical Literature

SEMEIA 62

Copyright © 1993 by the Society of Biblical Literature

All rights reserved. No part of this work may be reproduced or transmitted in any form or by any means, electronic or mechanical, including photocopying and recording, or by means of any information storage or retrieval system, except as may be expressly permitted by the 1976 Copyright Act or in writing from the publisher. Requests for permission should be addressed in writing to the Rights and Permissions Office, Society of Biblical Literature, 825 Houston Mill Road, Atlanta, GA 30329, USA.

ISSN 0095-571X
ISBN 1-58983-155-1

Printed in the United States of America
on acid-free paper

CONTENTS

Contributors to this Issue v

Introduction
    Robert C. Culley VII

I. ESSAYS

1. Textualizing Determinacy/Determining Textuality
    Richard Cooper 3

2. Psalm 102: A Complaint with a Difference
    Robert C. Culley 19

3. What Shall We Do with Judith?
   A Feminist Reassessment of a Biblical "Heroine"
    Pamela J. Milne 37

4. Textual Constraints, Ordinary Readings, and Critical
   Exegesis: An Androcritical Perspective
    Daniel Patte 59

5. Text and Contexts: Interpreting the Disciples in Mark
    Elizabeth Struthers Malbon 81

6. Wife and Sister through the Ages: Textual Determinacy
   and the History of Interpretation
    Robert B. Robinson 103

7. Reading Texts through Worlds, Worlds through Texts
    Vincent L. Wimbush 129

II. COMMENTS

8. The Role of the Text in the Reading Process
    Adele Berlin 143

9. The Challenge of Multicontextual Interpretation
    John Dominic Crossan 149

10. Textual Determinacy: A Response
    Burke O. Long 157

11. "Mirror, Mirror . . . ": Lacanian Reflections on Malbon's Mark
    Stephen D. Moore 165

CONTRIBUTORS TO THIS ISSUE

Adele Berlin
 Department of Hebrew and East
 Asian Languages and Literatures
 2106 Jimenez Hall
 University of Maryland at
 College Park, MD 20742

Richard Cooper
 1017 St. Joseph Blvd. East, # 1
 Montreal, Quebec H2J 1L2
 Canada

John Dominic Crossan
 Department of Religion
 DePaul University
 2323 North Seminary Avenue
 Chicago, IL 60614

Robert C. Culley
 Faculty of Religious Studies
 McGill University
 Montreal, Quebec H3A 2A7
 Canada

Burke O. Long
 Department of Religion
 Bowdoin College
 Brunswick, ME 04011

Elizabeth Struthers Malbon
 Department of Religion
 Virginia Polytechnic Institute
 and State University
 Blacksburg, VA 24061

Pamela J. Milne
 Department of Religious Studies
 University of Windsor
 Windsor, Ont N9B 3P4
 Canada

Stephen D. Moore
 Department of Religion
 Wichita State University
 Wichita, KS 67208

Daniel Patte
 Box 1704 Station B
 Department of Religious Studies
 Vanderbilt University
 Nashville, TN 37325

Robert B. Robinson
 Lutheran Theological Seminary at
 Philadelphia
 7301 Germantown Ave
 Philadelphia, PA 19119

Vincent L. Wimbush
 Union Theological Seminary
 3401 Broadway
 New York, NY 10027-5714

Introduction

Robert C. Culley
McGill University

This is the first of two volumes that will bear the title "Textual Determinacy." In choosing the term "textual determinacy," the editors wanted to raise the question of the relationship between texts and reading and the extent to which meaning is determined by texts or by the reading process. It is probably not a question of either/or but rather of an interplay between the two. If this is so, however, how should one describe that interplay? Some biblical scholars are already engaged in the discussion of these issues, and this has forced consideration of the matter in biblical studies. Behind this double question about text and reading lies a discussion of immense scope which runs through many disciplines.

Clearly, our two volumes will hardly treat this vast and important topic in any way sufficient and adequate to its scope, nor have we set out to do this. At this stage of the game, we seek only to encourage a widening and broadening of the discussion of text and reading already underway in biblical studies. As a consequence, the two volumes will be rather different from most other *Semeia* volumes in that they will be a bit looser and less focused. Our approach has been simply to invite a number of scholars to contribute essays treating the topic as they saw fit, except that we asked that a sample of biblical or cognate material be used to demonstrate or illustrate whatever approach they wished to present. Similarly, we have left those who provided comments relatively free to follow their own inclinations. In this way, we hope that the essays and comments in our two volumes will stimulate and encourage further conversations and exchanges, and debate and map out areas for future discussion.

The idea of two volumes on textual determinacy grew out of conversations between Robert Robinson and myself. A formal proposal was ultimately produced for the *Semeia* Board. We began with the observation that recent developments in critical theory (particularly deconstruction, reader response criticism, and certain forms of feminist criticism) raised in an acute fashion a crucial issue, which we stated in the following way.

> To what extent and in what manner do texts determine and control their own interpretation and to what extent and in what manner is meaning determined by factors lying outside the text in the reading process?

This way of formulating the question distinguishes and highlights, at least for purposes of discussion, two foci: the text and the process of reading. Do texts have meaning or are texts given meaning through the process of reading?

In the rest of this introduction, I will try to offer some further comments on our central question. Here I will be speaking for myself and not my co-editor. His turn will come in the introduction to the second volume. We have worked closely on the preparation of the proposal and the development of both volumes; it is only in the introductions that we will be presenting our own perceptions of the topic of textual determinacy.

This first volume has seven contributions and four comments. The views expressed are diverse and I will not make any effort to summarize and relate them to each other. The point of the volumes is to encourage further consideration of a discussion already underway and it would be premature to begin to sum up such a wide-ranging topic at this stage. At least it would be so for me, since I am still trying to sort out in my own mind the complexities of the problems posed by a consideration of the relationship between text and reading. Two things should be mentioned about the present volume. First, the essay by Richard Cooper is different from the others. He is not in biblical studies but primarily a philosopher of religion, although with an interest in literature and the arts. Since one of his major preoccupations over the past several years has been literary theory, he was invited to comment on the topic of "textual determinacy" from the perspective of his own reading in this field. Second, as I have just indicated, the persons who provided comments were given a very free hand as to how they could respond. They were encouraged to comment on the topic of the volume in whatever way they wished, using any, all, or none of the papers they received. Because, as sometimes happens with *Semeia* volumes, some essays were unavoidably late, each of those who provided comments lacked one or two essays from the complete set of papers but, since they were free to choose how to respond, we simply went ahead rather than delay the volume.

As far as the general issue of the text and the reading process is concerned, I can only note a few of my own perceptions. They will not illuminate the topic itself in any profound way but can only indicate how I came to be interested in it. I will begin with the obvious comment that biblical studies has changed rather rapidly during the past several decades. Change is normal and to be expected in any discipline over time. On the other hand, what we have experienced recently in biblical studies seems to go beyond the kind of change and development usually anticipated in a discipline, since some rather significant shifts have taken place. It would be nice, at this point, if I could provide a review of the state of biblical studies showing how and why we have come to the point where we feel the need to ask: do texts have meaning or are they given meaning? I will not, however, attempt to do this, and in fact I doubt that I will ever be ready to do so. One of the reasons the idea of two volumes on textual determinacy caught my interest was that I am still in the process of trying to sort out what I am doing in my own work and where this fits into what I perceive to be the larger picture. Recently, in a study of action in biblical narrative (1992), I did try, more for my own edification than anything else, to identify tentatively the kind of views of text and reading that I was working with. For me this was a preliminary step to further reflection and discussion.

Nevertheless, it is easy enough for me to illustrate some of the recent changes in biblical studies simply by referring to what has happened during my own career in biblical studies. In the days when I began to study the Hebrew Bible (1952, beginning my undergraduate studies in Arts), and for several years after that, one was not conscious of substantial choices when it came to a critical perspective on the biblical text. The bundle of approaches known as historical criticism appeared to be the only option and indeed offered more than sufficient range and scope for anyone. And it seemed to be a reasonable and natural option. How else would one set out to read an ancient text? The ancient Near East, then, provided the major context within which to read the Bible. It is rather ironic that I was studying on a campus where Northrop Frye was regularly giving lectures on the Bible to undergraduates. I was only vaguely aware of his work. At a later point, I can recall having a conversation about Frye with a friend doing doctoral studies in English in which he sought to explain to me Frye's approach. It was very difficult for me at that time to see how it could be helpful for the study of the Bible. As I later discovered, Frye thought exactly the same thing about historical criticism.

Later in my doctoral studies, after many lunch hours listening to doctoral candidates in English discuss the intricacies of Frye's literary theory, it began to dawn on me slowly that it was not unreasonable to read the Bible as a text, because that is what it was. Of course, Frye's context for reading the Bible was not the ancient Near East but rather a verbal universe, as he called it, made up of all literature. While pursuing my interest in oral literature, I began to encounter various kinds of structural analysis, still other ways of doing textual study.

A few years on the *Semeia* Board made it clear that choices as to how one could study the Bible were emerging. Not only could one carry out historical criticism, with or without newer experiments with sociology and anthropology, but it was also possible to pursue a range of text-oriented studies, including various literary and structuralist analyses. Some were even prepared to argue that a shift from an historical perspective to a textual perspective amounted to a change of paradigms in biblical studies. For scholars who said this, there was a clear choice: either you used an historical approach or you used a textual approach. The two could not be related easily to each other. While all this was going on, Brevard Childs was developing another approach, or to be more precise, trying to restate the oldest approach to the Bible, a reading of it as the text of a religious community. He proposed that the relevant starting point for a critical study of the biblical text should be a perception of the Bible as a religious text—an approach he described as canonical—rather than from historical or literary studies. Characteristically, I have continued to try to muddle through by keeping all three approaches (historical, textual, and religious/theological) in some sort of relationship, a strategy which could be construed as the result of insight or confusion.

By the time I returned to the *Semeia* Board, perspectives like poststructuralism, feminism, ideological criticism, and postmodernism were not uncommon in the volumes we produced. These offered still other ways of dealing with texts, and ways that were quite often construed as substantial challenges to previous approaches like historical and literary (including structuralist). It is interesting to note that, from the perspective of some of these newer approaches, historical and literary studies were viewed not as two different options but rather related approaches working with very similar assumptions.

While what I have just said simply expresses my own perception of some of the changes in biblical studies over the past few decades, our thinking (Robinson's and mine) about the topic of textual determinacy was prompted more directly by the recent perspectives just mentioned, which have raised the issues of text and reading in a very acute fashion. Perhaps I could illustrate this briefly by referring to the "Introduction" to *Semeia* 51 by Gary Phillips. The title of this volume is: *Poststructural Criticism and the Bible: Text/History/Discourse* (see also the more recent, related volume, *Semeia* 54, *Poststructuralism as Exegesis* by David Jobling and Stephen D. Moore). Phillips argues that a poststructural perspective, at least as reflected in the essays in his *Semeia* volume, demands that both structuralism and historical criticism be seen in relation to the ideological and institutional agendas, usually unrecognized and unacknowledged, that lie behind their practice. This means "questions of *institutional control and power*—over reading methods; over hirings and promotions; over production and dissemination of knowledge to guild members, etc." (2). Thus, both the critic and criticism are deliberately placed in the context of the religious and academic institutions within which they function. What is at issue is the connection between the practice of power and control that operates within institutions and the theory and practice of criticism carried on within them. The point is to show that what is accepted by critics as normal and derived from common sense is actually a set of constructs generated by arrangements of power and control within the institutions in which critics work.

Phillips expresses the central question of the essays in his volume as follows: "how are exegetes to think the question of the nature of the text, of history, of discourse, of praxis informed variously by feminist theory, deconstruction, ideological critique, liberation theology, postmodern aesthetics?" (3). The various perspectives he mentions are conceived of as discourses within which it is difficult to distinguish notions of text and critical comment (4). These "discursive strategies" even seek to surmount the "interpretation/text dichotomy which has framed (and continues to exert enormous influence over) our modern ways of reading the biblical text and our interpretive discourses about it" (4).

This brief reference to the views of Phillips illustrates the extent to which poststructuralists perceive their work as a radical and fundamental challenge to historical criticism, the dominant approach for over a century, and also to structural analysis which by definition bears a special relationship to "poststructural" approaches. Even the question posed for our volumes on textual determinacy distinguishes text and reading, text and interpretation, a dichotomy that poststructuralist critics want to challenge, although as Jacques Derrida has suggested, one does not dispense with dichotomies but uses them. Then too, the overt demand for change within the institutions to which critics are linked and within which they do their work adds a particular dimension to critical studies and presents a challenge that does not usually emerge when one simply shifts back and forth between historical, literary, structuralist, and religious perspectives.

Now I am quite prepared to take the questions raised by poststructuralist and ideological critics quite seriously, but interrogation needs to go both ways. In other words, there are a number of issues in need of clarification and discussion among those who work with poststructuralism, feminism, ideological criticism, and postmodernism, and I am sure that these scholars would agree to this. For example, feminist and ideological criticism is not necessarily compatible with poststructuralist and postmodernist perspectives. How are universal ethical claims about the rights of the individual to be linked with the non-totalizing penchant of poststructualism? I am not suggesting that it is not possible to relate ideological and postructuralist perspectives. A scholar like Linda Hutcheon does relate the two in her *The Politics of Postmodernism*. She implies, however, that the relationship is not straightforward when she argues that even though "the postmodern has no effective theory of agency that enables a move into political *action,* it does work to turn its inevitable ideological grounding into a site of de-naturalizing critique" (3).

I ended my own contribution to this volume by indicating that I was not sure how I wanted to proceed from what I was doing with the biblical text into higher perspectives and strategies. It is not that I do not have any ideas of what direction I would like to go but that I am not yet sure of how I want to move from more limited to larger spheres of discussion and how one relates perspectives at both levels. There are a number of interesting possibilities here. For example, in his reflections on culture and its varied components (such as law, religion, art, and the like), Clifford Geertz has opted for a pluralism that he works out in terms of a notion of spheres of "local knowledge" which interact or can be seen in interaction with each other. In his view, one must begin with and give serious attention to the particular example, but at the same time be aware that there is a larger context consisting of many particular examples. "The problem of integration of cultural life," he observes, "becomes one of making it possible for people inhabiting different worlds to have a genuine, and reciprocal, impact upon one another" (161).

Another slant is offered by Fredric Jameson. He seeks to hold together allegiance to a total vision (for him, Marxism) with a notion of pluralism that entertains spheres of validity, other world views, or different critical languages. In terms of method, he puts it this way:

> I have found it possible without any great inconsistency to respect both the methodological imperative implicit in the concept of totality or totalization, and the quite different attention of a "symptomal" analysis to discontinuities, rifts, actions at a distance, within a merely apparently unified cultural text (56-57).

In making these comments, I only want to indicate that future discussions will need to move in several directions. It will be especially interesting to see how all parties in the discussion will be able to offer critiques of other positions but also to develop critiques of their own positions, and especially how poststructuralist and ideological critics, who conceive of themselves so forcefully as instruments of critical analysis of other positions, can develop within their own thinking mechanisms for self-critique.

WORKS CONSULTED

Geertz, Clifford
    1983   *Local Knowledge: Further Essays in Interpretive Anthropology*. New York: Basic.

Hutcheon, Linda
    1989   *The Politics of Postmodernism*. London: Routledge.

Jameson, Fredric
    1981   *The Political Unconscious: Narrative as a Socially Symbolic Act*. Ithaca: Cornell University Press.

I
ESSAYS

Textualizing Determinacy/
Determining Textuality

Richard Cooper
Montreal

ABSTRACT

This article surveys some of the major contemporary views in general literary theory on the relation between determinate and/or determinable meaning and the constitution of a set of mutually coherent utterances as a text. The dynamics of the process of coherence is conceptualized as textuality. The paper examines the problematic and relative status of these definitions through first an exposition of the development of dominant patterns of theory in literary studies and the human sciences and, secondly, through a philosophical exploration of some of the implications of these ways of theorizing on the practice of interpretation.

TEXTUALIZING DETERMINACY

In her recent major philosophical study *Metaphysics as a Guide to Morals* (1992), Iris Murdoch lumps the whole complex of literary, social scientific, and philosophical writings that have proliferated in France since the 1960s under the rubric "structuralism." Structuralism, poststructuralism, and postmodernism are thus assimilated into a huge monolithic movement which she sees as constituting a dominant contemporary form of determinism. Since in these ways of thinking, according to Murdoch, the whole of reality as self-referential structure is internally determined, there can be nothing beyond it to which it points or alludes; there can, by dint of the total play of the system itself, be no "transcendental signified." Murdoch sets up this system as a polemical object against which she advances her counterview. However unfair one may think Murdoch's characterization of "structuralism" is, it does have the merit of getting to the center of a major issue in contemporary philosophy, literary theory, and by extension biblical studies, that is, the question of how an individual reader or an "interpretive community" is able to assent that a text means what s/he or they think or say that it means. How, in other words, is the determination of referential meaning possible?

It is to be noted that the idea of reference itself is not in question; rather, the manner in which referring functions is brought under scrutiny.

The failure to clarify sufficiently this distinction results in Murdoch's rather odd assimilation of structuralist and poststructuralist thought. At the same time, however, what might be initially taken as Murdoch's confusion does reveal some of the continuities between these two tendencies that are often overlooked. If under the most general view structuralist codes "refer" to an intrinsic system which they mediate, the poststructuralist emphasis on the contextualization—historical, sociological, anthropological, philosophical, etc. —of encoded systems really removes the methodological procedure to a further stage without necessarily affecting its paradigmatic status as an analytic tool. That, in fact, this removal does problematize the code-system model of reference is perhaps the chief distinguishing trait of poststructuralist ways of thinking. A concrete analogy from postmodernist architecture would be the way in which traditional decorative details are added on to—and hence problematize—the simple, clear structures of modernist buildings. Conflicting codes are juxtaposed with the result that the systems they mediate are ironically relativized. Encoded systems thus are reduced to larger and more complex codes which may through conjunction or disjunction refer to other larger and more complex codes. The distinction between code and system has been problematized in much the same way that Saussure's distinction between signifier and signified is problematized in Derrida's early writing. Codes refer to other codes, and the idea of system is the relatively illusory, though not nugatory, effect of the process of encoding. From this it follows that there is a shift in attention from the synchronic, morphological structure of systems to their diachronic grammar.

As is well known, in the period following World War II literary studies, particularly in North America, underwent a major shift from concern with the historical, biographical, and social background of texts to their quality as literary artifacts in and of themselves. A generation of American scholars was reared under the aegis of the New Criticism. It could be argued that the most influential work in this development was Wellek and Warren's *Theory of Literature*, a study which reveals the contribution of European methods of *explication de texte*, Russian and Prague formalism, and philosophical phenomenology to what might be called the textualization of literary studies. That there were English-language precedents in the modernism of Pound and Eliot and the practical criticism of I.A. Richards which also prepared the way for the New Criticism is indisputable. What only later became obvious because it was a contextual rather than a textual matter was the conservative bent of the New Criticism in its early stages. The association of a number of the major new critics with the Agrarian and Fugitive movements in poetry and their sympathy with the South and traditional, aristocratic values meant that literary studies in American universities and their influence on intellectual but not strictly academic journals such as *The Kenyan Review* provided a politically anodyne climate during the period of the Cold War and McCarthyism. During the 1960s this picture changed to a certain extent. Still, within the intellectual hegemony structuralism was able to reinvest some of the interest accruing from the New Criticism as well as to provide a more rigorous analytical support for its concern with the primacy of the text. Only with the advent of an internal critique of French structuralism by writers like Roland Barthes in the late 1960s and the philosophical skepticism influenced by Marx, Nietzsche, Freud, and Heidegger and applied to structures of intellectual power and dominance by thinkers like Foucault and Derrida was the problematic status of the model of code and system raised. Along with this questioning went that of the relationships between text and context.

That a certain priority has been attributed in poststructuralism to texts over contexts is not only due to the structuralist origins of poststructuralist thinking, but rather more importantly to the difficulty of conceptualizing contextuality outside of and over against textual means of accessibility. This is obvious enough for the documentary sciences, but also has logical ramifications, particularly in the thought of Derrida. For if there is a kind of grammar that not only encodes, but determines all human thought, then there is *per consequens* a sequencing which accommodates developments, changes, transitions, tensions, and contradictions in the unfolding of human discourse; and this is best thought of at the level of the largest meaningful unit beyond the morpheme, word, or isolated sentence, namely, the text. Thus, contextuality comes to be internally defined as textuality. The process of determining meaning is inherently textual, not contextual in the sense of being extrinsic to the sequencing of the extended utterance. At first this seems counter-intuitive. Without making the textual formation explicit, however, a context could not be thought or uttered. Wittgenstein said as much in the last aphorism of the *Tractatus*: "Wovon man nicht sprechen kann, darüber muss man schweigen" (150). Derrida goes beyond Wittgenstein in making "writing" rather than speech the ultimate determinant of all communication. He does this by following out the logic of the textual thesis to its conclusion. If there were no *archiécriture*, there could be no possibility of contextual silence.

It can, of course, be argued that positions such as that of Derrida are metaphysically reductionist. Arguments of this sort are not usually especially interesting or informative. It is more productive to consider some of the ambiguities to which grammatology and, more generally, the theory of textual grammar give rise. The theory of a grammar of discourses, which then narrows down to a theory of the grammar of textuality, owes its philosophical underpinnings to Wittgenstein's efforts to delineate the interface between logical structures, on the one hand, and language-games and life-forms, on the other. There is really little direct influence of Wittgenstein on French poststructuralist thinkers, though there are interesting parallel developments. The move from what are essentially the logico-linguistic analyses of structuralism to a reflective critique of how these analyses impinge upon, mirror, and distort the areas of investigation in the human sciences and philosophy appears to follow the same trajectory. One needs, nonetheless, to get a firm grasp on what a theory of textual grammar signifies. In a certain sense, grammar functions here as a metaphor. Textualized phenomena are viewed as conforming to a relatively limited set of rules of permutation which are adduced for descriptive purposes but which at certain stages of development tend to assume a normative, or prescriptive, status. One might then, for example, speak of a "grammar" of genres in which certain generic forms, such as epic, drama, lyric, and prose narrative, are observed to follow respective sets of formal rules, as well as to admit of internal variations and cross-generic fertilization. The history of literature amply demonstrates the spontaneous emergence of genres, their subsequent codification, and periods of the blurring of the boundaries between genres with the ascent of hybrid generic forms. There is a close analogy here to the history of grammar proper, the exception being that grammar is at once both much more rigid and much more fluid: rigid within the limits of its basic transformational operations, fluid in the possibilities of actualized expression. Grammatical fluidity is the result of the temporal and cultural situation of the speaking, writing subject. For instance, in English grammar there has within the last twenty years been a noticeable alteration in the number reference of third-person pronouns. This has been due to feminists' concern with sexist language. Whereas formerly "everyone" was in prescriptive grammar expected to be the antecedent of the masculine singular pronoun "he," it is now usual to use "he or she" or, because of the awkwardness and verbosity of this expression, the plural "they." The fact that previously in colloquial English plural pronouns with singular antecedents had not been uncommon no doubt paved the way for this latter usage which is, strictly speaking, a solecism. But, then, solecisms are often the most interesting aspects of the study of grammar. Indeed, one might say they are what grammar is for, if not of; just as fallacies in reasoning are a central part of logic. Moreover, the most interesting fallacies, such as those involving the so-called "law" of excluded middle, may not be fallacies at all, but issues of undecidability. Logic and grammar feed upon undecidability and ambiguity. Contrary to the Enlightenment tradition of clarity and rationality, but not contradictory to it, as in the case of some kinds of Romanticism, what poststructuralist thought has done is to scrutinize the tendency of the Western intellectual tradition to dichotomize and to calculate through the organization of dichotomous patterns. A textualized grammar and a grammar of textuality facilitate focusing on the interface of and interactions among descriptive and prescriptive rules and actual utterance, between *langue* and *parole*, form and content, text and context. For each of these pairs, there is not an easy acceptance of the duality, but a questioning of the nature of the relationships and interaction that makes possible the distinction in the first place.

So much seems clear. Legitimate doubts arise when one considers the extent to which a grammar of textuality can be carried. Derrida in his earlier work, by specifically narrowing down a grammar of textuality into what he called "grammatology" with its basis in *différance* and *écriture*, carried the project to the very limits of the tradition of Western metaphysics, with the result that the foundational assumptions of that tradition were systemically "deconstructed," always of course still within the boundaries of that discussion, so that there is a large sphere, but still a sphere, out of which one could not and would not wish to exit. At this level, where the *meta* of metaphysics seems to be chiefly a grammatical device, the ambiguity of the order of distinctions points to what may be the arbitrariness or randomness of the process of determination.

THE AGE OF METACRITIQUE

In surveying the main trends in literary studies during the past decade or so, certainly a major consideration is the shift in governing models from one that is based on language (in the sense of structural linguistics) to one that is based on a particular concept of textuality. The above discussion has attempted to outline some of the characteristics of this shift. Chiefly to be noted is a tension whereby, on the one hand, the social and cultural impingements upon linguistic formations demand attention while, on the other, a hypercritical awareness necessitates the articulation of an analytic model that does not naïvely assume a rigidly dichotomous situation in which the subjective and the objective, the inside and the outside, culture and nature, text and context, etc. subsist in opposition to one another. As an extension of an already dominant linguistic model, the textual model by stressing the dynamic, non-synchronous elements within a relatively bounded whole supplied a workable alternative. The theorization of such a model, then, as what I am calling a grammar of textuality, has tended to stabilize and provide a rationale for its dominant position. That there could be other models, and in future no doubt will be, goes without saying; what I am emphasizing is that there is a kind of historical and cultural logic at work here. In this way, there is a sort of determinacy to the development of the textual model, though it can only be conceived of as the relative, textualized determinacy that the theory of a grammar of textuality presupposes. There is a circle here, but it may be no more vicious than the dichotomizing alternative. An informative analogy is afforded in philosophy by the difficulties that arise in the debate over freedom and determinism: the only productive option seems to be some form of compatibilism.

The shift to the textual model has also meant the revival of hermeneutics as the discipline of interpretation. What chiefly characterized the forms of twentieth-century hermeneutical endeavor is the coalescence of the interpretive sciences and the various stands of critical philosophy, from neo-Kantianism to the Frankfurt School. This tendency was strengthened by the so-called "hermeneutics of suspicion," as exemplified in various ways by Marx, Nietzsche, and Freud. The illusion of a separate, objective relationship between "text" and interpreter had already been dispelled in these thinkers by the recognition of the mutually influencing interaction between the interpreter and the interpreted. Indeed, the process or "discourse" of interpreting became the focus of attention. The notion of discourse as text—as a bounded and reproducible congeries of utterances—implies a flexible schema of analytic rules, or methodology, for engaging in interpretation. That discourse in the sense of Benveniste's distinction between *discours* and *récit* can also have a more specific meaning than "text" should be stressed since the word bears something of this connotation in Foucault's work and it is one of the things that separates Foucault's thought from Derrida's.

On the overview, the names of Foucault and Derrida preside over the entire field of literary studies, and of those other disciplines that rely upon a text-interpretive model, in the 1970s and 80s. It is perhaps only in the 1990s, when attempts are being made to extend the areas of investigative procedure, that something of the measure of that influence can be taken. Initially, of course, in literary studies Derrida exerted the greater influence because of the closer proximity of his concerns to the subject matter as well as to the reading and interpretive procedures that had been fostered by the New Criticism and structuralism. Especially in North America, Derrida made his entrée through language and literature departments. This gave a certain slant to "Deconstructionism" which it could be argued unduly formalized some of Derrida's highly complex and tentative concerns, particularly those within the areas of phenomenology and the history of philosophy. On the general level, it was sometimes difficult to distinguish in the 1970s literary deconstructionism from a hermeneutics of suspicion applied to texts. Within the spread of Derridean thinking into the social sciences, however, and the intense if somewhat unfortunate debate between constructivism and essentialism, a wider and one might say juster appreciation of Derrida's concerns arose. Paralleling this development was the expansion, largely through politically motivated concerns, of a preoccupation with social, psychological, and cultural dimensions that inhere within literary works. Specialized studies of gender, sexuality, class, and ethnicity involved not only a jockeying for legitimation of hitherto ignored areas of study, but also a calling into question of the legitimacy of the texts that formed the canon of the dominant Western "humanist" tradition. Since literary deconstructionism provided a limited though useful means of testing the limits of legitimation—largely through the use of the exclusion-inclusion paradigm—a need was perceived for a more detailed, developmental model that could explicate the dynamics, ruses, and ambiguities of the history of power formations and conflicts. Foucault's detailed investigations of the history and structure of institutions through an analytic of discursive practices was ready to hand as such a model. The 1980s then, over the whole realm of the human sciences, might be thought of as the decade of Foucault.

Except for the last two volumes of *The History of Sexuality* (1984 [E.T. 1985, 1986]), Foucault's researches concentrated on the period between the seventeenth century and the present. From the beginning, in *Folie et déraison* (1961 [E.T. 1965]), he was preoccupied with the mutual shaping of theoretical discourse and interested practice. There is a kind of spiraling of weighted influences which bears upon the determination of epistemological perspectives. The realization of the ways in which epistemologies have been slanted through the progressive elaboration, rejection, and alteration of discursive practices provides a means of both describing and critiquing hypostatized ideas that function as power controls. Reason, the self-reflective subject, "man," and sexuality, as well as teaching hospitals (health and sanity) and the prison system (surveillance and discipline), are examples of the institutionalization of such ideas. Over a period of more than twenty years Foucault refined a series of detailed methods for analyzing the interaction of power and knowledge in the construction of these dominant ideational formations. The lateral tracing of correspondences between theory and practice within delimited chronological periods is what Foucault called archaeology, while he denominated the discernment of linear filiations between one period and another genealogy. Through intensive archival research (the synchronic, or archaeological, level) plotted on a grid that is calibrated to account for subtle shifts and changes (the diachronic, or genealogical, level), Foucault elaborated a method of research that he believed gave substance to Nietzsche's distinction between merely chronological and effective history (*wirkliche Historie*) (Foucault 1977:152-57).

That on Foucault's reading hypostatized ideas are epistemologically relative and often determined by non-epistemological concerns and in turn influence those concerns places him within the tradition of the hermeneutics of suspicion, as his acknowledged debt to Nietzsche and Heidegger indicates. This analysis of the ways in which power/knowledge formations are constructed reinforces both epistemological and social and cultural relativity. Finally, Foucault's own political commitments, which he constantly assessed critically, ensured that he did not dissociate himself through naïve "objectivity" from the matter of his investigations. In this way, Foucault, while basing his research on the critical and interpretive reading of specific texts, helped to foster the deconstruction of the dichotomized text/interpreter model, along with the dichotomies between subject and object, text and context that both determine it and follow in its wake. Within this perspective of bounded relativity, the impetus towards totalizing theory and the recitation of a "master narrative" (Lyotard) is frustrated. Certainly, the refusal of a "*grand récit*" in favor of localized histories with their contradictions and "points of resistance" explains to some extent Foucault's preference for a discursive-textual over a narrative-textual set of explanatory models. It also accounts for his popularity with, if not exploitation by, most of the theorists of postmodernism. A lingering suspicion, against which admittedly most of the evidence weighs, that Derrida entertains more than a passing infatuation with the *grand récit* of the history of Western metaphysics, much as it might be said Heidegger did, perhaps suggests a reason for the ascendancy of Foucault over Derrida in the 1980s when the problematization of political commitment, the questioning of ideological investment, and the shifting of social and disciplinary boundaries resulted in a proliferation of conflicting narratives and a hyperawareness of the critical and ironic relativity of the emergent perspectives. At this point postmodernism emerges.

The huge subject of postmodernism involves the confluences of practices in architecture, the visual arts, music, and literature with a number of the theoretical concerns of poststructuralist thinking. Among the latter are the models of textuality and intertextuality developed by deconstructionism, reception theory, and reader-response criticism; the displacement of the privileged position of the subject/author/interpreter, sometimes referred to as the "death" of the author; a re-emphasis on the diachronic dimension of creation and interpretation; a reassessment of the thought of the "masters of suspicion" (Marx, Nietzsche, and Freud) from the perspective of a surface-versus-depth model of interpretation in

Althusser, Derrida, and Lacan, for example; and the strategic privileging of *écriture* over the apparent immediacy of direct communication. These characteristics of the postmodernist scene find exemplification in the arts in a kind of baroque exuberance of media and detail fused onto a linear minimalism of repetitive spatial and temporal motifs, as in the musical compositions of Glass, Reich, or Adams or the so-called magic realism of Latin American novels. The deprivileging of the subject position of both author and interpreter results in a sort of Nietzschean perspectivism of shifting positionalities, and this in turn induces an ironic and critical attitude both within the work of art itself and in its consumer. This decentered, heterogeneous congeries of perspectives and interpretive options gives rise to the contestation of monological systems and teleological narratives. The contestation is often formulated in terms of ideology critique (as, for example, by Jameson), but there is also, as Linda Hutcheon (1989:2; 1991:70, 134) has pointed out, by the very nature of the opposition *qua* opposition, an element of complicity in the critique. A relativizing, perspectivist critique outfaces a monolithic system by bringing to light the ideological determinants of that system which escape explanation or justification within the system. To be consistent, however, ideology critique must then turn its guns upon itself. The standoff that results need not produce disillusionment or despair, particularly if ideology critique can exploit the perspective of irony and, indeed, this it seems to have done fairly successfully in its postmodernist form.

Within the realm of literary studies in the 1980s and 90s, the flourishing of numerous theoretical perspectives coming out of poststructuralist thought in the human sciences has combined with more specifically literary interests, such as semiotics, the study of narrative, reader-response criticism, genre studies, and the study of rhetoric and poetics, to produce a rich field of interacting and often conflicting theoretical-practical ways of reading and interpreting texts. While within each area of interest a tendency towards systematization is observable, there has been nonetheless a pragmatic and experimental attitude to adopting models and protocols not only from other areas of literary research, but also from other disciplines. More and more, the study of literature and literary theory (significantly, no longer "literary criticism") has come to be thought of as belonging to the wider field of cultural studies. The origins of this transdisciplinary movement go back, no doubt, to the radical university politics of the 1960s. Those politics, far from being defused, as was sometimes said, in the 1970s, actually underwent a series of transformations through particularization and elaboration by groups of scholars owing allegiance to specific social, cultural, sexual, and political identities. These changes can be easily documented by noting the changes in organization of the programs of the annual conventions of the Modern Language Association of America between the mid-1960s and the early 1990s. Certainly in the forefront of the restructuring process was the women's movement; and it is perhaps instructive to note how an indirect left-wing radicalism here tactically displaced the more overtly Marxian-inspired politics of the sixties while subsuming many of its practical concerns. Diversification and attention to immediate concrete issues have resulted in a complex network of centered interests within an overall decentered structure. Indeed, the question now moves to if and how the boundaries of the general structure can be drawn. Nor should it pass without noting that this way of imaging the affiliations among areas of interest is comparable to poststructuralist models of texts and to Foucault's concentration on localized histories as opposed to teleological history.

It is perhaps inevitable that the historical context of texts should return as a question in the discourse of literary studies. This is due not only to cross-disciplinary fertilization, but also to the problematization of the ways in which texts from the past discursively represent a range of contexts. What the New Criticism of the 1950s naïvely excluded returns in a sophisticated form in the New Historicism of the 1980s. The term "new historicism" was given currency by Stephen Greenblatt, whose *Renaissance Self-Fashioning* (1980) is generally taken as the programmatic work in this area of literary and cultural studies, though Greenblatt now prefers to call his way of working a "poetics of culture" (Greenblatt 1989). New historicist historiography attempts a shift in perspective analogous to that in the writing of history at the end of the nineteenth century. Totalizing, teleological schemes are eschewed in favor of a painstaking collection of archival evidence from diverse fields; emergent pictures in the form of local histories are compared and the contradictions, tensions, and aporiai among them highlighted. The influence of Foucault on the New Historicism is evident here, as it is in the playing off of the historian's "present" against the documents and artifacts of the past, with a consequent problematization of both past and present. Clifford Geertz's anthropological method of "thick description," which has certain affinities with the use of phenomenological procedures in the social sciences, is also employed as a way of eliciting the complex interweaving of the texture of historical narrative.

Though stretching across the political spectrum, new historicist writing, like most of the other methods and tendencies described in this article, has a definite bent towards the left. It is closely associated in Britain with the Marxian cultural materialism that descends from the highly influential work of Raymond Williams (Dollimore and Sinfield; Dollimore). These trends mark out the boundaries of rethinking Marxism in the light of poststructuralism and postmodernism. The notions of hypostatized history and a teleological schema have been replaced by analytic models for investigating the interrelations and conflicts among systems, discourses, and practices which can be read as though they were texts or œuvres and whose often covert investments, biases, contradictions, and inconsistencies can be elucidated. As Fredric Jameson (1991) has argued, the dimension of Utopia is not lost, but projected critically and problematically upon a receding horizon. The sense of a special kind of postmodernist irony, characterized by Jameson as being dominantly pastiche-like, emerges: one plays with the idea of the possible combinations of the pieces of the historical jigsaw puzzle. As has already been observed, the main paradigm shift in the New Historicism, as in much poststructuralist literary and cultural theory, is the replacement of a "depth" model by one that focuses on surface connections and interplay (Jameson:12).

Determining Textuality

In broad outlines, then, a picture has been sketched of the interweaving trajectories in the network of literary theory over the past couple of decades. What is chiefly observable is the problematization of the idea of a discrete literary field as such. The dislocation of disciplinary boundaries, the theoretical justification of limited fields of inquiry, the formation of often ideologically influenced positionalities, and a sense of fragmentation that yet retains a certain ironic coherence are all aspects of a larger problematization of the processes of determination and referentiality. This entire situation can be illustrated synecdochally by the recent interest in chaos theory in mathematics and its application to semantic paradoxes of self-referentiality. The paradoxes are resolved through invoking a dynamic process of truth values to escape the circle imposed by a strict binary logic of either true or false (Stewart 1993). The substitution of dynamic, polyvalent models of analysis for static, two-valued ones affects not only the processes of reading and interpretation in literature and the human sciences, but also the ways of conceptualizing the determination of meaning. That the phase "determination of meaning" is ambiguous is no accident, for it points to the multi-leveled process whereby meaning (minimally understood as a paraphrasable content that can be more or less consensually agreed upon) is both posited within and can be elicited from a limited linguistic field (a text, say). Simplistic models of the extraction of the contents from a container have yielded to more complex models of networks of shifting and interacting determinants, much as binary logical systems have, without being replaced, been supplemented and problematized by polyvalent logics.

The determinants of meaning may be thought of as both external and internal to a text, but they are given only by the text and by what the text as an intertextual phenomenon may give rise to. The textual constitution of meaning as well as its intertextual positionality can present problems for interpretation, but there are limits to the validity of particular interpretations. These limits are imposed by the larger network thrown, as it were, over the network of the text by the skills, experiences, and knowledge of individual interpreters and historical interpretive communities, as also by the conflicts into which they may enter. No longer is it sufficient to think of an interpretation as being either right or wrong, true or false. Rather, it is a question of relative degree. For example, to use the language of the analysis of paradoxes of self-referentiality, on a scale of 0 to 1, an interpretation may have a truth value of 0.7, though for each discrete point on the scale (e.g. 0.712345...) there is an infinite series of values. A paradox arises only when the value is 0.5, but then the interpretation is half-true, half-false. Of course, the degree to which interpretations are assessed is relative, but bounded. I may want to say that Shakespeare's *Macbeth* is really about the administration of Lyndon Johnson. Instead of immediately dismissing this interpretive statement, perhaps one ought to consider what I or a theater director might want to do with it. In this light, it might be considered 0.1 true; that is, as an interpretation it is 90 percent false but 10 percent true. The element of doubt has entered here through the pragmatic consideration that readers of *Macbeth* in the second half of the twentieth century are situated in a different position in a constructed historical narrative from readers of the play in the early years of the seventeenth century. This somewhat far-fetched example points to much more subtle instances of the flexibility, but not arbitrariness—except in some ultimate metaphysical or mathematical sense—of the determination of meaning.

A concrete illustration of the productive problematization of textual interpretive fields can be drawn from the discussion of the canonical status of a corpus of texts. In literary studies there has been in recent years considerable debate over the teaching of a fixed curriculum of valued texts. For reasons arising from a situation of cultural hegemony, this has been particularly true in the study of English Literature. In fact, the idea of a canon of English Literature is of rather recent invention, being concurrent with the emergence of departments of English in universities at the end of the nineteenth century. These departments displaced the centrality of the curriculum of classical studies, probably for reasons not very remote from national, imperial, and commercial expansion in the nineteenth century. So, on the one hand, the idea of an English canon is indebted to the precedent of an established body of texts in Greek and

Latin, while on the other a pragmatic boostering of a vernacular, national culture suggests a specific investment of authority.

The idea of a canon *per se*, however, is most probably chiefly empowered by the example of the biblical, and especially Christian, canon. If canons are really about the imposing of authority, then the stronger and more universal the authority, the more authoritative are the texts comprising the canon. So long as divine sanction is unquestioned, the status of the canon commands allegiance. In theory, at least, that is how the situation looks, but the analysis of the actual practice of the formation of canons reveals a somewhat different picture. In fact, there is, insofar as the subject can be traced, considerable debate over what should be included in the canon. And, in the end, the imposition of a canon is a matter of fiat, whatever justifications may be given, such as language (Judaism), a tradition of orthodox faith (Christianity), direct divine revelation (Islam), or venerable antiquity (Hinduism). It could be argued that what is really at stake is not any putative authority residing in the individual texts that make up the canon but a constructed narrative of how the texts cohere that constitutes the value and, hence, the power function of the canon. One can observe here the textual phenomenon of a network of actual texts being formed and thus determined by an ideal narrative that in turn, though it may never be instantiated in an actual text, is itself determined by textuality. There is a circle here, and the circle must maintain itself for as long as it exerts authority, for any text that does not conform to the master narrative must either be excluded or subjected to an inferior status. But it also follows that when there is a general questioning of authority and the breakdown of authoritative structures, the circulation of invested textual power gets diffused. In this case, contestation and confrontation occur, and these result in both strongly opposing positions and calls for mediation, unless of course an unquestioned authority is able to assert itself. The history of the Reformation and the rise of twentieth-century fundamentalists provide but two examples of this occurrence.

When national or cultural authority replaces religious authority in the formation of canons—as one might say of "laws" in general—the pattern remains the same, though there is at once a wider diffusion of power and a stronger impetus to reaction because of the removal in all but the most extreme cases of absolute sanctions. This situation has arisen in most academic institutions in the so-called First World during the last quarter of the twentieth century, a time at which, owing to a diffusion process in power structures that itself probably arose from the lateral effects of competitive capitalism and liberal democracy, previously marginalized groups have gained access to power. It may be that contestation over the status of academic canons and curricula is extremely productive of new insights and developments; or it may be—and it often looks this way—that endless debilitating standoffs are engendered. One way of trying to come to grips with this dilemma is to think in terms of the scale for resolving paradoxes of self-referentiality. It should of course be stressed that this is merely a heuristic device, but it can lead to clearer thinking about the subject. For example, if we were to position (arbitrarily) advocates of a closed canon at 0.7 and those of an open canon at 0.3, the occasion for extended, if often difficult, debate and a possible reversal of positions arises. The reverse allocation of values is equally possible, as is any other asymmetrical placing of values on the scale. What is to be avoided is the position of no canon at all or nothing but the canon (0 or 1)—an unreal situation in any case—or the possible, but completely unproductive 0.5/0.5 position, which results in an unending deadlock.

These procedures may be useful in thinking about and assessing the valencies and transformations through which articulatable structures of meaning—i.e., limited coherent wholes, whether these be individual texts, œuvres, canons, "master" narratives, or socio-economic and political organizations—pass. They do, however, rely upon fundamental relativistic models of which it has been the argument of this paper the textual model has occupied a particularly privileged position at a certain time in history, so much so that even our idea of history is thoroughly textualized. Basic relativism requires the possibility of other models: dynamic mathematical or physical ones seem a likely eventuality—even in the realm of texts. What makes no sense is the idea of an absolute model without any relations, for there the absolute is truly a fiction, though not necessarily a non-functioning one. Biblical theologians and advocates of a rigidly closed canon in whatever field should carefully weigh the implications of the following propositions: the absolute can only be saved relationally; a text and *a fortiori* textuality are only the effects of relatively bounded systems of coherencies; relativity can only be meaningfully measured by a set of mutually relative points of reference; chaos, in the mathematical sense, is "[s]tochastic behaviour occuring in a deterministic system" (Stewart 1989:17).

Works Consulted

NOTE: An extensive bibliography of all the works drawn upon for this article is not feasible. The items listed below are the most directly relevant. Readers who wish an overview should consult the anthologies of readings edited by Harari and Adams and Searle.

Adams, Hazard and Leroy Searle, eds.
    1986   *Critical Theory since 1965.* Tallahasee, University Presses of Florida.

Derrida, Jacques
    1976   *Of Grammatology.* Trans. Gayatri Chakravorty Spivak. Baltimore: The Johns Hopkins University Press.
    1978   *Writing and Difference.* Trans. Alan Bass. Chicago: University of Chicago Press.

Dollimore, Jonathan
    1991   *Sexual Dissidence: Augustine to Wilde, Freud to Foucault.* Oxford: Clarendon.

Dollimore, Jonathan and Alan Sinfield, eds.
    1985   *Political Shakespeare: New Essays in Cultural Materialism.* Manchester: Manchester University Press.

Foucault, Michel
    1965   *Madness and Civilization: A History of Insanity in the Age of Reason.* Trans. Richard Howard. New York: Vintage.
    1977   "Nietzsche, Genealogy, History." Pp. 139-64 in *Language, Counter-Memory, Practice: Selected Essays and Interviews.* Ed. Donald F. Bouchard. Trans. Donald F. Bouchard and Sherry Simon. Ithaca: Cornell University Press.
    1978   *The History of Sexuality.* Vol. 1: *An Introduction.* Trans. Robert Hurley. New York: Vintage. (Orig. pub.: *La Volonté de Savoir.* Paris: Gallimard, 1976.)
    1985   *The Use of Pleasure. The History of Sexuality.* Vol. 2. Trans. Robert Hurley. New York: Pantheon.
    1986   *The Care of the Self. The History of Sexuality.* Vol. 3. Trans. Robert Hurley. New York: Pantheon.

Greenblatt, Stephen
    1980   *Renaissance Self-Fashioning.* Chicago: University of Chicago Press.
    1989   "Towards a Poetics of Culture." Pp. 1-14 in *The New Historicism.* Ed. H. Aram Veeser. New York and London: Routledge.

Harari, Josué, ed.
1979   *Textual Strategies: Perspectives in Post-Structuralist Criticism*. Ithaca: Cornell University Press.

Hutcheon, Linda
1988   *A Poetics of Postmodernism: History, Theory, Fiction*. New York and London: Routledge.
1989   *The Politics of Postmodernism*. New York and London: Routledge.
1991   *Splitting Images: Contemporary Canadian Ironies*. Toronto: Oxford University Press

Jameson, Fredric
1991   *Postmodernism, or, The Cultural Logic of Late Capitalism*. Durham, NC: Duke University Press.

Lyotard, Jean-François
1984   *The Postmodern Condition: A Report on Knowledge*. Trans. Geoff Bennington and Brian Massumi. Minneapolis: University of Minnesota Press.

Murdoch, Iris
1992   *Metaphysics as a Guide to Morals*. London: Chatto and Windus.

Stewart, Ian
1989   *Does God Play Dice? The Mathematics of Chaos*. London: Penguin. (Orig. pub.: Basil Blackwell).
1993   "A Partly True Story." *Scientific American*. 268/2 (February 1993): 110-12.

Wellek, René and Austin Warren
1956   *Theory of Literature*. 3rd ed. New York: Harcourt, Brace and World.

Wittgenstein, Ludwig
1961   *Tractatus Logico-Philosophicus*. Trans. D.F. Pears and B.F. McGuinness. London: Routledge and Kegan Paul.

PSALM 102
A COMPLAINT WITH A DIFFERENCE

Robert C. Culley
McGill University, Montreal

ABSTRACT

In this study the questions of text and the reading process will be engaged at a relatively low level. Psalm 102 will be considered primarily from the point of view of its traditional and composite nature. The psalm as a whole works on three levels (the individual, the people, and the cosmos) yet the relationship of these is not finally resolved. Thus the text imposes limits for reflection by the clusters of imagery used, yet remains open in inviting the reader to explore the possibilities of relating these basic elements in different ways.

In the study of texts, questions about the nature of text and the process of reading are fundamental, but, like all fundamental questions, they are incredibly complex. Understandably, answers are many and opinions numerous. A whole range of perspectives and points of view are available. Questions about text and reading are especially significant because they lead quite readily to larger issues about the nature of language, and these lead in turn to reflection on the nature and status of reality. Does language in any way describe reality? How may it be said to do this? Then too there is the function of language. What is the power of language? Does it work for good through its ability to disclose new possibilities for human existence or for ill through its power to manipulate and exploit? In between the relatively limited task (still daunting enough) of reading a single text and the broader task of reflecting on the genuinely fundamental—in the sense that they are really world-view questions—issues of the nature of reality, lie a number of intervening steps, spheres of influence, and levels, all with their own perspectives and dimensions.

In this study I will be engaging the questions of text and the reading process at relatively low levels. I will be considering a specific text, Psalm 102, and viewing it as part of a specific collection, the Hebrew Bible. This will first require some comments on the Hebrew Bible as a whole, from the point of view of what kind of text it is, and here I will be looking at two features in particular, its traditionality and its composite nature. These comments will provide a partial perspective on the question of the nature of the biblical text that in turn can function as a tentative framework for reading Psalm 102. With regard to these two characteristics, traditional and composite, Psalm 102 furnishes an interesting case for discussion. This psalm contains language and ideas typical of the complaint psalms of the individual, which I will call traditional. It also contains, in the middle of the psalm, an abrupt shift to an announcement about Zion, rather untypical of complaints. It may be an example of a composite text.

My comments on the biblical text as a whole, in preparation for the study of Psalm 102, will be arranged under two headings: text and reading process.

1. *Text*. In a recent study of repeated and varied patterns in biblical narrative (Culley, 1992), I tried in the introduction to formulate the view of the biblical text that lay behind my approach. I did this largely to try to bring to my own consciousness some of the assumptions about the nature of the biblical text which I had been employing in my work. I described the Hebrew Bible this way: an ancient, religious text that is both traditional and composite. Text is the central notion: the Bible is primarily a text, an item of language. But this text, the Bible, has three striking characteristics: the text is very old, it has functioned as a religious text, and it is a traditional composite. Thus, the Bible is not just a text like other texts. It combines features rarely found together in other texts: ancient, religious, and traditional-composite. The Bible is something of a special case. It will be seen that this particular way of describing the notion of text will have implications for discussing the reading process.

For the study of Psalm 102, this general perception of the biblical text will lie behind what is done, although my attention will be directed particularly to two of the features: the text as traditional (highly conventional) and the text as composite (an interweaving of different sources and traditions). The religious dimension will be touched on at a later point. What is said in the following paragraphs about traditional and composite will in large part summarize what I have discussed more fully in my study of biblical narrative, *Themes and Variations* (1992:12-23).

When I say that the Hebrew Bible is traditional, I simply mean that we can usefully compare much of what is found in biblical writings to material studied by scholars of folklore and oral tradition (see the comments of Niditch, 1987:xiii-xiv). I am not arguing that the Hebrew Bible, or any particular part of it, is folklore as such or stems directly from oral tradition, only that the Bible is *like* this kind of material in some important ways and may even have roots in it. Much of the Bible has probably come from a scribal period when writing was being used to record, transmit, and produce important texts. In an age of scribal activity, one can imagine an interplay between the oral and the written as well as a continuation in written works of much of the language, style, and forms developed in an oral period (Culley, 1976, 1986; Lord, 1960). Thus, when I proposed in my study of biblical narrative that it was appropriate to describe much of biblical narrative as traditional, I was suggesting that a great deal of the conventional subject matter, language, style, and structure may have originated in oral tradition and been carried over into a scribal period. Texts like Homer and Beowulf have been portrayed in these terms and labelled "oral-derived" texts (see recently, Foley, 1991:xv). More needs to be said about oral and scribal.

Oral literature exists essentially in performance and is frequently characterized by stability and change (for further discussion of these issues, see Culley, 1976, 1986, 1992). Stability refers to the fact that oral literature is often highly conventional, marked by repeated use of traditional language, images, and structures. But change is an equally important feature of performance in that, more commonly than not, no two versions are exactly the same. With no "original version," stories and poems exist in oral tradition as a bundle of versions, or multiforms. Given this situation, oral artists play a double role. First, they are custodians of tradition who preserve and pass on the familiar stories and songs known to their audiences. Second, these poets are not just passive guardians of tradition but active contributors to an evolving process, in that artists are able to explore and bring out the various potentialities of the tradition, both taking advantage of and contributing to its multiform nature. Loyalty to tradition is combined with freedom to enhance.

What of scribal literature? When writing is used to record old and familiar poems and stories or incorporate them into larger written works or collections, it may be, as I have just suggested, that traditional language, images, and structures familiar to artists and audiences of an oral period can continue to inform the style of written texts. In other words, there may not have been a sharp break between oral and written; rather the use of writing may have been exploited to develop texts in ways not possible in oral tradition. If this were so, then scribes bear some similarity to oral poets in the sense that stability and change would still characterize their work which would display both a loyalty to received tradition and a freedom to vary and enhance it. Indeed, the use of writing in the production of texts would allow much more freedom to explore and develop the complexity of the traditions. Texts consisting of old and new material could be constructed, thus producing a composite text, a rather unusual kind of text characterized by a variety of voices.

Now, to be sure, what I have just said about the oral and scribal background of biblical texts is pretty much a guess, because we know so little in detail about how the biblical material came into existence. But it is an educated guess. I am making some rather general suggestions on the basis of what we know about oral tradition. It does not strike me as improbable that biblical texts are close to an oral background, at least closer to this than they are to modern literature, and most agree that the Bible is composite due in large part to scribal activity.

The complaint psalms offer a good example of what I mean by traditional texts. I will use "complaint psalms" as a designation for the whole group (but see Broyles:27 where he suggests "laments" as the title for the overall category). They form a group of poems in which one can distinguish a certain amount of common language and content, as Gunkel had already recognized (1966:172-265). For example, the plight of the sufferer in these psalms is often described in terms of some or all of the following three issues: physical deterioration (symptoms, danger of death, and sometimes the anger of the deity), isolation from family and friends, and enemies. Sometimes these elements are expressed in typical language and imagery. To call the complaint psalms traditional texts is simply to recognize the presence of this kind of common or traditional material, which, as I have suggested above, may reflect their oral and scribal background. If this were so, they can be called oral-derived texts.

The psalms are less obviously composite than the narrative texts but there are instances among the psalms where material may have been added or psalms joined together reflecting ongoing scribal activity. Psalm 102 may be just such a psalm. I would be prepared to consider the section on the restoration of Zion as an addition or insertion. However, it is not necessary to know this for certain because my interest does not lie primarily in identifying two separate texts and linking them to different historical settings or chronological stages, even though it is not unreasonable to do so. My interest lies in treating Psalm 102 as a single text but remaining open to the possibility of discerning different voices. In other words, my view of text as traditional and composite means trying to take seriously both coherence and difference as important characteristics of text which need to be accounted for by readers.

I have argued, then, that it is helpful to see the Bible in general and Psalm 102 in particular as a traditional-composite text and to give weight to both the elements: the notion of text on the one hand and traditional composite on the other. But why bother discussing the oral and scribal background to the text, which as I have already indicated remains speculative to a significant degree? For one thing, it has not been unusual for scholars to speak of conventional language in the complaint psalms (Kraus, 1988:49; Broyles: 26; Gelander). By specifying the particular kind of conventional language (oral-derived), one is able to give more precise content to the term "conventional," at least to the extent that some interesting questions can then be posed about text and reading. However, the important issue is not so much the desire to fill in the historical background of the growth of the text as it is to propose a concept of text that can function as a kind of working hypothesis, partial though it may be, for analysis of biblical texts, and here we are concerned particularly with Psalm 102 (Culley, 1992:12-45, especially 44). This model of text, even though it is tentative, is able to provoke questions that might otherwise not be asked.

In other words, our notion of text governs how we read, what we look for, what we notice, and what we ignore. For example, historical criticism is inclined to conceive of the Bible as an intricate composite exhibiting evidence of different sources and various stages of growth (however this may be conceived). By and large these elements become the texts to be studied rather than the whole. Much of the recent literary study of the biblical text views the Bible as a unified text, whether this means treating it as an organic whole or simply as a text which should be treated as a whole. To state it in a much oversimplified way, one could say that historical criticism gives priority to finding differences in order to find different texts to study but that a literary approach looks for similarities that reinforce and strengthen the impression of a single, unified text.

As I have indicated, by attempting to work with the notion of a traditional-composite text I want to take seriously both the notion of text as a whole and the notion of the text as a traditional-composite, which means trying to take both coherence and difference into account. It may be added that recent stances and strategies like ideological, postmodern, and feminist often search for differences that will undercut impressions of coherence or even assume that texts are by definition in conflict with themselves. While I agree that looking for difference is crucial step, in my view difference and similarity are so closely related that we do not find one except through the other.

2. *The Reading Process.* If the Hebrew Bible can be described as traditional and composite and if a biblical text like Psalm 102 may be usefully approached from this point of view, what are the implications for the reading process? The reader may be involved in two ways, one related to the traditional nature of texts and one related to the composite nature of texts. It was noted that the complaint psalms of the individual can be called traditional because they have much in common, sharing the same form as well as similar language and content. Since these psalms are so closely related to each other, one could say that to read one complaint psalm is in a real sense to become engaged in reading them all. The group as a whole offers a body of language and imagery appropriate to complaint. The individual complaint psalm represents, so to speak, a single

expression of some of the possibilities of the tradition as a whole. Of course, the "tradition" only exists in the ensemble of individual examples and must be deduced from the group as a whole. What is more, the rather small group of complaint psalms that remains in the Bible only reflect what must have been a richer tradition of complaint psalm composition.

From my point of view, there is need to keep both levels in mind. On the one hand, it is important to see what kind of general picture emerges from the common language of the group of complaints as a whole, that is, the tradition (or what remains to us of the tradition). On the other hand, it is equally important to examine the individual psalms to see how they have made use of the tradition: what they have included, left out, or added, what slant they have put on the tradition. It is possible to take a further step. One of the remarkable characteristics of the psalms is that they are terse, rarely filling out or developing their statements or images. To what extent did hearing or reading an individual psalm depend upon a knowledge of the larger tradition from which one can fill out the rather laconic verses of any particular psalm?

The relationship of the individual psalm to its traditional group has been touched on in some recent scholarship. In two previous studies of my own, one on Psalm 88 and one on Psalm 3 (Culley, 1988, 1991), I tried to use the whole group of individual complaints as a primary context within which to read the psalms in question, and in the article on Psalm 3 the common language was described as traditional language. There, it was suggested that the complaint psalms are governed by a rescue pattern in which we encounter a sufferer appealing for, and indeed seeming to expect, rescue. If the complaints form a group reflecting traditional language, then the task of reading, or at least an important aspect of this task, can be understood in terms of how these psalms are both similar to and yet different from each other as complaints. In this way, attention needs to be directed toward two levels (the group and the individual psalm) and toward how they are related to each other. The focus then shifts back and forth from the tradition as reflected in the group as a whole to the psalm as a particular expression of the tradition that develops its own articulation of the tradition.

Two other biblical scholars have recently alluded to the implications of the presence of traditional or conventional language in complaint psalms. Broyles has noted the presence of conventional language but also the degree of selection and variety of motifs (27). In this connection, he has remarked on how some psalms appear to be in tension with the traditional ideas expressed by others (83). In commenting on the relationship between individual psalms and the tradition, he has suggested that conventional language can function as a kind of shorthand used by poets to evoke the whole tradition (26). Gelander has pointed to the presence of a conventional pattern in Psalm 5, although he argues that through selection of and deviations from conventional language, the psalm reflects a significant measure of originality, which he interprets as the reflections of a personal experience lying behind the poem (315).

There is also some important discussion outside biblical studies that can be mentioned at this point. In a number of publications over the past ten years or so, John Miles Foley has sought to work out the implications of the oral-derived nature of texts for readers (1987, 1991, 1992). While the oral-formulaic theory of Parry and Lord did a great deal to identify oral diction in texts, one of the real difficulties experienced by those working with the approach was how one moved from simply recording formulas and other related features to the implications of all this for reading and interpreting texts. Foley offers some intriguing suggestions in this direction. He argues that "the so-called 'stock phraseology' is invested with a crucially important poetic function: it explains the momentary action in terms of the larger characterization, the present in terms of the timeless or unchanging" (1987:193). In other words, the traditional diction found in any single poem evokes the larger body of traditional language associated with the kind of poetry in question, familiar to both performers and audiences. The stock phrases become metonyms, as he calls them, for the larger traditional network. Meaning, then, exists "at the interface of text and tradition" (195). Thus the audience plays a role. In a sense they perform the text by evoking their knowledge of the fuller tradition through the appearance of the traditional elements occurring in the individual poem.

I have mentioned the work of Foley simply to show that there is a developing discussion on how to read traditional texts. My attempts to link the individual complaint psalms to their tradition as expressed by the complaints as a group bears some relationship to this discussion, which has stimulated my thinking at more than one point.

Turning to the composite nature of traditional texts, we encounter another issue. If the use of writing in a scribal period permitted the construction of composite texts in which different elements of traditional material could be brought together, then reading composite texts demands a great deal from readers since they are invited to work out the relationship between the different components of a given text. This applies to Psalm 102 where a complaint tradition is set beside an announcement of restoration for Zion. If the notion of a composite *text* (that is, a text which happens to be composite) is to be taken seriously, then one must be prepared to recognize both similarities and differences in order to see how some elements form links that hold the text together and some emerge as separate voices struggling to maintain their distinct perspective. Thus, the resultant tensions remain important features of text.

Finally, just a word on the religious dimension. The complaint psalms are prayers, which is an usual form of discourse. Prayers attempt to address a deity and in doing so seek to speak across the fundamental dividing line between the human and the divine, a separation characteristic of the world view of ancient Israel, and indeed many other religious traditions. But more than this, as a group of traditional psalms, the complaints offer a network of common language and imagery that contributes to this world view by expressing an understanding of the sufferer, and through this an understanding of the human condition. The tradition reflected in the complaints does not appear to present a closed and complete perspective with a fixed and final form. Rather, the tradition appears to be more like a cluster of language and images, the openness of which permits and even encourages exploration of the potential of the tradition. Indeed, the individual poems appear to be doing just this, through selection and variation of elements in the tradition. Thus, the complex relationship between any poem and its group.

We turn now to Psalm 102. I said that I wanted to treat this psalm as a single text but this does not mean assuming it to be an organic unity, since the psalm presents us with a juxtaposition of two rather distinct perspectives: a complaint of an individual and an announcement of the restoration of Zion. Actually, as will be seen, there is a third. The psalm could be a composite but it is not necessary to make a final decision. The real issue concerns how these two perspectives can be related to each other in the present text. What happens when they are set together in the same poem? For purposes of discussion it will be useful to begin treating these two elements separately before asking how they may be related.

The complaint of the individual appears in two sections: vv. 2-12 and 24-28, where one encounters some of the elements found in other complaint psalms. As noted earlier, the difficulty of the sufferer can be described in terms of three aspects: (1) physical deterioration, (2) isolation from family and friends, and (3) enemies, although all three elements are by no means present in all complaint psalms and can be expressed in rather different language and imagery. These three are echoed in Psalm 102.

Generally, physical deterioration includes physical symptoms, danger of death, and in some instances the anger of Yahweh. In Psalm 102 the symptoms enumerated are the following: the sufferer's bones are burning (v. 4b); his heart has been stricken and withers (v. 5a if the text is correct here); and bone sticks to flesh (v. 6). In addition, he has difficulty with food (vv. 5b, 10a).

While no direct and explicit reference to the danger of death occurs, there are clear indications that the subject is a major preoccupation. This is expressed in two images: the shortening of days and the withering of vegetation. The phrase "my days" appears four times in the psalm. It is found at the beginning and end of a section describing the suffering of the speaker (vv. 4-12). In the first instance, the sufferer complains that his days have come to an end in smoke, or like smoke (v. 4a). At the end of the section he laments that his days are like an outstretched shadow. Following the section about the restoration of Zion, the complaint language appears to resume in v. 24, which contains the phrase "my days." This is a difficult verse and changes are often suggested. As it stands, it seems to say that Yahweh has afflicted the sufferer's strength and shortened his days. The last appearance of the phrase "my days" occurs in the following verse (v.25) when the sufferer, in the only direct appeal for help, asks: "do not take me up in the midst of my days." Beyond this, vv. 24 and 25 are addressed to someone other than the deity.

Alongside this imagery of the premature end of the speaker's days, or life, there are two references to withering or drying up. His heart has dried out like vegetation (v. 5) and then, more forcefully (v. 12), he has dried out, withered like vegetation.

The direct cause of the sufferer's troubles, his physical distress, and his expectation of death is clearly stated in v. 11. It comes from Yahweh who in his anger and wrath has picked him up and thrown him down. The anger of Yahweh is mentioned only here in the psalm. This may imply that the suffering is a punishment for sin but it is not said so explicitly. Nor do sin and punishment become issues in the resolution of the problem of the sufferer.

Apart from physical deterioration, another element found in some complaint psalms is the isolation from everyone, even family and friends. This is not mentioned directly in this psalm. But what is the imagery about the birds (in the wilderness, in the ruins, and alone on the roof) meant to suggest? Perhaps, the isolation of the sufferer (Broyles takes it this way, 106 and 209). Since the imagery is unique to this psalm, we cannot be certain.

Finally, alongside the physical deterioration, including danger of death and anger of Yahweh, and the possible reference to isolation, there is mention of enemies (v. 9). Enemies are perhaps the most common element in the description of suffering in complaint psalms, but in this psalm enemies are only referred to in this one verse, where they are pictured as persons who insult the sufferer and "swear by him," whatever that means.

Psalm 102, then, does fit to some extent the pattern of the other complaints, although it goes its own way. I have just proposed, for example, that the figure of the birds may be a rather different way of expressing the isolation of the sufferer.

A more striking instance of how this psalm follows its own course may be seen in the way death is depicted. In other psalms, death is frequently described in spatial imagery. Death is going to the pit or sinking into the waters as, for example, in Psalm 8 or the opening line of Psalm 130: "Out of the depths, I cry to you." To be in a state of death is to be separated from the deity (Psalm 6). In Psalm 102, however, the imagery has to do with time: "my days." I have just noted that the phrase "my days" comes up four times in the complaint part of the poem. The psalmist portrays his days, or span of life, as though they were dissolving in smoke, stretching out like a declining shadow, being shortened, and being stopped short of the normal course.

The theme of time is developed in two further ways. First of all, the days, or lifetime, of the speaker, already in danger of being shortened, are set beside the "years," or the span of Yahweh's existence. Just before the section on the restoration of Zion begins, it is said: "my days are like a shadow that is stretched out" (v. 12) and this is followed in the next line by the statement: "You, Yahweh sit forever" (v. 13). This contrast is also found in v. 25: "Do not take me up in the midst of my days, your years are throughout all generations." This perception is reinforced a few lines later when it is asserted that, while heaven and earth may pass away, Yahweh will remain (v. 27). And it is added that "your years will not end" (v. 28).

This theme of time, expressed as a contrast between a brief span (the human condition) and an endless span (the divine existence), is bolstered by means of a transposition to another pair of contrasting ideas, permanence and impermanence, which has been woven into the time imagery. When it says in v. 4 that "my days have come to an end in smoke," the notion of time, "my days," is qualified by the image of smoke, which is insubstantial and impermanent. Beyond this, the image of vegetation that withers appears twice: once applied to the heart (v. 5) and once used of the sufferer (v. 12b): "I have dried out like vegetation" (v. 12b). At the end of the poem, the creation imagery pictures the heavens and the earth passing away while Yahweh remains. This event is described in terms of a garment which wears out. Here too, the contrast of permanence and impermanence is added to the notion of time.

As we have seen, then, the complaint section of Psalm 102 offers some of the usual traditional elements in the description of suffering but steers the notion of death in a different direction by using imagery of time and developing it so that human life in its brevity and impermanence is contrasted to the endless span of Yahweh's existence. What does this do? Is this shift of perspective offered as a response to the problem of suffering? Certainly to place the suffering of an individual human within the broad perspective of creation and endless of span of existence reserved for the deity would modify the significance of human suffering, reducing its ultimate importance appreciably. If the significance of human suffering is thus qualified, then one might say that the idea of rescue is also modified. Rescue would become an adjustment of perspective on the part of the sufferer rather than direct intervention by the deity. When rescue is understood in this way, it may be that one should not expect a deliverance from suffering and early death because such is the human condition. This would, of course, also adjust the purpose and function of the prayer. In fact, the direct appeals usually found in other complaint psalms calling on Yahweh to heal, save, and rescue are absent in Psalm 102. The only direct appeal is in v. 25: "Do not lift me up in the middle of life." The prayer for direct help still remains but in less forceful form and enclosed in the cosmic perspective which I have just described.

We may now consider the other section of the psalm, vv. 14-23, which introduces the theme of the restoration of Zion. The very first verse announces, in a direct address to Yahweh: "You will arise, you will comfort Zion" and proclaims that the time is near. One might almost expect this kind of statement to come as an announcement from Yahweh rather than from someone who is addressing Yahweh. But what will this restoration mean?

Further explanation comes in vv. 16 and 17. The nations and kings of the earth are brought into the picture and it is said about them that they will fear (many change this to "see") Yahweh's name and Yahweh's glory and that his glory will be shown when he builds Zion. On one level, this could point to the actual rebuilding of the city of Jerusalem which was left in ruins by the Babylonians who also carried off a portion of the population into captivity, and this rebuilding eventually took place. But these verses also recall in some ways chapter 40 of Isaiah where, with different language, it is announced that, with the return to Zion, the glory of Yahweh will appear for all to see. The emphasis at the beginning of this Isaiah chapter rests on comforting (different verb than Psalm 102:14) the people in exile and leading them back to a waiting Zion. Still, the appearance of Yahweh's glory in both Psalm 102 and Isaiah 40 suggests a dramatic intervention, and in Psalm 102 it is clear that the nations will see (or fear) the glory of Yahweh which will appear when Zion is built. Just what this would mean is not spelled out.

The next few verses (vv. 18-22) turn to the people. The rebuilding will be the answer to the prayer of the "naked one," and in v. 21 the "prisoner" and also "those slated for death" are mentioned. Verse 19 calls for this announcement to be written down for a future generation, a people not yet born, so that, one assumes, this future generation will witness the events and also possess written testimony to the fact that it had been announced in advance. It is asserted that Yahweh will look down, hear the cry of the prisoner, and release those slated for death. This fact will be proclaimed in Zion and praised in Jerusalem when, according to v. 23, peoples and kingdoms gather together to worship Yahweh. This last verse brings to mind the poem found both in Isaiah 2 and Micah 4 when many peoples decide to come to Mount Zion. In this poem, the coming of the people to Zion will occur in the last days when peace will reign and war will be no more, a time when the problem of human conflict will be at last resolved. This picture depicts the advent of a new age, but one which still remains within history. The building or rebuilding of Zion is not a part of this picture.

Now, this announcement section of Psalm 102 (vv. 14-23) presents a rather compressed picture of future events in and around Zion. Some things are clear. There will be a comforting and building of Zion accompanied by the appearance of the glory of Yahweh. There will be a response to the cry of the prisoners and an emancipation of the doomed. The peoples will recognize what is happening and will come to Zion to worship. However, because the images in these verses are so compressed, the full picture is not fully clear and we are left uncertain of the exact relationship of the elements to each other and the precise import of the details. Strangely enough the condensation and the resulting fuzziness does not seem to lessen the force of the portrayal all that much. One may wonder whether this brief cluster of images draws a larger body of traditional material on the topic of Zion just as the complaint language in the other parts of the psalm may have evoked the larger complaint tradition. The similarities to Isaiah 2 and 40 may suggest that some traditional language and imagery about Zion exists, involving a number of issues and adaptable to different situations. In any case, in Psalm 102 we have a small block of material on the topic of the restoration of Zion.

Now that both sections of the psalm have been reviewed, something needs to be said about what happens when they are put together. I have suggested that we have two clusters of language gathered around two themes, the complaint of a suffering individual and the restoration of Zion, but, as we have seen, there is a third theme, Yahweh and creation (permanence/impermanence), which has been introduced within the complaint section. It is difficult to judge whether or not this might also represent a stream of traditional language. In any event, we may speak of three important themes in the psalm, two of which appear to draw on traditional language. How are these themes related to each other as part of the same text and what kind of challenge does this offer to the reader?

Before dealing with this question, two brief comments may be added in order to pick up a couple minor items left out of the discussion so far. The first concerns the way I have divided the psalm in the previous discussion. My assumption has been that vv. 2-12 and vv.24-28, the sections before and after the Zion section (vv. 14-23), belong together as a complaint. I did this largely because complaint language starts again in vv. 24 and 25 (both verses contain difficulties) but also because the themes of time and permanence/transience initiated in vv. 2-12 also resume in vv. 24-28. Gunkel, for one, has proposed another possibility for this psalm (1968).

Second, a brief comment is appropriate at this point on vv. 1, 13, and 29, which have not been mentioned up to this point. The first verse appears to be a title declaring that the speaker is a sufferer pouring out his troubles before Yahweh. If this is a title, it functions as the earliest extant commentary on the psalm and indicates that the author considered that the dominant issue in the psalm was complaint. Verse 13 is on the border between the complaint and the Zion section. It can be read as the last verse of the complaint, contrasting the transience of the speaker to the permanence of Yahweh. But it could also be read as the start of the section on Zion. Therefore it functions well as a transition between the complaint and the announcement. Verse 29 introduces a sudden shift in topic. After vv. 27 and 28, which speak of creation passing away but Yahweh remaining, v. 29 appears to return to the perspective of the Zion section. The descendants of the present generation of Yahweh's servants (v. 15) will dwell in Zion, one assumes peacefully, although this is not said.

In returning to the question posed above about the three themes of suffering, restoration, and creation, it is interesting that the clusters of language and imagery gathered around suffering and restoration both involve a rescue pattern, one that is frequently found in biblical literature. In Hebrew narrative, rescue is, perhaps, the most common narrative pattern (Culley, 1992). This pattern traces the movement from a situation in which a person or persons find themselves in difficulty to their rescue by Yahweh. This pattern can be worked out both in terms of individuals and in terms of groups, such as the religious community as a whole or some part of it. The most obvious instance of a rescue pattern, in this case involving the people as a whole, is the exodus story, and this amounts to a rather long and elaborate narrative. Many other examples, varying considerably in length and complexity, can be cited: the Joseph story, the stories in Judges, and the miracle stories in the Elijah and Elisha narratives.

While a narrative leads listeners or readers through all the steps of the pattern, from the initial difficult situation to rescue, prayers for help like the complaint psalms view the pattern from a fixed position: a sufferer stands in a difficult situation and appeals for help, that is, looks ahead to a potential rescue. The sufferer clearly wants Yahweh to complete the pattern by intervening to rescue and moving the victim from a negative to a positive situation. Thus, to offer a prayer for help presumes a rescue pattern, and the complaint psalms as a group with their shared, traditional language play out some of the possibilities of this pattern. As we have seen, Psalm 102 assumes the traditional rescue pattern but appears to modify it by placing the human perspective within the context of the divine perspective, yet without really resolving the one into the other. This move has the effect of reducing the significance of direct intervention and immediate rescue, although the perspective can still shift between two levels: the difficulty of the sufferer on the human plane and the deity as the everlasting creator on a cosmological plane. It is interesting that the cosmological level does not include a cosmological rescue pattern, even though language and imagery was available in the traditions of Ancient Israel. Either the conflict view of creation where Yahweh battles the monsters or the vision of Yahweh, the warrior, coming to deal with his enemies in a final battle could have been employed.

The verses on the restoration of Zion also imply a rescue pattern. The situation of Zion (both city and people) is clearly a difficult one in which there is need of Yahweh's intervention. Here, however, the fixed point of the speaker is different. It is not at the stage of an appeal for help but further on in the pattern where an announcement is made that the appeal is going to be answered and that intervention is certain and immanent. In this picture of rescue, no modification is introduced, as in the complaint sections, invoking a higher and broader perspective that would invite a reinterpretation of the notion of rescue. The focus of the material is on joyous anticipation of the rescue of the religious community, a restoration that will occur on the historical plane.

The psalm as a whole, then, works on three important levels: the individual, the people, and the cosmos, and the first two of these involve rescue. The first and last of these levels, as we have seen, fall within the complaint sections. The complaint first develops the picture of a suffering individual on the human plane, which includes physical deterioration, danger of death and isolation, with brief references to enemies and divine anger. Then, this picture is related to a vast cosmological perspective that affirms Yahweh's abiding presence even after creation passes away. The Zion section introduces another plane that lies between the other two and focuses on the religious community, the collective, which includes a brief reference to the nations and kings, at least an acknowledgement that the world is shared with other peoples.

Now, these three levels have emerged in this psalm but their relationship to each other does not appear to me to be resolved. In other words, the levels, which form a hierarchy of individual, community, and cosmos, are juxtaposed, yet they maintain a certain distinctness from each other. The poem does not indicate unambiguously how they are to be related to one another. That is to say, while the evocation of a cosmological level may appear to provide a resolution of potential problems with the rescue pattern at the lower levels, it is not clear to me that Psalm 102 points clearly in this direction. Rather, it seems to leave the questions open at each level. At the same time, by virtue of the psalm's traditional and composite nature, it has lateral relationships with the broader, traditional clusters of language and imagery related to complaint and Zion. In this way, the text invites readers to reflect on the specific way complaint language was used here, but also on the other explorations found in other psalms. One might say the same for the Zion language, although on a more limited scale.

A reader, then, is called upon to think about several perspectives of the problem of rescue. Vertically, there are the levels of the suffering individual and the suffering community, along with how these may be viewed from an ultimate, cosmological perspective. The three perspectives remain sufficiently independent that they are free to qualify and modify each other, perhaps suggesting the incompleteness of any one without the others. Laterally, there are the related traditions of complaint and Zion to which the individual psalm is related, within which there is further interaction. This complex and multidimensional vision presented by the text invites readers to explore its possibilities, engage with the interplay of similarities and differences, and consider how one may fill in relationships among the various elements inside and outside the text. At this point, one is already deeply engaged with the religious or theological dimension.

In this view, texts like Psalm 102 are not completely open. The language of the text and its various clusters of imagery have provided a focus of attention, set bounds within which reflection can take place. At the same time, the relationships between these elements are not precisely determined within the text nor the relationships which function laterally to larger traditions. The reader is invited to be active in pursuing the possibilities of the elements that the text has presented.

Now, having considered Psalm 102 and its immediate context in the Hebrew Bible, how can this discussion be related to larger questions of text and reading that I spoke of at the beginning? I am not sure. It is a big jump from some texts to all texts, and I suppose that I am content to stay for the moment at lower levels and let broader discussions form an important background.

WORKS CONSULTED

Aejmelaeus, Anneli
    1986   *The Traditional Prayer in the Psalms.* BZAW 167. Berlin: de Gruyter.

Broyles, Craig C.
    1989   *The Conflict of Faith and Experience in the Psalms.* JSOTSup 52. Sheffield: Sheffield Academic Press.

Culley, Robert C.
    1976   "Oral Tradition and Old Testament Studies." *Semeia* 5:1-31.
    1986   "Oral Tradition and Biblical Studies." *Oral Tradition* 1:30-65.
    1988   "Psalm 88 Among the Complaints." Pp. 289-302 in *Ascribe to the Lord: Biblical and Other Studies in Memory of Peter C. Craigie.* Ed. Lyle Eslinger and Glen Taylor. JSOT Sup. Series 67. Sheffield: JSOT Press.
    1991   "Psalm 3: Content, Context, and Coherence." Pp 29-30 in *Text, Methode, und Grammatik: Wolfgang Richter zum 65. Geburtstag.* Ed. Walter Gross, Irsigler Hubert, and Theodor Seidl. St. Ottilien: EOS Verlag.
    1992   *Themes and Variations: A Study of Action in Biblical Narrative.* Semeia Studies. Atlanta, GA: Scholars.

Foley, John Miles
    1987   "Reading the Oral Traditional Text: Aesthetics of Creation and Response." Pp. 185-211 in *Comparative Research on Oral Traditions: A Memorial for Milman Parry.* Ed. John Miles Foley. Columbus, OH: Slavica.
    1991   *Immanent Art: From Structure to Meaning in Oral Traditional Epic.* Bloomington: Indiana University Press.
    1992   "Word-Power, Performance, and Tradition." *Journal of American Folklore* 105:276-301.

Gelander, Shamai
    1992   "Convention and Originality: Identification of the Situation in the Psalms." *Vetus Testamentum* 42:302-16.

Gunkel, Hermann
    1966   *Einleitung in die Psalmen.* Göttingen: Vandenhoek & Ruprecht.
    1968   *Die Psalmen.* Göttingen: Vandenhoek & Ruprecht.

Kraus, Hans-Joachim
    1988   *Psalms 1-59: A Commentary.* Trans. Hilton C. Oswald. Minneapolis: Augsburg.

Lord, Albert B.
   1960   *The Singer of Tales*. Harvard Studies in Comparative Literature 24. Cambridge: Harvard University Press.

Niditch, Susan
   1987   *Underdogs and Tricksters: A Prelude to Biblical Folklore*. San Francisco: Harper & Row.

WHAT SHALL WE DO WITH JUDITH?
A FEMINIST REASSESSMENT OF A BIBLICAL "HEROINE"

Pamela J. Milne
University of Windsor

ABSTRACT

The book of Judith tells a dramatic tale about sacrilegious arrogance, doubt, faith, and the unrivalled power of Israel's god. It is also a tale of a woman's courage, daring, and piety. Whether the story's depiction of woman should be regarded as positive or negative, feminist or patriarchal, is at issue in many recent analyses of Judith. The remarkable diversity, even polarization, of views raises the question of the respective roles of reader and text in the production of meaning. If, as Mieke Bal suggests, meaning is a readerly product but based on the elaboration of the possibilities of the text, both readers and texts must be held accountable. Feminist and pro-feminist readers of Judith can be held accountable for the assumptions they bring to the text about feminism and sexual politics, while the text can be held more accountable for the genre expectations it promotes.

INTRODUCTION: ONE JUDITH AND ANOTHER

Once upon a time, a young academic named Judith wanted to learn the oral history of a major development which had occurred in her field some decades earlier. She decided to invite four prominent senior scholars (all male), knowledgeable about this oral history, to dinner at a local restaurant. All accepted her invitation and Judith proceeded to make the necessary arrangements and reservation. The four men and Judith arrived at the restaurant at the appointed time and were shown to their table by the maitre d'. As the group arrived at the table, it became apparent that it was a table for four, not for five. Before anyone could draw the problem to the attention of the maitre d', one of the men mused (in all seriousness), "Oh, what shall we do with Judith?" Immediately, Judith stepped up behind one of the four chairs and said, "Why don't we put her here!"

When I began to think about the book of Judith and to read numerous feminist analyses of the story, my academic colleague's experience came to mind again. The more I reflected on her experience, the more it provided insight for me into aspects of the biblical story of Judith I found problematic as a feminist reader.

For one thing, Judith's dinner experience with her four male companions confirmed that, no matter how central a woman might be to the action of the plot, she can remain marginal relative to the dominant male perspective. Judith had conceived the idea of an oral history session; she had decided on a list of participants; she had invited them to dinner; she had done all the organization; *and* she was paying for the dinner. Nevertheless, she was perceived by her guests as the one lacking a place at the table. The question, "What shall *we* do with Judith?" classified the actors in the drama in terms of "us" and "her" clearly along gender lines. It rendered Judith anomalous and marginalized in her own play.

Our modern Judith, being the quick-witted feminist that she is, was able to reclaim her place immediately. She highlighted and undercut the gender division by speaking of herself as an object in the third person while asserting her subjectivity by placing herself within her male colleague's "we": "Why don't *we* put *her* here!"

As an actor in the drama, Judith was able to respond as she did, but would the same thing be possible for a narrative character like the biblical Judith? Like my colleague, Judith, in the company of four men, the biblical Judith appears as the sole active and named female character among Jewish leaders and elders and foreign generals and soldiers. How does she fare in such a context? Is she controlled by the author/narrator of the story (by the text) or by the reader who reads her story, or by both? Is she a feminist character or can she be seen as one by a feminist or pro-feminist reader? Or is she a character who embodies a thoroughly patriarchal idea and/or ideal of woman?

BIBLICAL TEXTS AND INTERPRETATIONS: THE DILEMMA FOR FEMINIST READERS

It is virtually axiomatic in feminist circles that the bible has played a significant role in the oppression of women in Western society. Nineteenth-century American feminists lobbying for women's suffrage often found themselves confronted by opponents who used the bible as the principal weapon in their war against equal rights for women. As a result, several prominent feminists devoted considerable intellectual energy to studying what the bible had to say about women, and how it was used against women, while they worked for political change.

For many, such as Lucy Stone, Antoinette Brown and the Grimké sisters, Sarah and Angelina, their feminist activism was deeply rooted in their religious beliefs. They shared the conviction that inaccurate translations and biased interpretations produced by male clergy, not the biblical text itself, were the source of the bible's oppressive impact on women.

However, others, like Matilda Joslyn Gage and Elizabeth Cady Stanton, were convinced that the problem went beyond sexist interpretations of the bible to the biblical text itself. By the end of the nineteenth century, long before the advent of structuralism, poststructuralism or postmodernism, a feminist biblical criticism had emerged which made the bible and its interpretation a political issue.

Feminist biblical criticism seems to have faded early in the twentieth century shortly after the publication of Cady Stanton's *The Woman's Bible*. It began to reappear in the 1960s and had become a vital and energetic pursuit by the mid-70s. Most of the studies produced during this period proceeded from the assumption that, for the most part, the patriarchal or misogynist bias of readers/interpreters had produced anti-woman interpretations not well-rooted in the biblical text. The early work of Phyllis Trible (1973; 1978) is typical of this approach. Trible argued that "the intentionality of biblical faith ... is neither to create nor to perpetuate patriarchy but rather to function as salvation for both men and women...." (1973:31) Through close readings of individual texts such as Genesis 2-3, using the techniques of rhetorical criticism, Trible sought to recover the liberating intention of the biblical authors and to challenge the misinterpretations produced by male readers over the centuries.

In the 1980s feminist scholars began to express more doubts about rescuing the "intentionality" of all biblical texts from the charge of sexism and misogyny. Scholars like Esther Fuchs (1985; 1988; 1989) began to explore the subtle literary devices and strategies through which biblical texts gave expression to the patriarchy of Israelite and/or Christian societies. Even Trible turned her attention to a group of biblical texts which narrated stories of such horrific acts of terror against women that no feminist reading could reclaim them as positive, liberating texts for women (1984). When confronted with narratives about the rape, mutilation, and murder of women, Trible's strategy as a reader was to focus on the female victims of violence and to identify with them *in memoriam* to them.

Feminist biblical scholarship, like much other biblical scholarship, has shifted focus somewhat in the last few years from historical and theological questions about authors and their intentions toward more literary questions about texts and readers. The work of Mieke Bal, who analyzes biblical texts as a narratologist, has been especially influential at the theoretical level. As a literary theorist, Bal is acutely aware of current interest in the question of the reader and the reader's role in the production of meaning. Bal's own position is one which holds the text and the reader in tension. In her understanding of narratology, meaning is a readerly product but is based on an elaboration of the possibilities of the text (1989:17).

Drawing on the work of Ernst van Alphen, Bal holds that meaning is a dynamic process comprised of two "moments." The text is the provider of meaning in the first moment, while in the second moment, "the reader formulates an ordering and reworking of the collection of possible meanings offered by the text" (Bal, 1989:14).

What interests Bal most, especially when dealing with a religious document like the bible, which has been and continues to be used to shape social reality in the Western world, are the ethical responsibility for, and the political consequences of, reading. The central issue is one of power. On the one hand it makes a difference whether the reader is a woman, black, poor and/or old, or a man, white, middle-class and/or middle-aged. White, middle-class, middle-aged men have dominated the reading of biblical texts to the virtual exclusion of others whose readings have been regarded as marginal or deviant. On the other hand, even when women become readers of the bible, they find biblical texts more disturbing because of the distribution of power in the text's "pre-text," the historical, biographical, and ideological reality from which the text emerges (1989:14, 16). For Bal, neither the text nor the reader is innocent.

Holding both the text and the reader accountable for meaning, as Bal attempts to do, would appear to be a very useful political strategy for feminists to adopt when dealing with the bible. Holding the text accountable will allow us to understand the multiple ways it has promoted and continues to promote the denigration and oppression of women. Holding the reader accountable will help us ensure that "normativity" of white, middle-class, middle-aged, male interpretations no longer goes unchallenged.

The following examination of the book of Judith, and in particular of its central female character, attempts to adopt a politicized feminist stance which holds both reader and text accountable for meaning. It does so by first assessing recent studies of the narrative character, Judith, in light of the concept of feminism and sexual politics espoused by the reader/interpreter. It then moves to the text and asks what expectations are created for the reader by the genre of the story, and how these expectations affect the degree to which Judith can be expected to function in a positive way for women.

THE BOOK OF JUDITH IN RECENT FEMINIST INTERPRETATION

The book of Judith is generally dated to the last third of the second century BCE and is thought to have been written by a Palestinian Jew, probably a Pharisee. For a variety of reasons, it was included in the Septuagint but not in the Hebrew canon (Moore, 1985:67-71; 86-93). A central motif in this apocryphal text, the killing of an enemy general by a woman, seems to have been modeled on parts of the Jael and Deborah stories in Judges 4-5 (White).

The story has a literary setting several hundred years earlier than its date of composition. It takes place in the time of Nebuchadnezzar who is depicted as the king of Assyria, not of Babylon. This, and numerous other historically inaccurate details, led most scholars since the Reformation to read Judith as a fictional story, not as an historical record.

As a story, the book of Judith is quite good, having high drama, intrigue, suspense, and a lot of sexual innuendo. The character, Judith, who is regarded by most interpreters as the story's heroine, does not make an appearance until chapter 8, half way through the book. She enters the story at a crucial point when the people of her town, Bethulia, are about to surrender to the Assyrian forces led by Holofernes. Judith, a pious, beautiful and religiously observant widow, convinces the town officials not to surrender until she has had an opportunity to work on the problem. On the pretense of wanting to assist the Assyrians, Judith is able to infiltrate the enemy camp. She wins the confidence of the general who is captivated by her beauty and intends to sexually seduce her. Judith avoids falling prey to Holofernes' seduction, decapitates him while he is in a drunken stupor and safely returns to Bethulia. The demise of their leader causes panic to spread among the Assyrian forces with the result that the Israelites are able to attack and destroy them.

The obviously dangerous and daring role played by Judith in delivering Israel from the threat of annihilation has drawn the attention of many feminist and pro-feminist analysts interested in the depiction of women in the biblical tradition. What I find particularly noteworthy is the diversity to be found in their assessments of the character of Judith with respect to whether she represents a positive or negative depiction of, and model for, women. Some find in the story as a whole, and in the character of Judith, very positive, strongly feminist elements; others are positively disposed to the story but are more cautious about the extent to which they would identify feminist elements; still others find the story not only not feminist but dangerously patriarchal, and Judith a classic *femme fatale*, not a feminist heroine.

The two most positive assessments of Judith come from George Nickelsburg and Carey Moore. Both men have described Judith as a feminist heroine in a feminist story. The strongest statement is from Nickelsburg who concluded that:

> The book of Judith is especially striking for its feminism. In creating a protagonist the author has chosen a woman, who calls to mind the Israelite heroines of the past - Judith - "the Jewess." As the narrative unfolds, Judith is

consistently depicted as superior to the men with whom she is associated: Uzziah and the elders; the Assyrian army and their general (108).

Nickelsburg concedes that "some passages seem to be saying that God's power is operative through the weakest of human agents, that is, a woman," and that her "use of deceit and specifically of her sexuality may seem offensive and chauvinistic," but contends that for the author of Judith it is just the opposite (108).

In a similar vein, Carey Moore, in his major commentary on the text (1985), has a section entitled, "The Heroine's Character." Two thirds of this are devoted to a review of interpretations of Judith, ranging from early fathers of the church to moralists of Victorian England. He demonstrates that the Judith character has always given rise to divergent, even conflicting assessments. Clement of Rome, for example, praised Judith as a brave and godly woman, while men like Tertullian and Ambrose were impressed by her self-imposed celibacy. "Clearly," Moore writes, "Judith was their type of woman." But it was a different matter for the values and priorities of Victorian England. Moore quotes Edwin Bissell's views that Judith's character is not simply objectionable from a literary point of view, but even more so from a moral standpoint. "Clearly," Moore writes, "Judith was not Bissell's kind of lady" (1985:64-65).

Moore's own view is that the book of Judith takes a "pro-feminist stance" and this may provide a partial explanation for the work's exclusion from the canon by men who found it too radical (1992:65). In support of this, Moore quotes approvingly from Patricia Montley who regards Judith as the archetypal androgyne who embodies, yet somehow transcends, the male/female dichotomy. According to Moore, what makes Judith's androgyny so unusual and fascinating is that her:

> "masculinity" and "feminity" [sic] are sequential rather than simultaneous. That is, as a widow she is asexual; in Bethulia with the elders, Judith plays the man; in the Assyrian camp, she acts the woman until she resumes her manly role by cutting off Holofernes' head; then back in Bethulia she continues to act the man until the defeat of the Assyrian army, after which she reverts permanently to the asexuality of her widowhood (1985:65).

Moore concludes, again quoting Montley, that Judith is "the feminist's kind of person," because she is "a heroine who rises above the sexism of her author's culture" (1985:65).

Nickelsburg and Moore are not known as feminist scholars, though both may endeavour to incorporate the results of feminist scholarship in their work, but Elisabeth Schüssler Fiorenza is a leading feminist biblical scholar. She, too, views Judith in a very positive light and quotes approvingly the passage by Nickelsburg cited above. According to Fiorenza, the book is an heroic biography built on feminist irony which highlights

Judith's guileful remarks, her enticing beauty, and her treacherous planning. Judith, herself, is "a woman who fights with a woman's weapons, yet far from being defined by her 'femininity,' she uses it to her own ends" (117).

A somewhat more reserved, but nonetheless positive assessment of this story, can be found in the writings of scholars such as John Craghan and Toni Craven. While not arguing that Judith is either a feminist heroine or a feminist's heroine, they argue that there are at least elements in the story and/or the character of Judith that may be viewed positively by feminists.

For Craghan, Judith (along with Esther and Ruth) provides us with a paradigm for human liberation (1982a). Liberation in the book of Judith, he claims, means the de-deification of Nebuchadnezzar, accomplished by Judith, a female warrior. Judith "sets out to rescue the male, using the most effective weapon, viz., beauty" (1982a:13).[1] The sexual element is more pronounced in the Judith story than in either Esther or Ruth. Craghan argues, however, that even in Judith the sexual element is not there for its own sake but rather is subsumed under the category of liberation. "In Judith," he writes, "the sexual element is so pronounced because it is *the* military weapon" (1982a:17). In his concluding comments, Craghan develops this theme of sexual violence further. He says that:

> Even as a guest, one can be and is expected to employ violence. In terms of sexual qualities they must be exploited to the full since they are the weapons par excellence (1982a:18).

Toni Craven's primary interest is in the rhetorical structure of the book of Judith, and her major contribution was to show the structural unity and intricate literary design of the text. But, as a feminist, Craven is also interested in the image of woman projected by the character, Judith. Like Moore, she thinks at least one reason for the book's exclusion from the canon was the radicalness of its central female character. She speculates that, had the gender of Judith and Achior been reversed, the book would have had a much better chance of being included in the Hebrew canon. However, despite the fact that her own study of Judith has identified occasional breaks with patriarchy in the story, she concludes that it would be groundless to suggest that the author was an ancient feminist and she does not even raise the possibility that Judith could be considered a feminist character (117, 121-22).

The work of Amy-Jill Levine moves another step away from identifying Judith as a feminist heroine. Levine still identifies Judith as a heroine

---

[1] It is not clear whether the male to which Craghan refers is the male deity, Yahweh, or the male community, Israel. I think it is the latter.

but her Judith is far from a feminist heroine. She agrees with commentators who see Judith as a metaphor for the community of Israel, pointing out that elsewhere Israel is metaphorically represented by female figures such as the bride, the whore, and the widow. With her name meaning "Jewess" and her status as a widow, Judith seems to be a classic metaphor for the community. As the only named female character, she speaks and acts in the public sphere, and seems to relativize the normative cultural constructions of the community, especially the construction of the role of women within it.

But, as woman, Judith remains Other, both to the male-defined world and to women within it. Her very public activity creates a crisis in the world of Israelite patriarchy. According to Levine, Judith:

> . . . endangers hierarchical oppositions of gender, race, and class, muddles conventional gender characteristics and dismantles their claim to universality, and so threatens the status quo (17).

Judith, she claims, "transforms the social roles of the Israelite women" who "like the sword-brandishing (13:6-8) and head-bearing (13:15) Judith, become both graphically and by their actions phallic women" (24).

To alleviate this crisis for patriarchy Judith must be reinscribed into the androcentric norm. By the end of the story this has happened. Levine shows how the narrative, in its final form, constrains, contains, domesticates Judith and renders her kosher. Judith represents Israel, but only incompletely. Her role as protector-avenger is a male role according to Israelite social norms and she makes this clear by identifying with her male ancestor, Simeon, in her reference to the story of the rape of Dinah in Genesis 34 (Jdt 9:2-4). This, according to Levine, renders her unable to represent Israel fully and certainly unable to represent Israelite women. "Were Judith fully to embody Israel," she argues, "then the traditional representation of the deity as the (male) savior of the female-figured community would be challenged. Were all women to be like Judith, not only Holofernes would lose his head" (19).

Through this separation of Judith from corporate Israel and from Jewish women, Levine argues, the "text's patriarchal ethos" is preserved. Judith is returned to female normalcy through such moves as her return to the private sphere and resumption of the traditional wife/widow role, her submission to priestly ministrations and the relinquishing of her Assyrian booty (19, 26-28).

Before moving on to the next step in feminist analysis, we can reflect on the important change which has taken place in the years between Nickelsburg and Levine in the way the feminist question is addressed to this text. Nickelsburg's comment that the book is striking for its feminism assumes an understanding of feminism in which women are seen to be superior to men. Judith, he concludes, is consistently depicted as "superior" to the men with whom she is associated. While it is true that such an understanding may characterize some forms of feminism, it is by no means the case that it characterizes all, or even most, definitions. More typically, feminism is defined in feminist literature in ways which emphasize the human equality of women and men and the need to make this equality a reality in social, political, economic and religious realms. Furthermore, Nickelsburg seems to equate a few non-stereotypical female behaviours with feminism and interprets the stereotypical presentations of female deceitfulness and seductive sexuality as being virtual feminist tools.

Moore's interpretation is perhaps even more problematic than Nickelsburg's. One cannot really discern whether Judith is or is not Moore's kind of person. But, as was the case for Nickelsburg, we can know something about his understanding of feminism. For Moore, the book has a "pro-feminist" stance and Judith is a "feminist's kind of person" because she is not really a woman but an "archetypal androgyne" who transcends masculinity and femininity, who begins and ends as an asexual and who merely "plays" or "acts" male and female roles in between. Whereas Nickelsburg might have found some support for his underlying notion of feminism as female ascendancy, Moore would be harder pressed to find any feminist theoretical support for his view which seems to negate femaleness completely.

Needless to say, I am troubled by these views, both because of the assumptions they make about feminism and because of the conclusions they reach about what constitutes feminist writing and a feminist character. Fiorenza's position is, therefore, also problematic for me, insofar as she accepts Nickelsburg's analysis. Beyond this, however, she appears to accept uncritically the idea that "femininity," "female beauty and behaviour" are a woman's weapons. She finds positive value in Judith's efforts to resist being "defined by her femininity" and circumscribed by her "female beauty and behavior." These qualities are contrasted with Judith's "intelligent wisdom, observant piety, shrewd observation and faithful dedication" which mark Judith's "real power." Fiorenza intends to show the irony which can result when men underestimate women, but in doing so she reinforces a hierarchical dualism which separates femininity from intelligence and associates femininity with deceitfulness. If feminist irony does exist here, it has been lost on centuries of interpreters who have been more prone to seeing the patriarchal glee of a powerful enemy brought low by a mere woman. Craghan, for example, links his presentation of Judith as a female warrior,[2] whose sexuality is a military weapon, with the idea that powerlessness is "God's most potent weapon" (1982a:18).

I begin to be more comfortable with Craven's discussion of Judith. Probably most women who attempt to be both feminists and biblical scholars have, at some time in their lives, hoped that some of the female characters in the biblical material would turn out to be feminist characters who provide positive images of and for women. But I agree with Craven that Judith is not, ultimately, a character who breaks the bounds of patriarchy. Personally, I would go much further than Craven to argue that we must not isolate fragments from this story and read them as feminist nuggets. By focusing on the occasional breaks in the boundaries of patriarchy we risk not seeing the price the female character might have to pay for such transgressions. Rather, we must carefully assess the impact of the whole book to determine what messages it conveys about women and femininity.

Levine's article has provided a solid beginning for an overall assessment of the Judith story. She has shown us how dangerously patriarchal the Judith narrative really is and how narrative control is exercised over the central female character so that she *cannot* be a feminist's kind of person. Her study helps us to see the censure exercised toward challenges to patriarchally defined female roles and modes of femininity. Although Levine herself does not pursue this line of analysis, she does move us away from the "quest for the feminist heroine" and toward a more critical feminist analysis of the whole text.

Betsy Merideth takes this kind of feminist analysis a step forward when she examines biblical representations of gender and the politics of sexuality in narratives about Delilah and Judith. Drawing upon the work of Mieke Bal, Merideth looks at how these two women characters use their sexuality to harm a man. She argues that, even though Judith is presented as clearly on the side of God and has the reader's sympathy, and even though commentators tend to overlook her use of sexual deceit to focus on her chastity and valuable contribution to saving the nation, we cannot assume that the story of Judith is a positive one for women. In Judith, beauty and deceit go together so that, at one level, the story inevitably carries the clear message that a "woman's beauty and sexuality are dangerous to men because women use their attractiveness to deceive, harm and kill men" (76). Even though Judith's behaviour has generally been interpreted positively by male interpreters, the story as a whole not only does not benefit women, it carries an anti-woman ideology, albeit

---

[2] The word "warrior" is read as a masculine form here in the same way as are words like "doctor" and "professor" when modified by the adjective, "female."

one sublimated and domesticated because, according to Merideth, Judith kills with the approval of her community (76).

I concur with Merideth's conclusions, except for her contention that Judith kills with the approval of her community. In fact, Judith receives the community approval for her deed only after she has done it (Jdt 13:20). Prior to that she has only the permission of Uzziah, the magistrates and elders to make an effort to deliver her town from the Assyrians (Jdt 8:32-35). I would argue that the anti-woman ideology is sublimated and domesticated by having Judith kill Holofernes as an instrument of the deity. This renders her action not only approved by, but subordinated to, the control of the male deity.

The importance of Merideth's comments on the use of beauty and sexuality, however, cannot be emphasized enough. In Judith, beauty and deceit are fashioned into a woman's weapon against men so successfully that she appears to some as a female warrior. While this may not be problematic for the character herself, it has serious consequences for the image of women it projects, and, hence, for the impact it has on women. A woman's sexuality and physical beauty are not external to her person but integral to it. Therefore, when a woman's beauty is observed by men, or when a woman expresses sexual interest in a man who has been thoroughly schooled in the dangers of the *femme fatale*, there is inevitable ambiguity, to the detriment of women.[3] In each and every instance a man must determine whether he is encountering a woman as a "woman" or a woman as a "female warrior."

Through the propaganda of the *femme fatale*/female warrior character, men are taught, above all, to fear women. The otherness of women is thereby emphasized and women become objects to be viewed suspiciously and trusted not at all.[4] Leonard Swidler, one of the first pro-feminist commentators on the text, highlighted the problematic nature of the image of woman projected by Judith in concluding that:

---

[3] The "female-warrior" text is not alone in making a problem out of women's beauty. In a discussion of wives in Genesis 10; 24; and 29, Ann Marmesh argues that not only must "a woman's kinship status be the right balance between incest and exogamy; she must also be beautiful; so beautiful that she would cause trouble for her husband. A woman's beauty thus becomes a negative quality; a deficit akin to barrenness" (51).

[4] The theme of woman as a danger to men is central to several other isolated texts, such as the story of Jael, Delilah, and Jezebel, as well as to the whole of the wisdom tradition from Proverbs to Ben Sira. An insightful presentation of the issue as it is expressed in Proverbs 1-9 has been given by Gale Yee. James Williams comments that Judith "captivates Holofernes and the Assyrians in a fashion reminiscent of the wisdom tradition's warnings against the beauty and wiles of the temptress, the 'alien woman'" (78).

> The moral of the Book of Judith is not that women are good creatures of God, but rather that God is so great that he can bring good out of evil; not that women are to be valued greatly, but rather that God is so great that he can humble Israel's enemies even through the lowliest of instruments, women— and the weapon women use against men, beguiling beauty and sex (114).

This theme has come to permeate Western culture, ironically obscuring the reality that men pose a much greater danger to women than women to men.

The Genre of the Judith Story and the Narrative Role of Judith

From the foregoing review it seems apparent that key assumptions about the nature of feminism and the politics of sexuality held by individual readers account in part for the diversity evident in scholarly assessments of the character, Judith. My own understanding of feminism differs greatly from that found in the works of Nickelsburg and Moore. It is one which insists on equity for women, while acknowledging women's concrete experience of oppression in a male-defined world. The ultimate goal of feminism, as I understand it, is to redefine and restructure society, and all its institutions, in ways which equitably reflect and sustain women's lives. I do not find the imagery of the *femme fatale* or the female warrior helpful in accomplishing this goal. For me, a feminist story would have to be one which promoted the equality of women, and a feminist character would have to be woman-centred and woman-defined.

When held accountable to this understanding of feminism, how does the story of Judith fare? The studies by Levine, Merideth, and Swidler implicitly assert that the text itself does not allow the possibility of regarding either Judith or her story as beneficial for women. In the space remaining I want to extend their feminist-critical work on characterization and sexual politics by examining how genre contributes to the construction of the story's anti-woman ideology.

The role of genre analysis in the hermeneutical process has been addressed cogently in the work of Mary Gerhart (1977, 1988, 1989). Gerhart argues that reading is always reading as genre. Thus genric[5] considerations are indispensable to the interpretation of texts. Since different genres give rise to different kinds of expectations, genric competence, that is the ability of readers to construct, identify, compare, test, retrieve, and critique genres, enables readers to render intelligible the

---

[5] The adjectival form "genric" is deliberately used rather than "generic" because the latter has come to connote non-specificity and commonalty. Gerhart uses "genric" to refer both to the taxonomic function of genre and to its productive function (1988:31, 41-42).

relationships between their experiences and the textual forms (1988; 1977:310, 312-314, 318).

The question of the genre of the book of Judith has been raised numerous times and many classification categories have been proposed. Beyond agreement that the story is fictional, however, no consensus has emerged. Carey Moore (1985:71-78) and Robert Doran (303) have summarized the proposals which include various types of apocalypse, novel and folktale. Both writers are inclined to think Judith is some form of folktale and both draw attention to the work of Mary P. Coote who classifies Judith as an epic rescue story, combining the folk motifs of the Faithful Wife/Widow and the Female Warrior. Moore prefers the classification "example story" to Coote's "epic rescue" while Doran simply notes that "one might quarrel with Coote's classification" without specifying an alternate suggestion. Doran seems to think that further exploration of the "traditional narrative qualities of the tale" is necessary before a more definitive classification can be made (Doran: 303).

The following analysis is an attempt to explore these traditional qualities and to evaluate Coote's suggestion that the book of Judith is a form of the epic genre. Coote's approach to genre classification is that of theme/motif analysis derived from western European folklore scholarship typified by the Finnish folklore school. This is the same approach to genre classification that influenced Hermann Gunkel and underlies biblical form criticism. In contrast to this, the approach adopted here will be based on an analysis of narrative surface structure. This approach is derived from the structuralist[6] work of the Russian folklorist, Vladimir Propp (Milne, 1988).

Propp sought to classify folktales on the basis of the smallest structural elements which remained constant in tales of the same type or genre (Milne, 1988:67-88). The two constant elements he isolated were "functions" and "roles." A function is an act of a tale role defined from the point of view of its significance for the course of the action (Propp: 21). Functions and roles are abstractions which must be "filled in" by concrete actions and characters. The role a character plays in a tale depends upon the functions she or he performs. The genre of a tale is determined by the particular set and sequence of functions and tale roles it employs.

Propp himself described the narrative structure of only one folktale type, the heroic fairy tale. His model of this genre contains thirty-one functions and seven tale roles. Others have developed narrative surface-structure models of different genres. Two such models relate to the epic genre, Aleksandr Skaftymov's model of the romantic epic and Heda

---

[6] Propp's opponents labelled his work "formalist," a designation he categorically rejected in favour of "structuralist" (Milne 1988: 26-29, 96-104).

Jason's model of the epic struggle (1981). If either of these models were able to describe or account for the structure of the Judith story, Coote's general epic classification would be corroborated, and a new perspective provided for a feminist assessment of the text.

JUDITH AS A ROMANTIC EPIC

Skaftymov's model of the romantic epic was a precursor of Propp's heroic fairy-tale model and is considerably less detailed. It has only three tale roles and just eight "episodes."[7] Six of the episodes may be identified in the Judith story, although not in the sequence outlined by Skaftymov. Judith 1:1-7:18 presents the attack of the Assyrian forces, moving from the general attack on uncooperative vassal states to the specific attack on the Israelite town of Bethulia. In Skaftymov's model, this could be described as episode 2, the enemy attacks. In the romantic epic, the enemy's strength is often presented as "superhuman" and in Judith there is repeated emphasis on the superhuman qualities of the Assryian king (Jdt 3:8) and on the immense power of the Assyrian forces (Jdt 2:11, 28; 4:2).

The dispirited and dejected response of the townspeople of Bethulia to the Assyrian threat (Jdt 7:19-32) corresponds to part of episode 3 in which the inhabitants and the ruler of a beleaguered city despair. But in Judith, only the inhabitants despair while the rulers still urge courage and confidence in God.

The introduction of Judith and the emphasis on her widowhood, a state which presumably increases the weakness she projects as a woman (Berg: 150; Moore, 1985:180), may constitute episode 1 in which the hero's initial weakness is described. In episode 4, the hero is called or arrives by chance to rescue the city. Judith takes up the challenge to "deliver Israel" in Jdt 8:9-9:14, but she neither arrives by chance nor is called. Furthermore, she does not present herself as the rescuer. Rather, it is the deity who will deliver Israel by her hand (Jdt 8:33; 9:7-14).

Judith 10:1-13:10, where Judith goes to the enemy camp and succeeds in killing Holofernes, may be described as episode 5 in which the hero sets out against the enemy and vanquishes him single-handedly. Again, however, this identification is weakened by repeated claims that it is the deity, not Judith, who is primarily responsible for killing Holofernes (Jdt 11:6, 16, 22; 12:4, 8; 13:4, 7). Similarly, episode 8, in which the ruler rewards the hero, might be identified in Jdt 15:8-16:18, but here, too, there is confusion about who is rewarded for the victory, Judith or the deity.

At least two episodes in the romantic epic model do not appear to be evident in the story of Judith. These are episodes 6 and 7 in which a victo-

---

7 Propp used the term "function" in place of the term "episode."

rious hero returns home but the populace does not believe that he has single-handedly vanquished the enemy. The hero must convince the populace that he has done so. In the Judith story, the townspeople of Bethulia are amazed when Judith returns with the severed head of Holofernes but they do not express any disbelief. In fact, they immediately bow down to worship their god, proclaiming their belief that he has mortified the enemy (Jdt 13:11-17).

Two of the three narrative roles in the romantic epic model can be filled easily and unambiguously with characters from the Judith story. The role of hero's adversary is played by the Assyrians, Nebuchadnezzar, Holofernes and his army, while the background roles are played by Uzziah, the elders and townspeople of Bethulia, Judith's maid, Manasseh, Joakim and the Israelite Council from Jerusalem.

It is more difficult to fill the hero role. At first glance, it appears Judith is the hero since she is the one who actually carries out the actions that lead to the defeat of the adversary. But she does not perform other functions ascribed to the hero, such as in episodes 6 and 7. Even when she does appear to perform the hero function, Judith claims not to, giving credit instead to the deity (Jdt 9:7-14; 11:6, 16, 22; 12:4, 8; 13:4-7; 16:1-8). The people, too, credit the deity with the victory (Jdt 13:17-19; 14:10). Given that the Assyrian king, Nebuchadnezzar, claims deity status for himself and that the ultimate military goal of the Assyrian army is to force all nations to worship their king as god (Jdt 3:8), the main adversarial relationship appears to be between Nebuchadnezzar and the god of Israel. The deity, therefore, seems to fill the hero role better than Judith. If the deity is considered the hero, there is no suitable role left for Judith.

While the romantic epic model is useful for describing some aspects of the Judith story, it is not able to account well for the whole tale. Hence it seems unlikely that Judith belongs to the romantic epic genre, though it does exhibit some similarities to this literary type.

JUDITH AS AN EPIC STRUGGLE

Heda Jason's model of the epic struggle genre is much more complex than Skaftymov's and closer to Propp's in its design. It has nine roles and twenty-two narrative functions.[8] It is a model which accounts for three

---

[8] Narrative Roles: 1.1 Hero; 1.2 Hero's community; 1.3 Messenger A (community's messenger); 1.4 Helper A (hero's helper in battle); 1.5 Helper B (helper-seducer on behalf of the hero); 1.6 Messenger B (hero's messenger); 2.1 Adversary; 2.2 Creator of Adversary; 2.3 Adversary's following.

Narrative Functions: 1 Creation of monster; 2 Mission of monster; 3 Initiative; 4 Demand for surrender; 5 Response to demand for surrender; 6 Summoning; 7 Proposal for struggle; 8 Advice; 9 Response to advice; 10 Mission of seduction; 11

forms of epic struggle, namely, cosmic struggles, struggles against monsters and human struggles. Therefore, not all functions will be relevant to any one form (Jason, 1981:55).

The core of the model is a struggle between a hero and an adversary. The struggle is often fought in two stages. In the first stage, the hero may lose to his adversary and then summon a weaker helper. One of the forms specifically mentioned by Jason has a male deity using the help of a female deity or human being. In the second stage, the adversary is overcome in a decisive battle with a helper's assistance (Jason, 1981:47-48).

The general plot outline of Judith would appear to be amenable to an analysis using this model. If it is an epic struggle, it is one in the human, not the cosmic or monster, realm. Thus, functions 1 and 2, which involve a monster, will not be found. Function 3, initiative, is the first to occur. In this function, the adversary takes the initiative for a clash with the hero. This occurs in Jdt 2:1-3:9 when Nebuchadnezzar takes the decision to avenge those who refused to assist him in his war against the Medes. He commissions Holofernes who sets out on a campaign against the western region to make every dialect and tribe call Nebuchadnezzar god. Function 4, demand for surrender, is not made explicit here but may be implicit in Jdt 2:10 and 2:21-3:9.

At the beginning of chap. 4, the Israelites learn of the horrors committed by the advancing Assyrian army, especially the sacking and destroying of sanctuaries (Jdt 4:1). The Israelites, fearing both for Jerusalem and for the Temple of their god (Jdt 4:2), prepare to resist the Assyrians (Jdt 4:4-15). This may be described as function 5, the response to the demand for surrender. The Israelite resistance is of two kinds: military and religious. As part of their religious preparation, they beg the deity to protect them. This section, Jdt 4:8-14, could be described in terms of Jason's functions 6, 8 and 9. Function 6, summoning, has messenger A summon the hero and/or the community. Here Joakim and the Council summon the community which, in turn, advises the hero to oppose the adversary, function 8. Function 9 occurs when the hero accepts the advice of the community to oppose the adversary. This function can be identified in 4:13 when the deity responds positively to the people's prayer. Function 8 may be repeated in Jdt 6:18-21, where the community of Bethulia urges the deity to oppose the adversary.

When Holofernes moves against Bethulia in Jdt 7, functions 3, 4 and 5 are repeated. This time the response to the crisis is both negative and positive: the people want to surrender (Jdt 7:23-28) but Uzziah wants to

---

Attempt at seduction; 12 Seduction; 13 Preparation for encounter; 14 First encounter; 15 Defeat; 16 Council; 17 Search for help; 18 Cry for help; 19 Help 20 Second encounter; 21 Victory; 22 Triumph.

resist a little longer (Jdt 7:30). Function 6 is repeated when Judith sends her maid to summon the three town elders (Jdt 8:10) and function 5 is repeated when she urges continued resistance (Jdt 8:11-17, 33).

In function 10, the community sends helper B, the helper-seducer, to seduce the adversary. This seems to occur when Judith volunteers her help and the elders accept her offer, though they are not aware of the particular means by which Judith will help (Jdt 8:32-35). This is made clear only in chap. 9 and only to the reader, not to the community. In chap. 10, Judith prepares for her mission of seduction, while in chaps. 11 and 12 she actually sets out upon it. Function 11, attempt at seduction, seems appropriately applied to chapters 10-12.

Holofernes succumbs to the seduction, function 12, in Jdt 12:16-13:4 and this leaves him vulnerable to a fatal attack by the hero through the hand of the helper, Judith. At this moment Judith again recalls that it is the deity who is about to use her hands to defeat the adversary (Jdt 13:4-5). Then she moves to attack Holofernes (Jdt 13:6-7). This can be both function 14, the first encounter between the hero and the adversary, and function 19, the helper extends help to the hero. In Jdt 13:8-10 the hero and helper overcome the adversary when Holofernes is decapitated and his head carried back to Bethulia. This is function 21, victory. The final function, 22, triumph, occurs in Jdt 13:14-20 when all the people bow down to worship their god, recognizing that he has defeated the enemy.

In the remaining chapters, functions 18-22 are repeated as Judith summons the men of Bethulia to help (Jdt 14:1-4), they take up arms (Jdt 14:11), attack and defeat the Assyrian army (Jdt 15:1-7), and celebrate the deity's victory in worship (Jdt 16:1-18). The Israelite men here fill the role of hero's helper in battle, helper A.

Jason's epic struggle model appears to account well for the plot structure in the Judith tale. The struggle revolves around the issue of who is god, the lord of Assyria or the lord of Israel. This issue is introduced in Jdt 3:8 and repeated frequently through the story (e.g., Jdt 5:21; 6:11-21; 8:20; 13:17, 19; 14:10; 16:1-18). Jason's model also accounts well for the characters in the story, particularly for the deity and Judith. On the basis of this narrative surface structural analysis, therefore, the Judith story appears to resemble strongly the epic struggle genre.

CONTRIBUTION TO A FEMINIST ANALYSIS

Understanding the roles individual characters play in the epic struggle genre provides us with another perspective from which to hold the text accountable with respect to the feminist or patriarchal meaning possibilities it promotes.

The application of both Skaftymov's and Jason's epic models to the text produced problems in assigning Judith the narrative role of hero. Using either model, the hero role was more easily assigned to the deity. This left Judith without a suitable role in the romantic epic genre but in the epic struggle genre her actions related closely to the functions performed by the helper-seducer role.[9]

In the epic struggle genre, Judith is a central character whose actions are crucial to the plot action. But her narrative role is that of helper, not of hero. Separating the centrality of her actions from the role she plays allows for a more precise feminist critique. Being central to the plot is no guarantee that a female character's role will be woman-centred and woman-serving. Casting Judith in the role of helper-seducer, serving the interests of the male characters, is one of the effective literary devices through which the text's anti-woman ideology (Merideth: 76) is communicated.

Even though Judith may act in some atypical ways, she is not a counter-cultural character, but remains very much a man's woman. Her name may call to mind the Israelite "heroines" of the past (Nickelsburg: 108), but Judith herself calls Israelite heroes to mind. She repeatedly identifies with male models like Abraham, Isaac, Jacob (Jdt 8:26), and Simeon (Jdt 9:2-4). More than this, however, she identifies *against* female characters when she ignores the plight of Dinah and the Shechemite women who are victims of rape and when she eradicates their individual identities (Jdt 9:2-4) (Levine: 18-19).[10] In short, the text presents Judith as the very antithesis of a woman-identified woman. Unlike our modern Judith at the dinner table, the character Judith in no way undercuts the gender division through her identification with male characters.

Moreover, as a "helper" (Clines: 27-32) the Judith character effectively reinforces the patriarchal ideology that women are inferior and secondary by repeatedly making self-effacing, even self-denigrating, statements. Not only does she attribute all her success to the deity, as has been noted in the structural analysis, but she makes a point of emphasizing the negative attitudes held by her Israelite/Jewish society toward women. In Jdt 9:9-10 she, not the narrator, draws attention to the added ignominy of being defeated by a woman. Lest the point be lost, it is repeated in Jdt 13:15 and

---

[9] Coote had also assigned the hero role to male characters, the deity and the men of Israel, while Judith was assigned the role of female warrior who rescues the social group (23-25).

[10] Moore suggests Judith speaks approvingly of Simeon's act because she found herself in a position analogous to Dinah's, namely, concerned about being raped. But her lack of concern for the Shechemite women seems to support Freedman's view that she is concerned not about being raped, but about killing Holofernes (Moore, 1985: 190-191).

16:5. In these places she describes herself not as *gunē*, "woman," but as *thēleia*, "female," a term which Moore points out is less honorific and can be applied to animals as well as humans (Moore, 1985:193, 232, 248). Along with this, Judith portrays her strategy against the enemy not in terms simply of clever outwitting but specifically in sexual terms with negative connotations: she uses the guile of her lips (Jdt 9:10), a beguiling tongue (literally, "a word and a deceit") (Jdt 9:13), her face to trick (Jdt 13:16), and her dress to beguile (Jdt 16:8).

In short, Judith is presented and, as a narrative character, presents herself virtually completely from a male, patriarchal perspective. She is a pious helpmate to the male deity who uses her as a female instrument to defeat the enemy forces. This female instrument chooses to use her beauty and wiles, a potential danger to all men, only against non-Israelite men. Among Israelite men she remains the model of male-defined sexual propriety. Judith is a character who does heroic deeds, but she does so in the role of the hero's helper and she does so in a way that represents the projection of a patriarchal stereotyped idea of a woman's dangerous sexual power. Because of this, she is a highly ambiguous character. On the one hand, the very fact that she is atypically active for a female biblical character leads some to see her as a feminist's kind of person. On the other hand, however, her very action is rooted in the dynamics of men's fear of women's sexuality and in the gender hierarchy that adds insult to the Assyrian injury.

So what *shall* we do with Judith? I would suggest that feminist readers reject any suggestion that she is a feminist heroine or a feminist's heroine. As a character Judith is, instead, a seductive helper who effectively promotes gynophobia, not equity, in a patriarchal narrative. Though she plays an important literary role in an epic struggle to liberate her people from the Assyrians, Judith liberates neither herself nor her countrywomen from the status quo of the biblical gender ideology.

WORKS CONSULTED

Alonso-Schökel, Luis
    1975   "Narrative Structures in the Book of Judith." Pp. 1-20 in *Protocol of the Eleventh Colloquy: 27 January 1974, The Center for Hermeneutical Studies in Hellenistic and Modern Culture*. Ed. Wilhelm Wuellner. Berkeley, CA: The Centre for Hermeneutical Studies in Hellenistic and Modern Culture.

Alphen, Ernst van
    1988   *Bij wijze van lezen: Verleiding en verzet van Willem Brakmans lezer*. Muiderberg: Coutinho.

Bal, Mieke
    1989   "Introduction." Pp. 11-24 in *Anti-Covenant: Counter-Reading Women's Lives in the Hebrew Bible*. Ed. Mieke Bal. Sheffield: Almond.

Banner, Lois W.
    1980   *Elizabeth Cady Stanton: A Radical for Woman's Rights*. Boston: Little, Brown and Company.

Bass, Dorothy C.
    1982   "Women's Studies and Biblical Studies: An Historical Perspective." *JSOT* 22:3-5.

Berg, Sandra
    1979   *The Book of Esther: Motifs, Themes and Structure*. Missoula: Scholars.

Clines, David
    1990   "What Does Eve Do to Help? and Other Irredeemably Androcentric Orientations in Genesis 1-2." Pp. 25-48 in *What Does Eve Do to Help? and Other Readerly Questions to the Old Testament*. Sheffield: Sheffield Academic.

Coote, Mary P.
    1975   "Response." Pp. 21-26 in *Protocol of the Eleventh Colloquy: 27 January 1974, The Center for Hermeneutical Studies in Hellenistic and Modern Culture*. Ed. Wilhelm Wuellner. Berkeley, CA: The Centre for Hermeneutical Studies in Hellenistic and Modern Culture.

Craghan, John
    1982a   "Esther, Judith, and Ruth: Paradigms for Human Liberation." *BTB* 12:11-19.
    1982b   "Judith Revisited." *BTB* 12:50-53.

Craven, Toni
    1983   *Artistry and Faith in the Book of Judith*. SBLDS 70. Chico, CA: Scholars.

Doran, Robert
1986 "Narrative Literature." Pp. 287-310 in *Early Judaism and Its Modern Interpreters*. Ed. Robert Kraft and George Nickelsburg. Atlanta, GA: Scholars.

Fuchs, Esther
1985 "The Literary Characterization of Mothers and Sexual Politics in the Hebrew Bible." Pp. 117-136 in *Feminist Perspectives on Biblical Scholarship*. Ed. Adele Yarbro Collins. Chico, CA: Scholars.
1988 "'For I Have the Way of Women': Deception, Gender and Ideology in Biblical Narrative." *Semeia* 42:68-83.
1989 "Marginalization, Ambiguity, Silencing: The Story of Jephthah's Daughter." *JFSR* 5:35-45.

Gage, Matilda J.
1980 *Woman, Church and State*. Reprint edition. Watertown, MA: Persephone.

Gerhart, Mary
1977 "Generic Studies: Their Renewed Importance in Religious and Literary Interpretations." *JAAR* 45:309-325.
1988 "Genric Competence in Biblical Hermeneutics." *Semeia* 43:29-44.
1989 "The Restoration of Biblical Narrative." *Semeia* 46:13-29.

Gifford, Carolyn De Swarte
1985 "American Women and the Bible: The Nature of Woman as a Hermeneutical Issue." Pp. 11-33 in *Feminist Perspectives on Biblical Scholarship*. Ed. Adele Yarbro Collins. Chico, CA: Scholars.

Gurko, Miriam
1976 *The Ladies of Seneca Falls: The Birth of the Woman's Rights Movement*. New York: Schocken.

Jason, Heda
1981 "Ilja of Murom and Tzar Kalin: A Proposal for A Model for the Narrative Structure of An Epic Struggle." Pp. 47-55 in *Slavica Hierosolymitana: Slavic Studies of the Hebrew University*. Ed. L Fleishman, O. Romen, and D. Segal. Jerusalem: Magnes.
1982 *The Fairy Tale of the Active Heroine: A Model of the Female Fairy Tale*. Jerusalem: The Israel Ethnographic Society.

Levine, Amy-Jill
1992 "Sacrifice and Salvation: Otherness and Domestication in the Book of Judith." Pp. 17-30 in *"No One Spoke Ill of Her": Essays on Judith*. Ed. James C. VanderKam. Early Judaism and Its Literature 2. Atlanta: Scholars.

Marmesh, Anne
1989 "Anti-Covenant." Pp. 43-60 in *Anti-Covenant: Counter-Reading Women's Lives in the Hebrew Bible*. Ed. Mieke Bal. Sheffield: Almond.

Merideth, Betsy
1989 "Desire and Danger: The Drama of Betrayal in Judges and Judith." Pp. 63-78 in *Anti-Covenant: Counter-Reading Women's Lives in the Hebrew Bible*. Ed. Mieke Bal. Sheffield: Almond.

Milne, Pamela J.
   1986   "Folktales and Fairy Tales: An Evaluation of Two Proppian Analyses." *JSOT* 34:35-60.
   1988   *Vladimir Propp and the Study of Structure in Hebrew Biblical Narrative.* Sheffield: Sheffield Academic.

Moore, Carey A.
   1985   *Judith: A New Translation with Introduction and Commentary.* AB 40. New York: Doubleday.
   1992   "Why Wasn't the Book of Judith Included in the Hebrew Bible?" Pp. 61-71 in *"No One Spoke Ill of Her": Essays on Judith.* Ed. James C. VanderKam. Early Judaism and Its Literature 2. Atlanta: Scholars.

Nickelsburg, George
   1981   *Jewish Literature Between the Bible and the Mishnah.* Philadelphia: Fortress.

Propp, Vladimir
   1968   *Morphology of the Folktale.* Austin: University of Texas Press.

Stanton, Elizabeth Cady and the Revising Committee
   1974   *The Woman's Bible.* Reprint edition. Seattle, WA: Coalition Task Force on Women and Religion.

Swidler, Leonard
   1979   *Biblical Affirmations of Woman.* Philadelphia: Westminster.

Trible, Phyllis
   1973   "Depatriarchalizing in Biblical Interpretation." *JAAR* 41:30-48.
   1978   *God and the Rhetoric of Sexuality.* Philadelphia: Fortress.
   1979   "Eve and Adam: Genesis 2-3 Reread." Pp. 74-83 in *Womanspirit Rising: A Feminist Reader in Religion.* Ed. Carol Christ and Judith Plaskow. New York: Harper and Row.
   1984   *Texts of Terror.* Philadelphia: Fortress.

White, Sidnie Anne
   1992   "In the Steps of Jael and Deborah: Judith as Heroine." Pp. 5-16 in *"No One Spoke Ill of Her": Essays on Judith.* Ed. James C. VanderKam. Early Judaism and Its Literature 2. Atlanta: Scholars.

Williams, James G.
   1982   *Women Recounted: Narrative Thinking and the God of Israel.* Sheffield: Almond.

Yee, Gale
   1989   "'I Have Perfumed My Bed with Myrrh': The Foreign Woman (ʾiššâ zārâ) in Proverbs 1-9." *JSOT* 43: 53-68.

Textual Constraints, Ordinary Readings, and Critical Exegeses: An Androcritical Perspective

Daniel Patte
Vanderbilt University

Critical production will risk developing in any direction at all and authorize itself to say almost anything. But this indispensable guard-rail has always only protected, it has never *opened* a reading." (Derrida:158)

ABSTRACT

This article examines the issue of textual determinacy from a male European-American perspective at once interested and critical. A dissolution of the subject/object dichotomy is proposed as a prerequisite to a new understanding and practice of textual interpretation. In search of a practice which would exhibit a dialectical understanding of subject and object and affirm the role of the ordinary reading in critical interpretation, the text of Matt 8:17 is presented as a case study, and several contradictory but equally legitimate readings of that text are examined.

An Androcritical Perspective on "Textual Determinacy"

The topic, "textual determinacy," is here considered from an *androcritical* perspective. As a male European-American exegete, I want to affirm the importance of acknowledging the role of textual constraints in the interpretation process, for two interrelated reasons: (1) an "interested" reason: without such an acknowledgement, critical exegesis would become impossible—something which would be a significant loss for me and other European-American males who have devoted our lives to the task of critical exegesis, because of our convictions that the performance of this task is beneficial to many; and (2) a "critical" reason: there is sufficient legitimate evidence to argue that textual constraints (plural!) play a determinative role in the process of interpretation; this affirmation is at least as plausible as alternate ones.

My argument in favor of stressing "textual determinacy"—and thus the a-contextual regulating role which a given text plays in its readings whatever might be the situation—is therefore contextual, and not universal. This is not a paradox! It is an effort to maintain in a dialectical tension two components of the process of critical interpretation: its interested, contextual character and its critical character. In the process, we have to acknowledge with Derrida that while "critical production" (or exegesis) has an important function, "it has never *opened* a reading," as ordinary readings do. Part of the problem with failing to maintain the dialectical tension mentioned above is that we misconceive the relationship between critical and ordinary readings, and as a consequence betray our vocation as critical exegetes.

My treatment of this topic is "interested" in that it reflects certain concerns of a specific interpretive community—that of *"andro's,"* i.e., male European-American exegetes. In brief, critical exegesis and its teaching are for us a vocation "for others" (in the service of others), because uncritical interpretations of the Bible, even though they might seem benign, soon become dangerous obscurantist interpretations that are destructive both for those who hold them and for those around them. Thus, practicing critical exegesis is an ethical responsibility and vocation which establishes our identity (our *ethos*) as critical scholars. Preserving and sustaining the possibility of carrying out this vocation is preserving and sustaining our community of male European-American critical exegetes and its perception of the seriousness of the problem posed by obscurantist readings of the Bible. In addition, for us, practicing critical exegesis is serving a broader community (including churches) in which, for better or for worse, European-American males are in positions of leadership; our exegetical practices are performed with the hope of transforming our broader community by helping to free it from its obscurantism. In sum, my argument is molded by my interests and concerns as a member of diverse interpretive communities in which European-American males play a significant role. By affirming the role of my interpretive community, I invoke Fish (1980) and further locate myself on the side of reader-response, poststructuralist, and postmodern critics (as well as of certain liberation critics).

Nevertheless, this inquiry also seeks to be *critical* (andro-*critical*), in two different senses. First, I consider the phenomenon "interpretation process" and its features (e.g., textual constraints) as an object to be critically studied by constructing and verifying a theoretical model of it as a universal phenomenon. This semiotic "critical" investigation (to which I simply allude here; it follows semioticians, and especially Greimas and Courtés, 1978, Eng. 1982) seeks to establish a theoretical basis for a set of critical methods and procedures to be used in exegetical studies. Second, my reflections are an exercise in self-criticism; they are "critical" of any male European-American exegetical discourses which do not acknowledge their "andro" character. Thus, I acknowledge that my theoretical model of the universal phenomenon of interpretation, a semiotic model, is itself culturally-bound and, consciously or not, developed for the sake of my group. This theoretical model is important for me (us), because it provides a basis for interpretive practices, aimed at addressing issues that are of particular concern for male European-American exegetes in the present pluralistic situation.

Overcoming The Subject/Object Dichotomy as an Ethical Imperative

These introductory statements have many implications for envisioning our practices and our ethical responsibility as critical exegetes. Thus, it is important that these statements be perceived as clear and sensible, a perception which depends in part upon the perspective from which they are read. I know that my affirmation—according to which the importance of textual constraints is to be acknowledged because of the interested character of critical exegeses—will be viewed as confused or even as self-contradictory, as long as one considers *the subject/object relation to be a dichotomy*: an interpretation is *either* subjective *or* objective; one gives a marked priority *either* to the role of readers (as reader-response, post-structural, and postmodern critics do) *or* to the role of texts and their constraints (as most other critics do by offering "objective" descriptions of the text and its features or of its historical or literary context). Yet, my opening statements make sense when one considers *the subject/object relation to be a dialectic*: a critical interpretation is *both* subjective *and* objective;[1] *both* interested *and* critical; *both* a reflection of the readers' interests, concerns, and contexts, *and* a submission to textual constraints.

Of course, this dialectical view is nothing new. It is already implied in Troelsch's principle of criticism according to which a (historical) critical judgment can only claim a higher degree of probability than other judgments (see Troeltsch 1914; Harvey:14-15), and is reinforced by the acknowledgment that any methodological theory is culturally-bound (e.g., Harvey:68-101; Patte 1990:1-17), as the history of scholarship exemplifies. This dialectical view is further acknowledged when the polysemy of texts and the legitimacy of a plurality of critical methodologies are affirmed—this twofold affirmation, first made in the context of parable studies (see Tolbert:1978, and her bibliography), applies to the study of any text. Thus, in the present age of methodological pluralism, we should

---

[1] The alternative complex category, neither subjective nor objective, is also plausible. I do not adopt it, because it is in total discontinuity with traditional exegetical practices.

readily respect "the dialectics between the rights of texts and the rights of their interpreters" (Eco, 1991:6). Yet, we often betray it, by overstressing one or the other of its poles. A costly betrayal, which vitiates our exegetical practices.

The dichotomous view of the subject/object relation has such a power upon us that, *in our practices*, we commonly contrast "subjective" uncritical readings with our "objective" critical exegeses. Of course, we theoretically know (following hermeneuticians such as Heidegger, Gadamer, and Ricoeur) that our critical exegeses necessarily reflect the hermeneutical circles in which we are caught and are therefore *both* subjective *and* objective (the dialectical view). Nevertheless, *in practice*, I and many of my colleagues deny the male European-American character of our critical exegeses, explicitly or implicitly positing them as authoritative descriptions of significant features of the text that should be "universally" acknowledged; our critical exegeses are objective and not subjective (the dichotomous view). We do so by overstressing the "rights of texts" and textual constraints (including constraints arising from the historical context of the text). For instance, we affirm at the outset of a critical study that certain significant features of the text, which drastically limit the field of possible legitimate interpretations, have been definitively established by (male European-American) scholarship and thus must be universally recognized as characteristics of the text which must be the basis of any legitimate interpretation. (The first sentence of Strecker [1988] is typical: "No proper exegesis of the Sermon on the Mount can ignore the results of more than two hundred years of historical-critical research into the New Testament"). Furthermore, we conceive of our critical exegetical work as an attempt to continue this scholarly work by seeking to demonstrate that other such features of the text should be (*universally!*) recognized as characteristics of the text which must be the basis of any interpretation that wants to have a claim to legitmacy. The rights of readers are thus minimized; it is posited at the outset that any interpretations which do not base themselves on these recognized characteristics of the text are illegitimate, whoever might be the readers, and whatever might be the contexts from which they read.

Becoming aware that this attitude is ethically problematic is a necessary first step. Minimizing the rights of readers leads us to exclude many actual readers and thus prevents us from being accountable toward many of those affected by our exegetical work; from the outset, our critical exegeses exclude as illegitimate all the readings which are not like ours. But this awareness, despite its importance, is not sufficient to help us correct this ethical problem. Indeed, our first impulse is to seek to correct this situation by overstressing the rights of readers at the expense of texts and their rights, implicitly or explicitly denying any significant difference between critical and ordinary readings, since both are hermeneutical, contextual interpretations. Then, in our practices, we end up giving priority to the subjective over the objective, perpetuating the dichotomous view of the relationship between subject and object, even though it is now reversed. This reversal could be a valid solution if it would resolve the ethical problem. But far from doing so, it perpetuates it, because it undermines the authority-power of all readings of the Bible—a situation which is acceptable for those (the elite) who do not depend upon this authority-power for survival, but which is potentially very destructive for those who do depend upon it (including the poor and the oppressed).

From this perspective, I can begin to clarify why the issue of the dialectic of the rights of texts and of the rights of their interpreters is of "interest" and "concern" for me, and why it should also be for other male European-American critical exegetes. It is a matter of accountability toward the guild and also toward those who are affected by our work.

We have good reasons (rooted in the Enlightenment) to want to make sure that biblical studies be "critical" and thus accountable to the guild. But former definitions of criticism are radically put into question by the fact that we now are in a period of methodological pluralism. Elucidating the respective roles of texts (textual constraints) and of interpreters in critical interpretations amounts to defining what is and what is not a "critical" interpretation, and thus promises to provide us with pluralistic, "multi-dimensional" definitions of "criticism," adapted to the present academic context, which will take the place of our traditional, "one-dimensional" definitions of criticism. It *may seem* that such a pluralistic conception of criticism would demand that one emphasize the role of readers and minimize the role of texts in the interpretation process. Yet, far from resolving the guild's uncertainties about the nature of critical studies, such attempts bring even more confusion.

The dialectic of the rights of texts and of interpreters also is an issue of accountability toward those affected by our critical exegetical work—an issue which urgently needs to be addressed in a period when our practices as male European-American exegetes are properly denounced as andro*centric* (e.g., Schüssler Fiorenza, 1983) and Euro*centric* (e.g., Felder) by women and other people whom we marginalize and in whose oppression we participate, with the good conscience which our good intentions give us. The root of this latter (ethical) problem *may seem* to be a denial of the role of interpreters and an overstressing of the rights of texts expressed in universalizing claims, according to which a critical interpretation elucidates textual features that everyone should recognize as significant. Thus, it once again *may seem* that the solution to this problem is a radical reader-response critical stance, affirming the role of readers so strongly that the role of textual constraints is minimized or denied. Yet, when we, male European-American critical exegetes, analyze our own work and its problematic character, it appears that such a solution merely duplicates the problem.

This is not the place to review the entirety of this analysis of our work, which shows that, far from being a part of the solution, denying or limiting the role of textual constraints is an intrinsic part of the ethical problem (see Patte, 1994). Yet, a brief reference to a few aspects of this analysis is necessary for understanding the importance of acknowledging the role of textual constraints in the process of interpretation—a process conceived as both subjective and objective.

Since Elisabeth Schüssler Fiorenza's presidential address at the 1987 SBL meeting (Schüssler Fiorenza, 1988), the issue of ethical accountability in biblical scholarship has not left me, again and again putting its disturbing question-mark upon my research and teaching activities. Her address convinced me that our male European-American exegetical work is ethically problematic in that it fails to be accountable toward many of those who are directly or indirectly affected by it. Thus, as long as we do not address this issue, our legitimate endeavors as male European-American critical exegetes cannot but be corrupted and turned into failures, even if we have the illusion of succeeding. But the nature of this problem and the practical changes it calls for remained elusive. After five years of running into dead-ends by pursuing wrong issues, or worse, by finding myself trapped in the quick-sand of contributing to the problem even as I strove to address it, at last I feel that I have found my bearings through the companionship of other male European-American critical exegetes. Together we begin to size up the problem—i.e., the androcentric and Eurocentric character of our critical exegetical *practices*—and thus to envision a solution, *"androcritical"* practices which are dialectical and include:

> (1) Accounting for the rights of interpreters by acknowledging the contextual and interested character of our work as well as by affirming its significance; in itself our vocation as male European-American critical biblical scholars is valuable; the problem is in the way we *practice* it (see Patte and Phillips, 1992); and,
>
> (2) Accounting for the rights of texts by acknowledging that they drastically limit our interpretations, as well as by affirming that they give legitimacy to a diversity of readings, including many of those which we reject or ignore, because texts have power upon readers and because this power is itself diversified.

But, it is one thing to recognize that critical exegetical practices need to have this androcritical and dialectical character, and quite another thing to conceive of such dialectical androcritical exegetical practices!

PAYING ATTENTION TO THE WAY WE "PRACTICE" CRITICAL STUDIES

Theoretical and methodological denunciations of the betrayal of the dialectical view and of its consequences are useful and necessary, yet they are clearly not sufficient for overcoming these problems. We need to pay attention to the ways in which we practice critical studies; our practices are often in tension (or contradiction) with the very theory that we strive to implement by developing new methodologies. A case in point is semiotic research, which "in theory" (and through its methodologies) advocates a dialectical view of the subject-object relation and of critical interpretation, but which "in practice" often ends up promoting a dichotomous view of this relation, by giving priority to one or the other dimension of the process of interpretation.

From the start, semiotic research has been a diversified effort to correct the imbalance resulting from overstressing the rights of texts. Thus, Eco elaborated upon the Peircean idea of "unlimited semiosis," in *Opera aperta* (1962, Eng. tr., *The Open Work*, 1989), then in *A Theory of Semiotics* (1976), *The Role of the Readers* (1979), and *Semiotics and the Philosophy of Language* (1984); Barthes sought to account for a multiplicity of legitimate readings by underscoring the multiplicity of codes that can be used in reading, in *S/Z* (1974) and other works; Greimas elucidated the multiplicity of meaning-producing "structures" involved in any communication "process," in his multifold reading of a tale by *Maupassant* (1976), then theoretically in *Semiotics and Language* (Greimas and Courtés), following Hjelmslev (1953 and 1971) who in his linguistic theory rigorously maintains a dialectic tension between "system" and "process" in any aspect of human communication.

Yet, these and other semiotic efforts to maintain a dialectic between the rights of texts and of interpreters do not succeed in communicating this point. They are perceived, despite their avowed intentions, as overstressing either the rights of texts (texts as objects)—as Greimas's work is often perceived—, or the rights of interpreters—as Eco's work is often perceived. Thus, poststructural, postmodern, and reader-response critics reject Greimas's work as logocentric and applaud Eco's, without taking note of the resolute efforts of both scholars to keep a balance between the rights of texts and their structures and the rights of interpreters. Thus, Eco rejects the accolades from such critics by publishing *The Limits of Interpre-*

tations. A part of the problem is with poststructural, postmodern, and reader-response critics: by denying any rights to texts (and objects), so as better to emphasize the rights of interpreters (and subjects), they presuppose a dichotomous view of the subject/object relation (either . . . or), which prevents them from appreciating Greimas's and Eco's efforts to maintain a dialectic between interpreters and texts, subjects and objects (both. . . and). Yet, another part of the problem is with the semioticians' practices: either the role of interpreters or that of texts is commonly overstressed when Eco's or Greimas's theory is *put into practice* by their respective followers and even by the masters themselves. As Parret emphasizes from the perspective of Greimas's school and as Eco (1991:23-43; 203-21) also does, the problem is that the entire issue of "pragmatics," including an examination of our own concrete practices, is never truly addressed by semioticians.

In sum, as long as one remains in the domain of theoretical and methodological discussions, one fails truly to address the problem of the dichotomous view of the subject/object relation. This view comes back surreptitiously in the interpretive practices based upon the methodological theories which purport to eradicate it.

This apparently contradictory outcome can be understood when one notes that the relationship between object and subject also finds expression in the relationships between methodological theory (objective) and practice (implementation by a subject in a specific situation); between critical exegesis (the use of critical methods) and hermeneutics (and vocational pursuits); between accountability to the guild and accountability toward those affected by our work (Schüssler Fiorenza, 1988; Patte, 1994); between critical exegesis and ordinary reading (West; Patte and Phillips, 1992). As long as these relationships of our practices are patterned according to a dichotomous view of the subject/object relation, the theoretical affirmation that this relation is dialectical and the affirmation that maintaining this dialectical view is an ethical imperative will be contradicted by our practices. In other words, our view of the relationship between the respective roles of texts and interpreters will truly be dialectical only insofar as the relationships between theoretical-methodological endeavors and exegetical practices, as well as between critical, academic, exegetical readings and ordinary, untrained, hermeneutical readings are themselves dialectic.

One can appreciate the drastic changes required by any effort to pattern our critical exegetical practices according to a dialectical view of the subject/object relation, when one recognizes that our common male European-American conception of the relationship between critical and ordinary readings embodies a dichotomous view. Accordingly, critical readings establish the range of legitimate readings of a text (if not "the" single legitimate reading of it); any ordinary (hermeneutical) reading which conforms to the norm established by critical readings is legitimate; other ordinary readings are illegitimate. Since most ordinary readings are not based upon critical readings, they are suspected of being illegitimate, until proven otherwise. Is not the fact that there are many, often contradictory, ordinary readings of the same text the proof that most ordinary readings are illegitimate? Is it not our task as (male European-American) critical exegetes to develop critical readings of biblical texts, so as to eradicate the wrong and misleading "ordinary" readings? This is, at the very least, the attitude we have toward the readings with which our students come into our classes. Is it not our role to help them overcome their childish or naive fundamentalist readings? In sum, according to our traditional practices, critical, objective readings are superior to ordinary, subjective readings. Despite our theoretical-methodological claims, our practices deny any subjectivity to critical readings, as if they did not reflect our concerns and interests as interpreters. Similarly, our practices deny any objectivity to ordinary readings, as if they did not reflect the role of the text in the interpretative process! Curiously, our practices reflect a doubly dichotomous view: concerning critical readings, this view denies the role of critical interpreters so as to emphasize the role of the text (since "textual evidence" is the basis for critical readings); concerning ordinary readings, it denies the rights of the text, so as to emphasize the (undue) role of the interpreters.

In order to have practices that reflect the dialectical view that we hold in our methodological theories, we would need not only to acknowledge the subjective (interested) character of our critical interpretations as male European-American exegetes, but also to affirm the role of the text in determining ordinary readings, so much so that ordinary readings would be presumed legitimate, until proven otherwise. For instance, this would mean that we would need to presume that the naive, fundamentalist readings with which our students come into our classes are basically legitimate, because these represent the way in which our students have been affected by the text—note the emphasis on the power of the text. Conversely, we would need to envision differently the task of critical exegesis, so that it might be both subjective and objective, by acknowledging the "interested" character of any "critical" reading.

These suggestions seem untenable, and totally unwarranted. Is this not in direct contradiction with our vocation as critical exegetes? Far from it! The affirmation of the basic legitimacy of ordinary readings resulting from the effect-power of a text upon its readers is actually a condition for fulfilling our vocation; without it, our critical interpretations become exclusive and destructive as much as fundamentalist and other obscurantist interpretations which they purport to overcome. This becomes clear in the South African context. As West and his white male South African colleagues (including Bernard Lategan and the Center For Contextual Hermeneutics he leads; see recent issues of the journal *Scriptura*) have emphasized, as long as their critical teaching of the Bible does not account for African ordinary readings, their teaching covertly or not so covertly promotes apartheid. In order to remedy this situation, they emphasize the contextual character of any interpretation; in this way, legitimacy can be recognized in African interpretations as much as in white male interpretations. Yet, contrary to what might at first appear to be the case, this is not a solution; as noted above, abandoning any distinction between ordinary and critical readings by affirming that critical readings are nothing else than contextual hermeneutical interpretations (as ordinary readings also are) amounts to depriving ordinary readings, here African interpretations, of their power-authority. Thus, more recently, these South African biblical scholars (e.g., West) study ordinary African readings of the Bible (including those in the "Independent Churches"), with open minds and with the expectation that these readings are basically legitimate.

For me, this investigation, which is just beginning, is a most helpful way of proceeding and provides us with a model for understanding in our own context the relationship between critical and ordinary readings and between the respective roles of texts and readers in an interpretive process. It might seem that those critical biblical scholars who study ordinary readings *with the expectation that they are basically legitimate* have abandoned their vocation as critical exegetes. Are they not playing the role of anthropologists or historians of religion, who adopt a positive attitude toward the "natives" and their religious practices? In a way, they are. Yet, I want to argue, their positive investigation of ordinary readings is an intrinsic part of the task of critical exegetes. Presuming that ordinary readings are legitimate until proven otherwise (rather than presuming that they are illegitimate) can be conceived as *an affirmation of the power of the text to affect readers in certain ways*. The fact that ordinary readings are often divergent and at times contradictory can readily be explained by the polysemy of any text, and especially of religious texts. In other words, far from offering a single set of textual constraints that would delimit a range of complementary legitimate interpretations, a text should be viewed as contributing to the production of several quite different legitimate interpretations through its different features—or, better, *through its several meaning-producing dimensions*. If the text is viewed as having this diversified power to affect readers in different ways through several of its dimensions, then it makes sense to presuppose that any ordinary reading, as a product of this process, is potentially legitimate: it reflects the meaning-producing dimension of the text which, for contextual reasons, was most immediately meaningful for certain ordinary readers.

Then, *the task of critical exegesis* appears in a new light. It can no longer be conceived as the elucidation of "the" legitimate (set of) interpretation(s) of a text, which would serve as a norm to determine the legitimacy or illegitimacy of ordinary readings, since all ordinary readings are presumed to be basically legitimate. Rather, its role would be *to demonstrate the legitimacy of ordinary readings, by elucidating the kind of meaning-producing dimension which is the basis of each given ordinary reading.* In the process, critical exegesis would also refine and complement the ordinary reading, by adducing appropriate textual evidence and by demanding that this reading be consistent with its own premise, that is, with the dimension which became central for it—a common problem with ordinary readings (as well as with critical readings!) is that in trying to affirm that they are "the" only true reading of a text, they become inconsistent by incorporating features from other dimensions privileged by other readings, or, on the contrary, in acknowledging their tentative and partial character they overlook other aspects of the dimension on which they are focussed.

This suggestion regarding the task of critical exegesis and its "horizontal" relationship with ordinary readings—it takes its starting point with ordinary readings and concludes by demonstrating their legitimacy—is impossible to justify fully in the limits of this essay. Male European-American critical exegetes might be especially surprised by it. Yet, as I discovered for myself, it becomes quite plausible as soon as one analyzes one's exegetical *practices,* including: why we choose to study a certain text rather than another one; why we choose a certain method; and why we choose to focus our study on certain issues regarding a text. Then, it becomes very difficult to deny that our critical exegeses find their starting points in "hunches" and "intuitions," which are ordinary readings that we seek to bring to critical understanding through our critical exegetical work. Do we not begin critical exegetical investigation by positing a "thesis" which is nothing else than the formal expression of our hunches!

In sum, the most difficult aspect of the above proposal concerns the affirmation that a text has several meaning-producing dimensions, each of which has the power to affect readers and thus to impose itself as that which expresses the central meaning of the text, and each of which can be that which is critically elucidated through the use of one or another critical method. This diversified "textual determinacy" is best explained through the discussion of different critical interpretations of a given text.

DIVERSIFIED TEXTUAL DETERMINACY: CRITICAL INTERPRETATIONS OF MATT. 8:17

For any given biblical text, there are quite a number of different *critical* interpretations, without speaking of the many ordinary readings of this text through the centuries (*Wirkungsgeschichte*). Should I say that all these critical interpretations, except for the one I happen to favor, are illegitimate, incorrect, or somehow "off the mark"? Am I for some reason the only one who knows how to use rigorously a certain critical method? Or, is the critical method that I use the only one which is truly critical? These rhetorical questions are enough to show the absurdity of the implicit claims we make when practicing critical exegesis as if its task were to establish "the" single true legitimate reading of a given text. Yet, these questions should not be taken as an expression of skepticism about the possibility of performing readings that are demonstrably based upon textual evidence—i.e., critical exegeses. Rather, my point is that several critical exegeses of a given text are legitimate even when they are conflicting, because through the use of different critical methods—or different implementations of methods—they describe distinct meaning-producing dimensions of this text.

Demonstrating the plausibility of this point would require considering in some detail a series of critical interpretations of a text which would, at first, seem to be "unambiguous," so as to show how each of the interpretations does focus on distinct meaning-producing dimensions of the given text. I cannot do so in the space of this essay (see Patte, 1995). Here I have to be content with alluding to (and not discussing in detail) critical interpretations of a text that is easily perceived as polysemic (rather than being perceived as unambiguous).

The text, the interpretations of which I propose to consider, is Matt 8:17 as a passage of the Gospel according to Matthew. Thus, the actual text being read is the Gospel of Matthew as a whole, with a focus on 8:17, as is done in redaction criticism (of various kinds), but also for instance in critical exegeses performed according to history of traditions, literary, and structural critical methods.

This passage, Matt 8:17, is soon perceived as polysemic, because it is the quotation of Is 53:4. Of course, this quotation is interpreted differently if one reads it in terms of different contexts in which it belonged or might have belonged: e.g., as a part of the book of Isaiah; of the Jewish traditions; of the pre-Matthean oral traditions which associated this quotation with events of Jesus' ministry (Kilpatrick:56-58); of an eventual collection of Scripture "Testimonies" fulfilled by Jesus, similar to the Qumran Testimonies (Strecker, 1962:49-50, 82-84); or of the special Matthean source, possibly targum-like ("targum" on Mark, Q, and other Jesus traditions [Bacon:475], or on the prophets [Baumstark:296-313]) eventually produced by a "school of Matthew" [Stendahl, and following him, Luz, 1989:78, 160-61]). This polysemy of the quotation of Is 53:4 in Matt 8:17 remains even if we limit our investigation to critical studies of Matt. 8:17 as a part of the entire Gospel as text. What is quoted in the Gospel of Matthew is not merely a verse of Isaiah, but this verse as interpreted and reinterpreted in the tradition(s) or the source(s) to which the author-redactor might have alluded in the very process of reinterpreting it once again.

More generally, because of its nature as a quotation, Matt 8:17 is an explicit signal of intertextuality. As such, it necessarily evokes a plurality of potential "meanings," by the very fact that it alludes to various possible other texts (contexts); it is *explicitly* polysemic—by contrast with other texts which might only be implicitly polysemic, yet no less polysemic. Thus, for my present purpose, I do not need to demonstrate further the polysemic character of this passage.

How do male European-American critical exegetes interpret such a text? While most acknowledge the potential polysemy of such a text (and the plurality of its dimensions), they traditionally consider this polysemy as a problem to be overcome: the redactor/author meant to convey something specific through this quotation! This tendency to abolish the polysemy of the text is found in one form or another in each of the critical studies discussed below; in effect, each seeks to establish "the" truly legitimate interpretation by collapsing upon a single dimension the features of the other dimensions, so as to reach a comprehensive, consistent, and coherent interpretation. By contrast, I want to argue that as long as one conceives the polysemy of a text (and the plurality of its dimensions) as a problem that can and should be overcome, one misrepresents the text. One fails to be truly critical when one attempts to deny the ambiguities of the text and to make the text univocal.

Matt 8:17, with its quotation of Is 53:4 as a signal of intertextuality, is overloaded with denotations and connotations resulting from its association with the prophet Isaiah and/or with Jewish and Christian traditions, which allow it simultaneously to partake of several semantic coherences of the text of the Gospel according to Matthew—i.e., of several of its various meaning-producing dimensions. For instance, the significance of the quotation is perceived quite differently, whether or not one concludes that Matt 8:17 evokes or does not evoke the early church's interpretations of Is 53:4 for understanding the cross (e.g., Acts 8:32-33 or 1 Peter 2:22-25). If Matt 8:17 evokes this church use of Is 53:4, it deliberately transfers to Jesus' ministry and his healings the vicarious character of Jesus's death—it is by his ministry, and not merely by his death, that Jesus has taken upon himself our transgressions (Schweizer, 1975:217-18), or alternatively, Matt 8:17 represents a rejection of a vicarious interpretation of Jesus' death (Patte, 1987:117). By contrast, if Matt 8:17 does not evoke the early church's interpretation of the cross, there is nothing of all this in this passage; the text does not connote "vicarious" suffering (Jesus does not take "upon himself" our infirmities and diseases, but takes them "away"); thus the relevant connotations are those related to other intertexts, such as those of Jewish traditions (Beare, 1981:211-12; Luz, 1990:19).

How did these scholars reach these divergent conclusions? Either of these connotations is plausible, for a text dated in the latter part of the first century! Despite the lack of explanation in these commentaries, it is clear that in each case it is a matter of consistency: in a given critical interpretation, implementing in a specific way one of the critical methods, the coherence one perceives in the Gospel (or at least in the immediate context of Matt 8:17) determines the decision regarding which intertextual connotations are relevant. In order to illustrate this point, let us briefly consider four possible critical exegeses of Matt 8:17.

1. *Traditional Redaction Critical Interpretation.* In redaction critical study as practiced by Strecker (1962) and Bornkamm, Barth, and Held, the formula quotations (including Matt 8:17) demonstrate what Strecker calls "the historical character" of the ministry of Jesus as Kyrios, that Matthew emphasizes all along (this is the "historicizing tendency" of Matthew; cf. Strecker, 1983); they establish the veracity of the various details of Jesus' life, here, of his healing ministry (Strecker, 1962:72, 85). The context of Matt 8:17 shows this quite clearly: despite his lowliness (cf. 8:18ff) which could be a sign of Jesus' humanity and weakness (against the claim that he is the Kyrios), Jesus is indeed shown to be the Kyrios with "all authority in heaven and on earth" by his healing ministry, as is confirmed by the fact that this ministry fulfills the prophecy of Is. 53:4 (Bornkamm, Barth, Held:263-64). Furthermore, the fulfillment quotations verify that Jesus is indeed the Kyrios, since he fulfills the prophecies, against the claim of the Jews who reject him (in the time of Matthew's church): through his healings, Jesus "takes away" the diseases and infirmities of people. Thus, the quotation of Is 53:4 in Matt 8:17 contributes to the apologetic defense of the Christian faith (of the church) against Judaism. Such an interpretation is focused upon a textual dimension which would be consistent with interpreting Matt 8:17 and its quotation of Is 53:4 in terms of (and by contrast with) the connotations it acquired in Jewish interpretations.

2. *A Narrative Critical Interpretation Focused on the Plot.* If, by contrast, we interpret Matt 8:17 following a narrative critical interpretation (comparable to Edwards and, for Mark, Kelber), and focus on the study of

the plot (as advocated by Moore:18-20)—a critical study focused on a different meaning-producing dimension—the formula quotation is read as an expression of the continuity of Jesus' ministry with the history of Israel, the prophets, and thus the Jews (rather than a polemic against the Jews, as above), and as an expression of Jesus' lowliness (rather than of his exaltation as Kyrios). Once again, this is part of a consistent and coherent reading of Matthew. A narrative reading which takes seriously into account the unfolding of the plot cannot but recognize that it is only after the resurrection that Jesus becomes the exalted Kyrios (Matt 28:18), and that during his ministry he is on the contrary characterized by his lowliness. Even when there are some previews of his exalted status or authority, the plot makes it clear that it is God's (and not Jesus'!) authority, power, and goodness which are manifested through Jesus's ministry. In brief, from this perspective, the formula that introduces the quotation of Is 53:4 in Matt 8:17, "This was to fulfill what was spoken by the prophet Isaiah," sets Jesus' healing ministry in continuity with the divine activity in the time of the prophets, as is also the case with the other formula quotations. The word of the prophet, as quoted, "He took our infirmities and bore our disease," is a flashback summary of the preceding healing stories, which calls attention to one of their points: in these stories, each time Jesus touches the sick person (the leper, Peter's mother in law), he becomes ritually unclean, as they were before their healing, and as they are no longer afterward (as the ritual that the leper must perform shows; cf. Matt 8:4). Thus, he becomes unclean in their place, he takes upon himself their infirmities and disease. Jesus' ministry has a vicarious character. Yet, note that this is not the case with all the healings: sometimes he heals without touching (by a word), and thus without becoming impure—namely, when people have great faith (the case of the centurion). This demonstrates that, in his healings, Jesus makes himself unclean for people only when they lack faith. Is it because, in such cases, he would somehow lack the power to heal them with a word? The nature miracles and exorcisms amply demonstrate that his word would be powerful enough. Thus, it is not by necessity that Jesus touches the sick and becomes unclean instead of them. It is *voluntarily*. This is further expressed in Matt 9:9-13. These latter verses not only show that Jesus becomes ritually unclean by interacting and eating with tax-collectors and sinners, but also that he does so voluntarily, as is expressed when Jesus quotes Hos 6:6; it is because Jesus makes God's will his own will, because he manifests mercy, compassion, good will, which are God's mercy, compassion, good will, that he takes upon himself the uncleanness of the sinners as well as of the sick who lack faith, that is, all Israel (cf. 8:10). It is in this vicarious and lowly way that Jesus is "God with us" during his ministry; not as the exalted Kyrios (as he will be only after his resurrection). Thus, a critical reading focused upon this specific narrative meaning-producing dimension would be consistent with interpreting 8:17 and its quotation of Is 53:4 in terms of (and by contrast with) the connotations it acquired in early Church interpretations of the cross.

3. *A Figurative Redaction Critical Interpretation.* When the semantic coherence of the text is perceived in its figurative dimension, the interpretation focuses upon the organization of the text in figurative units, marked for instance by "inclusions." This is in effect what Luz does in his commentary, which I take as an example. Thus, Matt 8:17 is located in a figurative unit which is marked by the inclusion between 4:23 and 9:35. Furthermore, the figures can be properly understood only when one takes into account the allusions to traditions and other texts that the implied readers might recognize. For these two reasons, it appears that Jesus's teaching (Matt 5-7) and healings (Matt 8-9) are closely related. Both underscore Jesus' fulfillment of the Scriptures, the Law and Prophets. Yet, in his teaching and his healings Jesus fulfills the Scriptures in a quite different way than Judaism (represented by the Pharisees and the Sadducees) does. By contrast with the scribes and Pharisees who do not have true righteousness, because they do not completely fulfill the Law, Jesus does completely fulfill the Law (cf., the Sermon); Jesus and those who follow his teaching (the implied readers) are those who are truly faithful to the Law. The Church appropriates for itself the Jewish Law, and therefore expropriates the Jews from the Law. Similarly, the fact that Jesus fulfills the prophecies shows that he totally submits himself to God's Plan for human history and fulfills it (so Luz). This shows that it is not only the Law but also the prophets which are now the Church's Scriptures. These Scriptures are no longer properly the Scriptures of the Jews, because they have not recognized in Jesus the fulfillment of the Scriptures. They are therefore dispossessed of the Scriptures, which are no longer theirs, but actually and properly the Church's. As Luz emphasizes, this is all that the formula quotation in 8:17 expresses. It should not be over-interpreted, as it is too often, so as to find in it a christological or theological point (Luz, 1989:162-63; 1990:18). The formula quotations as well as the other quotations do not add anything else to the text. They are content to underscore the main christological themes of the Gospel. They do not add anything beyond the affirmation that the Scriptures are now the property of the Church, and do not belong any longer to the Jews.

4. *A Thematic Structural Interpretation.* When the semantic coherence of the text is perceived in its structural semantic dimension, the thematic organization of the text becomes the key to the interpretation, as it is in

my commentary. The thematic unit in which Matt 8:17 is located is 8:1-9:34, whose theme is the acknowledgment of the true character of the authority or power of Jesus (Patte, 1987:109-111). Matt 8:1-17 forms a thematic sub-unit, which relates the healing of the leper by touching (8:1-4) to the healing of Peter's mother-in-law, also by touching (8:14-15) associated with healings-exorcisms "with a word" (8:16), and also relates the references to Scripture in both 8:4 and 8:17, which refer respectively to the fulfillment of the Law and to the fulfillment of a prophecy. As in the second reading ("plot"), one notes that Jesus takes upon himself the infirmity, the uncleanness of the sick when he heals by touching because of the weakness of their faith (a point which is made possible because of the ambiguity of the translation of the Hebrew of Is 53:4); one also notes that in other circumstances Jesus heals with a word—in the case of great faith, and also in the case when demonic powers (or natural power; cf. Matt 8:23-34) are involved.

The quotation is therefore part of a thematic unit which shows (1) that Jesus has indeed divine authority-power (2) but that the use of this power is strictly limited and defined by the specificity of the human situations, (3) so much limited by such situations that divine authority and divine power are manifested in discreet and ambiguous ways in human affairs (as was also the case in the history of Israel; cf. Matt 1:2-17; cf. 9:33), and thus (4) that the acknowledgment of this authority-power by human beings is in no way automatic or easy (cf. Matt 9:32-34). This interpretation is consistent with a similar study of the other quotations of Scripture in Matthew, which show that it is not at all self-evident that Jesus is the fulfillment of the prophecies or of Scriptural types; actually, more often than not, he is presented as a surprising, ambiguous fulfillment of the Scriptures (the Law as well as the prophets). This interpretation of the theme "fulfillment of Scriptures" (which cannot be summarized here; see Patte, 1987:16-135) applies to the quotation of Is 53:4 in Matt 8:17: it does express the continuity of Jesus' ministry with Israel and thus with Judaism, but in the same discreet and ambiguous way as God's authority and power are manifested in human affairs. The continuity between Jesus and Judaism is a fact, but it does not impose itself, it does not force the recognition and acknowledgment. So it is with God's authority-power; it does not impose itself, it does not force recognition and acknowledgment. This is so, because it is manifested as mercy, as goodness.

Concluding Remarks

The above examples of critical interpretations of Matt 8:17 through the use of different critical methods do not prove that any given biblical text is polysemic and that diverse critical interpretations elucidate different meaning-producing dimensions, each of which can be the basis of legitimate and coherent readings of a text. Yet, these examples show that such a view of the text as offering a plurality of textual constraints for ordinary as well as for critical readings is *at least as plausible as* the traditional presupposition embedded in our critical practices, according to which the text offers a single set of constraints, and *at least as plausible* as the postmodern presupposition according to which the reading process is primarily determined by the interpreters' contexts. This plausibility is enough for us, male European-American exegetes, to continue to carry out our vocation as critical exegetes, even though we have become aware that our interpretations are contextual. By recognizing the plausibility of a plurality of textual constraints, we can conceive our task as male European-American critical exegetes in a way which will be ethically accountable both to the guild and to those affected by our work: we can recognize that the goal of critical exegesis should be, is, and has always been the development of critical interpretations which demonstrate the legitimacy of (ordinary) readings by showing that they are actually based upon specific textual constraints or meaning-producing dimensions. By affirming the plausibility of a plurality of textual constraints, we male European-American exegetes are in a position to envision a very different kind of critical exegetical practice, which might be ethically responsible as well as academically and pedagogically sound. Such a critical exegetical practice would acknowledge that its role is not, and has never been, to provide a basis for ordinary readings ("it has never *opened* a reading," Derrida:158). Ordinary readings ground themselves upon the text; or better, they reflect how ordinary readers were affected by the text through one of its meaning-producing dimensions. Thus, the task of critical exegesis is not to evaluate whether or not an ordinary reading is legitimate (with the presupposition that it is illegitimate), but rather to elucidate the textual dimension which has been the basis of a given ordinary reading (with the presupposition that it is legitimate).

A new vision of our task. Fear and trembling. Something new on the horizon, which might change our ways. Who would have thought that an issue as abstract and as prosaic as "textual determinacy" contained the seeds of such changes!

Works Consulted

Bacon, Benjamin W.
    1930   *Studies in Matthew*. New York: Holt.

Barthes, Roland
    1974   *S/Z*. New York: Hill and Wang.

Baumstark, Anton
    1956   "Die Zitate des Matthäus-Evangeliums aus dem Zwölfprophetenbuch." *Bib* 37:296-313.

Beare, Francis W.
    1981   *The Gospel According to Matthew: Translation, Introduction, and Commentary*. San Francicso: Harper and Row.

Bornkamm, Gunther, Gerhard Barth, and Heinz J. Held
    1963   *Tradition and Interpretation in Matthew*. Trans. Percy Scott. Philadelphia: Westminster.

Derrida, Jacques
    1976   *Of Grammatology*. Baltimore: Johns Hopkins University Press.

Eco, Umberto
    1976   *A Theory of Semiotics*. Bloomington: Indiana University Press.
    1979   *The Role of the Reader: Explorations in the Semiotics of Texts*. Bloomington: Indiana University Press.
    1984   *Semiotics and the Philosophy of Language*. Bloomington: Indiana University Press.
    1989   *The Open Work*. Trans. Anna Cancogni. Cambridge: Harvard University Press.
    1990   *The Limits of Interpretation*. Bloomington: Indiana University Press.

Edwards, Richard A.
    1985   *Matthew and the Story of Jesus*. Philadelphia: Fortress.

Felder, Cain Hope, ed.
    1991   *Stony the Road We Trod: African American Biblical Interpretation*. Minneapolis: Fortress.

Fish, Stanley
    1980   *Is There a Text in This Class?: The Authority of Interpretative Communities*. Cambridge: Harvard University Press.

Greimas, Algirdas J.
    1976   *Maupassant: La Sémiotique du Texte: Exercices Practiques*. Paris: Seuil.

Greimas, Algirdas J. and Joseph Courtés
    1982   *Semiotics and Language: An Analytical Dictionary*. Trans. Larry Crist et al. Bloomington: Indiana University Press.

Harvey, Van A.
    1966   *The Historian and the Believer: The Morality of Historical Knowledge and Christian Belief*. Toronto: Macmillan.

Hjelmslev, Louis
    1953   *Prolegomena to a Theory of Language*. Trans. Francis J. Whitfield. Baltimore: Waverly.
    1971   *Essais Linguistiques*. Paris: Editions de Minuit.

Kelber, Werner H.
    1979   *Mark's Story of Jesus*. Philadelphia: Fortress.

Kilpatrick, George D.
    1946   *The Origins of the Gospel according to St. Matthew*. Oxford: Clarendon.

Luz, Ulrich
    1989   *Matthew 1-7: A Commentary*. Trans. Wilhelm C. Linss. Minneapolis: Augsburg.
    1990   *Das Evangelium nach Matthäus*. 2 Teilband, Mt. 8-17. Evangelisch-Katholischer Kommentar Zum Neuen Testament. Zurich/Neukirchen: Benziger and Neukirchener.

Moore, Stephen D.
    1989   *Literary Criticism and the Gospels: The Theoretical Challenge*. New Haven: Yale University Press.

Parret, Herman
    1983   *Semiotics and Pragmatics: An Evaluative Comparison of Conceptual Frameworks*. Philadelphia: John Benjamins Publishing.

Patte, Daniel
    1987   *The Gospel According to Matthew: A Structural Commentary on Matthew's Faith*. Minneapolis: Fortress.
    1990   *The Religious Dimensions of Biblical Texts: Greimas's Structural Semiotics and Biblical Exegesis*. Semeia Studies. Atlanta: Scholars.
    1994   *The Ethics of Biblical Interpretation: An Androcritical Perspective*. Minneapolis: Fortress.
    1995   *Discipleship According to the Sermon on the Mount: An Androcritical Multidimensional Exegesis*. Minneapolis: Fortress.

Patte, Daniel and Gary Phillips
    1992   "A Fundamental Condition for Ethical Accountability in the Teaching of the Bible by White Male Exegetes: Recovering and Claiming the Specificity of our Perpective." *Scriptura*: October, 1992.
    1994   *Teaching the Bible Otherwise: Can We be Responsible and Critical in A Pluralistic Context?* (forthcoming)

Schweizer, Eduard
   1975   *The Good News According to Matthew*. Trans. David E. Green. Atlanta: John Knox.

Schüssler Fiorenza, Elisabeth
   1983   *In Memory of Her: A Feminist Theological Reconstruction of Christian Origins*. New York: Crossroad.
   1988   "The Ethics of Biblical Interpretation: Decentering Biblical Scholarship." *JBL* 107:3-17.

Stendahl, Krister
   1968   *The School of St. Matthew and Its Use of the Old Testament*. Philadelphia: Fortress.

Strecker, Georg
   1962   *Der Weg der Gerichtigkeit: Untersuchung zur Theologie des Matthäus*. Göttingen: Vanenhoeck and Ruprecht.
   1983   "The Concept of History in Matthew." Pp. 67-84 in *Interpretation of Matthew*. Issues in Religion and Theology 3. Philadelphia: Fortress.
   1988   *The Sermon on the Mount: An Exegetical Commentary*. Trans. O.C. Dean, Jr. Nashville: Abingdon.

Tolbert, Mary Ann
   1979   *Perspectives on the Parables: An Approach to Multiple Interpretations*. Philadelphia: Fortress.

Troeltsch, Ernst
   1914   "Historiography." Pp. 716-23 in *The Encyclopedia of Religion and Ethics*. Ed. James Hastings. New York: Charles Scribner's Sons.

West, Gerald O.
   1991   *Biblical Hermeneutics of Liberation: Modes of Reading the Bible in the South African Context*. Pietermaritzburg: Cluster Publications.

TEXT AND CONTEXTS:
INTERPRETING THE DISCIPLES IN MARK

Elizabeth Struthers Malbon
Virginia Polytechnic Institute and State University

ABSTRACT

This paper approaches the topic of differing interpretations of a text by considering the differing contexts in which interpreters read it. A four-part typology of contextual foci of interpreters is presented, based on the intersection of two familiar distinctions: internal/external and literary/historical. The typology is applied to Werner Kelber's reading of the story of the disciples in Mark as presented primarily in *The Oral and the Written Gospel*. Following the suggestions of intellectual historian Dominick LaCapra, questions are raised about the possible "contextual saturation of the meaning of the text." An alternative reading of the story of the disciples in Mark is offered from the point of view of an alternative context. The conclusion suggests two images (advocacy and "complication") that give direction to the question of how to interrelate multiple readings of a single text resulting from multiple interpreters focusing on multiple contexts.[1]

It is a cliché, of course, to say that one must read the text in context, not use the text for a pretext. The cliché may indeed be true, but its view of truth is over-simplified, for a text has not one but many contexts. Different interpreters, focusing on one or another of these contexts, may come to conclusions that are mutually complementary or competitive. A more systematic understanding of the relations between a text and its contexts and between contextual foci and interpretive conclusions would aid us in evaluating interpretations and thus in interpreting texts. The present essay will propose a typology of contextual foci of interpreters and apply it to a significant work of New Testament scholarship: Werner Kelber's *The Oral and the Written Gospel*. Kelber's study is concerned (among other things) with interpreting the story of Jesus and the disciples as it unfolds in the Markan narrative, and that concern will serve as a "test case" for asking questions about the relation of text and contexts in the interpretive task.[2]

---

[1] It seems appropriate to note that the original (external historical) *context* of this paper was a session of the Structuralism and Exegesis Section of the SBL in 1985.

[2] The interpretation of the disciples in Mark serves as a test case for the application of redaction criticism for Black, who focuses on the work of Robert P. Meye,

I. A Typology of Contextual Foci of Interpreters

One must refer to the contexts of a text, not its singular context. As Dominick LaCapra persuasively argues: "For complex texts, one has a set of interacting contexts whose relations to one another are variable and problematic and whose relation to the text being investigated raises difficult issues in interpretation" (35). It would perhaps be an impossible task to enumerate all the contexts of a text, but a simplified typology of contextual foci may be of use in registering the different interests, approaches, and assumptions of interpreters of texts and their contexts.

The proposed typology of contextual foci of interpreters is the intersection or crossing of two familiar distinctions: internal/external and literary/historical. Murray Krieger's images of the text as mirror and the text as window (see also Petersen: 19) suggest metaphorically what is meant here by the "internal" and the "external" contexts of a text. When an interpreter focuses on the text's "internal" context (text as mirror) he or she looks to "the text itself"—its words and sentences, its characters and settings, its plot and action, its rhetoric and imagery—for the text's meaning and significance. When an interpreter focuses on the "external" context of a text (text as window) she or he looks through the text in some larger world—whether cultural, political, religious, or literary.[3] "Literary" and "historical" have often been characterized as two distinctive (if not opposing) approaches to texts. To focus on the "literary" context of a text is to concentrate more on how the text is read than on why it was written, more on function—perhaps in relation to the conventions of a genre—than on intention. To focus on the "historical" context of a text is to investigate its place in societal/cultural processes of continuity and change. The quotation marks enclosing the four main terms of the typology are intended to indicate the problematic nature of the terms and the impossibility of their pure manifestation except as abstractions.

Ernest Best, and Theodore J. Weeden, Sr., but discusses an extensive bibliography. Black's final appraisal is judicious but not surprising: Researchers' presuppositions predict their outcomes better than their stated methodologies do; redaction criticism has tended toward "methodological imperialism" and has sought to answer questions that are, by definition, unverifiable; a more synthetic interpretation—including historical, tradition, literary, authorial-theological (i.e., modified redaction), and reader-response criticism—is needed. See my review (Malbon, 1991b).

[3] With Krieger (28) and with Kelber (1987: esp. 121-27), I agree that both views of the text—as mirror and as window—are not only legitimate but necessary to the interpretive task in its fullest sense. The difficulty lies in relating the two views in a way that does justice to both. See also Kelber, 1985:32-34, and note 13 below.

Contextual Foci (of Interpreters)

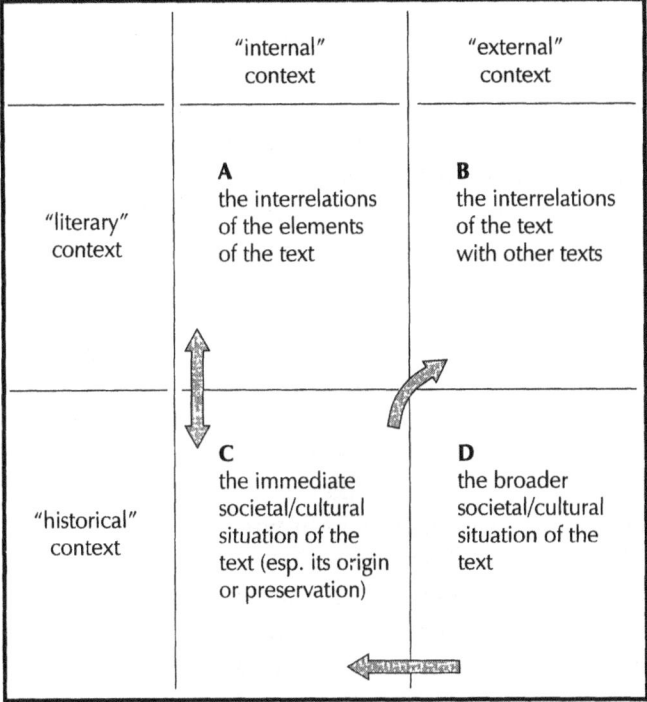

Arrows reflect relationships
in Werner H. Kelber, *The Oral and the Written Gospel*.

Crossing the "internal"/"external" distinction with the "literary"/"historical" distinction results in four contextual foci of interpreters of texts (see diagram): A, the interrelations of the elements of the text; B, the interrelations of the text with other texts; C, the immediate societal/cultural situation of the text (especially its origin and/or preservation); D, the broader societal/cultural situation of the text. It is here assumed (although it will not be discussed) that "the text" is an abstraction employed to refer to the communication process involving an author (real and implied), a text (variously transmitted), and an audience (real and implied).[4] The audience of particular concern here is the community of scholarly interpreters. The parentheses around "OF INTERPRETERS" in the title of the diagram indicates that the role of the interpreter (reader,

---

[4] Thus I am in agreement with Paul Armstrong that "A text is not an independent object which remains the same regardless of how it is construed. The literary work is not autonomous but 'heteronomous'" (11), that is, "paradoxically both dependent and independent, capable of taking on different shapes according to opposing hypotheses about how to configure it, but always transcending any particular interpreter's beliefs about it" (x).

literary critic, historian), although integrally involved with a text's multiple contexts, is not the focus of this typology. Yet it is important to note here that these are contextual foci *of interpreters*. The interpreter is omnipresent in interpretation. Thus we will need to return, in the concluding section, to a brief explicit consideration of the role of the interpreter in relation to text and contexts.[5] The immediate task is to apply this typology to the work of a real interpreter.

The title of Kelber's 1983 book, *The Oral and the Written Gospel*, suggests its underlying concern: the dynamic interaction of orality and textuality manifested in New Testament texts—especially Paul's letters and Mark's Gospel. This interaction is, for Kelber, a central element—and perhaps the central element—of the broader societal/cultural situation of the New Testament—a D focus. To indicate that Kelber is concerned with the "external"/"historical" context is not to identify linguistics with history, but only to point out that Kelber focuses on the interactions and shifts between linguistic media as they occur in time, in history. Although Kelber does, of course, concern himself with the interrelations of the elements of the text (A) of Mark—especially its characters—this does not appear to be his focal concern, and this observation seems even more true of *The Oral and the Written Gospel* than of his two earlier books, *The Kingdom in Mark* and *Mark's Story of Jesus*. Kelber's focal concern—in all three books in distinctive ways—is the immediate societal/cultural situation of the Markan text, especially its origin (C). The concluding chapters of *Kingdom* and *Mark's Story* very explicitly deal with the historical situation of the genesis of Mark's Gospel. The concluding chapter of *Oral and Written* shares this concern as well, but, in terms of contextual foci, it adds an interesting new twist: a focus on the genre of Mark, which entails examining the interrelation of the Markan text with other texts (B). For Kelber, Mark's genre—parable—is the only one appropriate for the occasion of its genesis. Thus Kelber ignores none of the contextual foci of the typology; but concerns for A and D seem to serve C, that is, the "internal"/"literary" context and the "external"/"historical" context seem primarily useful in clarifying the "internal"/"historical" context. B also serves C, that is, the "external"/"literary" context serves to clarify the "internal"/"historical" context; but one gets the feeling at the close of *Oral and Written* that genre (B) is becoming as intriguing to Kelber (and as

---

5 One might, of course, *focus* on the role of the interpreter, as reader-response critics do, or on the movement from the reader/interpreter's pre-understanding to explaining the text (perhaps from an A focus) to understanding (with a second focus on the role of the interpreter). On this latter option see Poland, especially the final discussion of Ricoeur. See also Armstrong, who presents a theory of "limited pluralism" in which conflicting readings of interpreters may be evaluated and appreciated without absolute claims to "truth" or "correctness."

focal) as genesis (C). This feeling is confirmed in Kelber's 1985 article, "Apostolic Tradition and the Form of the Gospel," which presents Mark's Gospel as "an anti-genre to the genre of a sayings tradition" (42), the parabolic reversal of "the revelation dialogue that has been embedded in 4:1-33" (42) and is exemplified by the Gospel of Thomas.

Although Kelber manifests awareness of multiple contexts, no interpreter can focus on everything at once. The arrows on the diagram suggest the ways in which these four contextual foci are interrelated for Kelber. The arrow moving from D to C indicates that the broader societal/cultural situation of the text forms the background for the immediate societal/cultural situation of the text (especially its origin), which is in the foreground for Kelber. The two-directional arrow between A and C represents the interaction between Kelber's interpretation of the text and his presentation of its immediate context, seen most clearly in his understanding of the polemical nature of both. The arrow from C to B suggests the movement of Kelber's concern from his primary focus (genesis) to his secondary—but increasingly important—focus (genre). Basically Kelber studies the relation of text (A) and history (D) in Mark and comes to an understanding of, firstly, Mark's genesis (C) and, secondly, Mark's genre (B).

This typology of contextual foci is intended to be descriptive not evaluative, although, clearly, judgments about what is the central thrust in a work are required in order to apply the typology. Now, having presented this (admittedly schematic) view of how various textual contexts are related, I do wish to pose some questions about all contextual readings. Again Kelber's contextual reading of the text of Mark will serve as an example.

II. QUESTIONS ABOUT CONTEXTUAL READINGS

I introduce my questions by reference to Dominick LaCapra's critique of the book by Allan Janik and Stephen Toulmin, *Wittgenstein's Vienna*. This book is "an exemplar of a contextualist approach to interpreting the meaning of an important text" (86)—Wittgenstein's *Tractatus Logico-Philosophicus*. But LaCapra raises questions about Janik and Toulmin's book based on his reading of Wittgenstein's book. LaCapra describes the goal of the former in this way: "The explicit intention of Janik and Toulmin is to relate the *Tractatus* (first published in 1921) to a precise context: fin-de-siècle Vienna. This context was characterized by a widespread cultural concern with the crisis of language and the problem of ethics. Their argument is that the ignorance of this context has led to significant distortion in the way the *Tractatus* has been read" (86). But LaCapra's judgment is as follows:

> In Janik and Toulmin's account, the idea that the *Tractatus* is essentially "ethical" rather than "logical" in meaning depends upon an extremely reductive interpretation of the text which, not surprisingly, coincides with an extremely reductive interpretation of the context. This dual reduction serves the interest of a fully unified interpretation. . . .
>
> In Janik and Toulmin, the context serves ultimately to saturate the text with meaning. The paradoxes and silences of the text are not questioned precisely because they are filled in or smoothed over by generous helpings of context, and the paradoxes of the context itself are transcended through a methodology that ties everything together (87-88).
>
> In a circular fashion, the notion of context as a synchronic whole, situated in time and place, further serves to bring about a coincidence between the author's intentions and the meaning of the text (91).

LaCapra complains that what Janik and Toulmin either seek or assume—"*the* context"—does not exist. No text has just one context; contexts are always plural, and they present the same problems and challenges as texts: they demand interpretation in themselves and in relation to other "more or less pertinent contexts" (95-96). LaCapra realizes that "it would of course be humanly impossible to treat adequately all these contexts," but he insists that "the awareness of the 'intertextual' horizon of any contextual reading serves both as the (recurrently displaced) ideal limit for research and as a check against unsubstantiated claims for the primordiality of any given context" (99). Thus LaCapra's point is "not to fault Janik and Toulmin for not being exhaustive" but "to question the concept of exhaustiveness, including the form it takes in Janik and Toulmin: that of contextual saturation of the meaning of a text" (99).

One way to test the relative importance of any one context is "to examine critically the extent to which it informs a reading of the text" (99), a task that LaCapra carries out in relation to *Wittgenstein's Vienna* and *Wittgenstein's Tractatus* (100-14). While LaCapra admits that "'contextualism' in the sense practiced by Janik and Toulmin . . . may seem liberating in contrast with a narrowly literary or 'history-of ideas' point of view" (114-15), he fears that it has limits of its own. The text should not "be identified with the self-enclosed, unique aesthetic object" (116) nor over-identified with "*the* context." "The relationship between text and context," LaCapra concludes, "would then become a question of 'intertextual' reading, which cannot be addressed on the basis of reductionist oversimplifications that convert the context into a fully unified or dominant structure saturating the text with a certain meaning. Meaning is indeed context-bound, but context is not itself bound in any simple or unproblematic way" (117).

Certainly Kelber does not believe that *the* simple, unproblematic context of Mark is to be sought, much less found. In fact, *The Oral and the Written Gospel* serves to awaken New Testament scholars to certain of Mark's multiple contexts that have been neglected. And certainly Kelber's work "informs a reading of the text" of Mark to a considerable extent. Yet it is instructive, as an example, to ask (1) whether Kelber's book tends toward the "contextual saturation of the meaning" of the Markan text and (2) what are the limits of the extent to which his work "informs a reading of the text." My questions are, thus, less pointed than LaCapra's questions; but, like his, they are raised in order to highlight general methodological assumptions and strategies as much as to critique specific interpretations.

Kelber is concerned to show how Mark stands out in its broader context: it confronts orality with textuality; it confronts tradition with parable. Of course Mark has both continuities and discontinuities with its historical/cultural context, as Kelber is aware. But the continuities seem under-explained (not quite *not* explained) by Kelber. It is a matter of the interpreter's *telos*, his or her end, in the sense of both *goal* and *conclusion*. If one reaches one's goal, conclusions seem in order. If one is interested especially in the relation of a text to a particular context, and one works out a reasonable interpretation of the text and a plausible reconstruction of the context, and the two fit together nicely, one may be tempted not to ask further questions of the text or the context (especially from the point of view of yet another context) that might upset that delicate balance. It seems very unlikely that Kelber had a fully worked out view of a Markan ("historical" or "external") context before working out a Markan exegesis. More probably, exegesis influenced understanding of the context as well as vice versa throughout the process of interpretation. It is the neatness of the final fit between the text and the focal context that gives pause and raises the question of the "contextual saturation of the meaning of the text."

In relation to Kelber's *Oral and Written* the problem is especially complex, for we may need to ask not only about the possible contextual saturation of the meaning of the text but also about the possible textual saturation of the meaning of the context! Does an understanding of the context of Mark as polemical (textuality vs. orality) lead to an understanding of the story of the Markan disciples as polemical? Or does the reading of the Markan story of the disciples as polemical influence the reading of the Markan context as polemical? Each of Kelber's three books asserts a polemical reading of the story of the disciples and a polemical reading of the Markan context—although the foundation for the polemic is different in each case. The disciples are portrayed negatively in Mark because they represent those who, in Mark's historical context, held the "wrong" eschatology (*Kingdom*), belonged to the "wrong" church (*Mark's Story*), employed the "wrong" linguistic medium (*Oral and Written*), and/or embraced the "wrong" genre (Kelber's 1985 article). In order to resolve this chicken-or-egg problem of Kelber's work, one would probably have to trace it back to the relation of text and context in Weeden's work on the disciples in Mark (1968, 1971) and from there back to Georgi's work on text and context in regard to the opponents of Paul in 2 Corinthians.[6]

A more important question would seem to be whether the mutual saturation (or especially "neat" fit) between text and focal context leads Kelber to misread some of his own cues. Kelber presents a rather thorough analysis of "Mark's Oral Legacy" (chapter 2), that is, the "oral forms and conventions" that "have gained admittance into the written document" even though "the pre-gospel transmission does not in itself account for the extant gospel" (44). On this basis it would seem more accurate to describe Mark as shaping and interpreting oral tradition, rather than opposing and rejecting it (see also Weeden, 1979:158-60). Furthermore, if (1) oral tradition is not completely rejected by Mark (as Kelber's discussion of its "oral legacy" would seem to suggest), and (2) the disciples in Mark represent oral tradition (as Kelber asserts explicitly), then (3) it would seem more consistent to argue that the disciples are *not* completely rejected but, rather, interpreted--in ways that preclude their simple idolization. As oral tradition is curtailed and contained but not eliminated, Kelber might well argue, so the disciples are critiqued and chastened but not discredited. But his understanding of the Markan context as polemical blocks such a reading. The argument can be made from a different angle as well. If, as Boomershine (1974) persuasively argues, the Gospel of Mark was intended to be told and heard, not read individually and silently, was Mark really as opposed to orality as Kelber suggests? It would appear, rather, that the author was presenting his own interpretation—written, to be sure, but written to be spoken—but his own interpretation of oral tradition for his own situation (see also Weeden, 1979:162-63). And, if this is true, an interpretation of the disciples as representatives of the opposed oral tradition loses crucial support.[7]

---

[6] Sharyn Dowd (6-24) traces the influence of Dieter Georgi's *Die Gegner des Paulus im 2. Korintherbrief* on Weeden's dissertation (1968, 1971), and then to Norman Perrin and his students. Kelber was a doctoral student of Perrin at Chicago and dedicated his first book (his revised dissertation) to him. See Kelber, 1985:26-28, 42, on Perrin and Weeden.

[7] Kelber's attempt to resolve this problem by distinguishing between primary orality (Mark's oral legacy) and secondary orality (the reading aloud of Mark's Gospel) is not convincing, even though the distinction itself is of interest (1983:217-18).

It is clear that Kelber does not present orality/textuality as "*the* context" of the Markan Gospel. Kelber comments, for example, that the "early and radical" shift from orality to textuality that Mark represents is "not fully accounted for without the stimulus of environmental factors," especially the destruction of the Temple in 70 C.E. (210). But the shift from orality to textuality that Kelber takes as an extremely important element of the Markan context he then depicts as essential and central to an understanding of the disciples. At one point Kelber presents the argument compactly:

> the relationship between Jesus and his disciples is constructed on the oral principle of *imitatio magistri*, or in Platonic terms on *mimesis*, which has as its chief concern the preservation of tradition.
> In Mark's gospel the twelve personify the principal, oral representatives of Jesus. They function in a mimetic process whose function is to assure continuity of tradition.... [However,] *Both the model of a mimetic relationship and the drama of failing discipleship are drawn with equal care by Mark.* This leads us to suggest that the dysfunctional role of the disciples narrates the breakdown of the mimetic process and casts a vote of censure against the guarantors of tradition. Oral representatives and oral mechanism have come under criticism (197, Kelber's emphasis).

Kelber's argument that his observations about orality and textuality are central to the search for the "original form" of the sayings of Jesus is more convincing than his argument that they are central to Mark's story of Jesus and the disciples.[8] (The contextual view of Mark from which I make this statement will be made explicit below.)

Yet it seems only fair to remind ourselves that, in his insistence that the distinction between the oral and the written be taken seriously, Kelber was, in 1983, almost a voice crying in the wilderness. This does not free his work from the danger of the contextual saturation of the meaning of the text, but it does raise the possibility of a certain degree of understandable over-compensation. The contextual saturation of the meaning of the text may be a built-in danger when one seeks to interpret a text and yet focuses not on the text itself (contextual focus A) but on the "internal"/"historical" context, especially the genesis of the text (C). *The Oral and the Written Gospel* is not immune to this danger, although Kelber is not unaware of it. The difficulty of the interpretive task makes the struggle all the more important. A theory of the text's genesis is no substitute for an interpretation of its significance. To explain the text's emergence in history is not to explain the text.

---

[8] One might also ask: Can there be a contextual saturation of the understanding of the *form* of the text as well as of its *meaning*? This question could be applied to Kelber's discussion of the gospel's form as parable. See Malbon, 1986b.

I have borrowed LaCapra's metaphor of "saturation" to speak of this danger. Concretizing this image may clarify its significance for the interpretive situation. When a sponge is saturated with water it does not really do a very good job of wiping off the kitchen table; it leaves a watery trail, and it cannot absorb any cleanser, should some be needed for a more thorough job. (Of course, a dry sponge, one that is totally unsaturated, is equally unsuited for this task.) Analogously, when a text like Mark's Gospel is saturated with meaning from one or another of its contexts, it does not function at its best either; it does not tell its story fully. If the questions a text raises tend to be quite completely answered by information from one of the text's "external" contexts, for example, then information from the text's "internal" relations may simply not be absorbed. Sometimes an interpreted text, like a sopping sponge, needs to be squeezed out.

A metaphor more often employed in discussing this issue is the hermeneutical "circle." Scholars of ancient literature and ancient history are accustomed to the problem of the circularity of analyzing the text for information about the context, then reconstructing the context on the basis of that analysis, and finally reinterpreting the text in terms of that reconstructed context. Kelber breaks out of this potentially vicious circle in an important way: he brings to his analysis of Mark significant information about the first-century context that could not be gleaned from Mark alone by the twentieth-century reader. But the hermeneutical circle spins in another way when Kelber relies heavily on this new contextual information either to answer or not to raise basic questions about the text itself, the interrelations of its elements, its characters, plot, etc. Then the relations between orality and textuality in a reconstructed context become *the key* to interpreting the relations between Jesus and the disciples in Mark. The questions the characters and plot of Mark present to the reader tend to be answered on the basis of the reconstructed context of its genesis, to the (relative) neglect of the context of its own interrelations. One way to break open the interpretive circle again is to move to another context. Such a move is my goal in the following section.

III. Questions About the Disciples in Mark

My questions about the disciples are raised from a different contextual focus from Kelber—from a focus on the interrelations of the elements of the text (A). And it may be that this different focus can suggest a reading of the story of the disciples in Mark that supplements, complements, and in some cases corrects the reading of Kelber.

My first question is in essence a restatement of my contextual focus: Do we not need, at some point, to read the text with primary reference to its own "internal" relations, as a check on readings of the text in close relation to "external" history or "external" literature (with their contingent dangers of contextual saturation of the meaning of the text)? Of course, reading the text with no reference to history or other texts is impossible; and, of course, focusing on the internal relations of the text has its own dangers. Yet there is still something to be said for preliminary investigations of the text and of history in relative isolation, so that the two may thereafter inform each other rather than risk forming or deforming each other initially. In terms of the Markan story of the disciples, my first question might be rephrased: Does not a reading of Mark with primary reference to its own "internal" relations suggest (for example) that two of the narrator's critical decisions must be interpreted together—the decision to end chapter 16 with questions about the disciples' future actions unanswered and the decision to include in chapter 13 Jesus's description of the disciples' future actions? And does not this reading serve as a check on readings (often made in close connection with a reconstructed historical context) of the Markan disciples as "failures"?

Readings of the disciples in Mark as "failures" (such as Kelber's) frequently include several interpretations of elements of chapters 13 and 16 not supported by a reading that focuses on the internal relations of the text. For example, the assumption that the disciples remain in Jerusalem is not shared by the Markan Jesus, whose message is not, "Tell the disciples and Peter to go to Galilee so they will see me," but rather, "Go, tell the disciples and Peter that I am going before them to the same place they are going—home, to Galilee; there they will see me as I told them earlier." Nor is the assumption that the disciples never hear of or respond to Jesus' resurrection supported by the narrator's choice to end the chronological narration with the women's fear and silence. Jesus' descriptions of the disciples' future responses, narrated proleptically in chapter 13, are not given as commandments that the disciples may or may not succeed in keeping, but as predictions: you *will* be beaten and you *will* stand before governors and kings for my sake, not you *should* stand. Were these projections judged to be inaccurate, it would not be the disciples who were discredited, but Jesus (*contra* Kelber, 1983:128; 1985:35-36, 39-40). And this is clearly not the case in Mark.

Based on a contextual focus on the interrelations of the elements of the text, one might say that the Markan Gospel has a double ending: the passion of the community (chap. 13) paralleling the passion of Jesus (chaps. 14-16) (see Malbon, 1986c: chap. 5). Or one might say, with Frank Kermode (1979:127-28), that Mark 13 is intercalated between 1-12 and

14-16 and, with most Markan interpreters, that intercalation serves an interpretive function. This arrangement of chapters 13 and 16 allows the narrator to suggest something very important about Jesus the teacher. The climactic teaching of Jesus is his teaching about suffering and death, about taking up one's cross for the sake of the other. But Jesus' lessons on this subject are not over until he dies, because talking about dying is not at all the same thing as dying. The disciples' learning cannot be complete until Jesus' teaching is complete. Reporting suffering and possibly death for the disciples (the completion of their learning) proleptically in chapter 13 rather than chronologically in chapter 16 has the crucial function of ending the gospel story dramatically with Jesus's death and resurrection. Thus the Markan hearers/readers are left to stand *with* the characters in the story (especially the women) at the empty tomb—face-to-face, as his followers were, with the challenge and the promise of Jesus's death.

My second question about the disciples that challenges the extent to which Kelber's book informs a reading of the text is this: In terms of the internal relations of the text, are not the disciples more closely related to the other Markan characters and to the readers than Kelber suggests? In Kelber's interpretation the reader is completely at odds with the disciples. More convincing is Robert Tannehill's view that the reader is intended to identify with the disciples (with their strengths first but later with their weaknesses), not just in chapter 16 but throughout the narrative, and Joanna Dewey's refinement of this view: the implied reader identifies both with the disciples and with Jesus; the implied reader's situation is that of the disciples, but his or her values are those of Jesus.

Furthermore, the relation between the disciples as characters within the narrative and the hearers/readers as respondents beyond the narrative is prepared for in the Markan Gospel by the relations between the disciples and other characters within the narrative. There is a movement outward from the disciples to the crowd; the crowd (*ochlos*) serves to complement the disciples in a composite portrait of the followers of Jesus. Jesus calls to himself both the disciples and the crowd, and both the disciples and the crowd follow Jesus. Jesus teaches and feeds both the disciples and the crowd—and also heals the crowd—and both the disciples and the crowd are amazed or astonished at Jesus. Again and again the crowd comes to Jesus; time after time the disciples go with Jesus. Jesus spends more time with the disciples and asks more assistance from them—in teaching, feeding, and other tasks. Yet the crowd crowds Jesus, and the disciples misunderstand discipleship. Although both the disciples and the crowd find themselves in opposition to Jewish leaders because they follow Jesus, in the end both abandon Jesus, who must then face the opposition of Jewish leaders alone. Both the disciples and the crowd are fallible followers. The encompassing movement from the disciples to the crowd within the narrative continues in the direction of the implied readers, as may be seen in the "whoever" statements of Jesus to his followers (most frequently the disciples but also the crowd): for example, whoever would come after me must deny self and take up his or her cross and follow me (8:34) (see Malbon, 1983: esp. 31-32, and Malbon, 1986a).

The relation of the disciples to other characters or character groups in Mark also has a direct bearing on the hearer/reader's relation to the disciples. According to Kelber, the disciples of Jesus are actually portrayed in Mark (by stages) as opponents of Jesus, along with the Jewish leaders and others; this is because they represent the opponents of the author of the Markan Gospel. My view is that the disciples are depicted first of all as "round" characters, in contrast to the demons and the Jewish leaders—who are "flat" characters on the negative side (see Malbon, 1989: esp. 275-81), and in contrast to the so-called "little people" (Rhoads and Michie, 129-35)—who are "flat characters on the positive side (for the classic discussion of "flat" and "round" characters see Forster). Whereas the hearer/reader might hiss the opponents and cheer the "little people," he or she would find more to identify with in the characterization of the disciples. If there is a connotative coloring to Mark's Gospel, the disciples represent neither white nor black but gray. The shading of the Gospel of Mark—and especially of its portrait of the disciples—is thus more subtle than that to which a polemical reading is sensitive. And the challenge of being a follower of Jesus is thus more intricately drawn. The Markan Gospel discredits not the disciples, but the view of discipleship as either exclusive or easy.

In Kelber's 1985 article, based on a 1982 paper at a conference on the theme of discipleship in the New Testament, this polemic between the disciples and the readers still stands. Kelber writes: "Nowhere in the canon does a text generate in readers as much alienation from the disciples as in this Gospel [of Mark]" (24); "*the full narrative impact* of the disciples' story is a negative one" (24); "Mark enforces discipleship that is discontinuous with the Twelve and also with the women" (36). Whereas Kelber seems to suggest that his view of the disciples challenges as too conservative (or traditional) the views of other interpreters (e.g., Petersen, Tannehill, and Boomershine; Kelber, 1985:34-37), Kelber's own understanding of Mark's narrative seems to me not radical enough. (Polemical is not the same thing as radical.) Kelber hears the Markan Gospel as an attack on the disciples as the claimed authorities of an esoteric group (1985: 41-42); I sense in it the pulling of the rug out from under any and all such groups, including the audience.⁹ Neither the disciples nor the hearers/readers can rest on their insider status; in this the two groups are alike, not different. Kelber's negative reading of the disciples and positive reading of the audience risks encouraging the readers' shared sense of superiority. I think Mark pulls the rug out from under us too.

However, in the conclusion to Kelber's 1988 article, "Narrative and Disclosure: Mechanisms of Concealing, Revealing, and Reveiling," there is a shift in the presupposed disciples/readers polemic. While the disciples are still viewed negatively (as chosen insiders who have made themselves outsiders), the readers' natural advantage over the disciples is questioned.

> In view of parabolic mystery at the peak of the narrative, the role reversal of the disciples from insiders to outsiders should have a chilling effect on us, the new insiders. In thinking that we are inside the narrative, we are perpetually reminded of what happens to insiders. It will not let us stay inside for long, if at all[.] And if we think we are inside, it is a sure sign that we are already outside (Kelber, 1988:17).

In such a situation, I would add, how can we be so sure that the disciples are irrevocably outsiders? Or that being inside and being outside are polemically opposed rather than connected in process and in mystery? In the conclusion to Kelber's 1991 address to the Bible in Ancient and Modern Media Group of the Society of Biblical Literature it is the absoluteness of the polemic between the oral and the written that is questioned. What is demanded, Kelber admits, is

> a new sensitivity toward the interworkings of Scripture [the written] and Logos [the oral] whereby each comes into its own by interaction with the other.
> What this suggests is that Scripture versus Logos, this great divide thesis, which pits oral tradition vis-a-vis the gospel text, cannot in the end supply the answer to the questions concerning tradition and gospel.... To grasp the overlaps and interfaces, we have to understand the hermeneutics of speech and writing, even if they rarely existed in a pure state. And yet, the longer one works with the strong thesis, the more we are aware of its character as a mastertrope. We need to force the dichotomy in order to erase it (14).

Would this new sensitivity to the interrelations of the oral and the written as media enable a less polemical interpretation of the interrelations of the disciples within and the readers of Mark's Gospel?

My questions about the disciples in Mark, directed here primarily to the conclusions concerning the disciples drawn by Kelber in his three books, serve to complicate his analysis. Can the disciples really serve as

---

⁹ Similarly, earlier Kelber heard in Mark a rejection of Jerusalem as the site of the parousia in favor of Galilee (Kelber, 1974), whereas I heard a rejection of the notion that the place of the parousia could be predicted (Malbon, 1986c).

vehicles for polemic if Markan patterns of characterization show them not as black or white but gray? Can the Markan Gospel really be said to lack discipleship fulfillment if chapter 13 is not forgotten in interpreting chapter 16?

Of course one could ask whether my reading of the disciples in Mark—barely sketched out here—tends toward the "contextual saturation of the meaning of the text." It would be a fair question, since the danger is inherent in the interpretive situation. It is, perhaps, somewhat more difficult to apply the metaphor of "contextual saturation" to an approach that focuses on the internal relations of the elements of the text since such an approach is sometimes accused of ignoring contexts altogether.[10] But, given that the internal relations of the elements of the text also comprise a context (A), what would characterize "contextual saturation" from this standpoint? Anachronism in interpretive strategies would seem to be the chief problem—reading the text in ways common enough in twentieth-century literary criticism but contra-indicated or undocumented in the ancient world. Eccentricity on the part of the interpreter could also be a means of "contextual saturation of the meaning of the text" from this standpoint—reading in one's own views more than reading out the text's views. But eccentricity and eisegesis are not the prerogatives only of those focusing on the internal relations of the text. I believe I could defend my reading of the disciples in Mark against the charges of anachronism and eccentricity, although the present essay is not the place to attempt this.[11] But I would certainly not see my own approach—or anyone's—as inherently protected from either the danger of contextual saturation of the meaning of the text or the opposite threat of contextual isolationism (ignoring too many relevant contexts).

---

[10] See the critique of "formalism" (which would appear to include interpretations focused on the interrelations of the elements of the text) presented by Poland. Poland argues that formalism in New Testament interpretation gains some of its strengths and some of its weaknesses from its borrowings from New Critical theory. For example: "Since New Critical theory is itself unclear about how a literary text is related to contexts of meaning outside of it, biblical scholars appropriating these critical assumptions may repeat these ambiguities in their own work" (160).

[11] In any such defense, the three criteria of validity presented by Armstrong would be of importance: (1) inclusiveness ("If understanding is a matter of fitting together parts into a whole, then that belief about their relations will be superior which can encompass the most elements in the configuration it projects" [13], (2) intersubjectivity ("Inasmuch as interpretation requires us to project beliefs, our reading becomes more credible if others assent to it or at least regard it as reasonable" [14]), (3) efficacy (that is, "the evaluation of a hypothesis or a presupposition on pragmatic grounds to see whether or not it has the power to lead to new discoveries and continued comprehension" [15]). Armstrong makes it clear that "these tests are capable of ruling out some interpretations as demonstrably illegitimate, although they cannot conclusively identify a single correct reading and must consequently allow genuine, irreconcilable hermeneutic conflict" (83).

I would argue, however, that a certain "pride of place" or "veto power"—to suggest metaphors for the initial and final roles—is appropriate to an interpretation with a contextual focus on the interrelations of the elements of the text, especially when one's goal is to interpret the text. When one's goal is to depict the history of Christian origins or the scope of ancient literary genres, the internal relations of individual texts, while still important, might well move into the background—although not too far into the background.[12] But when one claims to say what the text says, one must be willing to be guided not only by fruitful suggestions from multiple contexts but especially by the "internal"/"literary" context, the interrelations of the elements of the text.[13]

It is because of the multiple dimensions of texts and contexts and the human limits of their interpreters that a more systematic understanding of the relations between a text and its contexts and between contextual foci and interpretive conclusions is essential to the on-going process of evaluating interpretations and, more basically, interpreting texts. "In an ideal world," writes LaCapra, "each historian [or interpreter] would be responsible for the treatment of all problems from the most comprehensive of all possible perspectives. In the real world, certain choices must be made. Only when these choices are self-conscious and thought out can genuine cooperation among historians [or interpreters] with different emphases be undertaken in a noninvidious spirit" (67).

IV. TEXT, CONTEXTS, AND INTERPRETERS

A contextual reading in itself provides no guarantee of the adequacy of a textual interpretation. *The* context does not exist, and the text's mul-

---

[12] Questions about the internal relations of the elements of texts must not move too far into the background because assumptions are always being made about them. As Armstrong notes, "An appeal to origins cannot settle disputes about interpretation because in both arenas suppositions about part-whole relations are at stake. . . . A historical source seems self-evident to the critic only because it corroborates his or her sense of the whole that is the type of the story" (105). See also LaCapra's discussion of social history and intellectual history in the final essay of his book, *Rethinking Intellectual History*. "The difference between social and intellectual history is primarily one concerning the direction of interest. Social history uses texts to reconstruct a context or a past social reality. . . . Intellectual historians should, I think, try to provide good, close readings" (343-44).

[13] In his 1985 article Kelber would seem to agree: "That a gospel lives by its own internal logic is a principle of special relevance for discipleship, which is one of the most circumspectly plotted features in Mark. It may not be amiss, therefore, to withhold credence from any theory on Markan discipleship that has not seriously attempted to decode the full narrative pattern" (33). But, of course, one does not attempt "to decode the full narrative pattern" without presuppositions. See the note below. And yet, in the same article Kelber concludes: "the answer to Markan discipleship will in the last analysis come from the history of the tradition" (41).

tiple contexts seem to raise as many interpretive questions as they answer. Yet, to understand the text we must have contextual readings, and multiple contextual readings, and, in most cases, multiple contextual *readers*. Thus in considering the relation of text and contexts, we have concerned ourselves with the interrelations of the contextual foci *of interpreters*. The critical question is how to interrelate the multiple readings of a single text that result from multiple interpreters focusing on multiple contexts.[14] *The* answer, like *the* context, does not exist. But we may try out a couple of images that give direction.[15]

The first image is advocacy, and it comes from the legal field. Perhaps we interpreters are like attorneys defending our clients (our contextual foci or contextual readings), always dedicated to our own clients' best interests. One obvious advantage of this metaphor is that it makes room for areas of expertise; if one wanted to argue an interpretive case concerning orality and textuality, one would surely retain Kelber as a consultant! Another useful application of the metaphor is this: just as attorneys have limited free choice of their clients (specialty, location, financial needs or desires dictate accepting some clients; others may be assigned by the court system), so many interpreters select their contextual foci neither at random nor with perfect freedom and fully conscious deliberation (I doubt that the feeling of being "drawn" by one's approach—or one's text—is rare). In addition, the image of advocacy suggests the strength of the bond between an interpreter and his or her contextual focus. But the legal analogy breaks down in the end. Scholarly debates, although sometimes heated, are not basically adversarial situations. To suggest that one contextual focus or one contextual reading could be adjudicated "innocent" and another "guilty" assumes not only an acknowledged judge and jury of interpretation but also *a* standard that all are sworn to uphold: *the* (right, best, whatever) context. In fact, it may make more sense to conceive of the text as the client of all its interpreters, in which case our common advocacy defuses our adversarial relations. Thus the advocacy image is inadequate.

A second image that might provide direction as we struggle to interrelate multiple contexts and multiple interpretations of the text is

---

[14] Of course, the multiple and differing presuppositions of interpreters is an equally critical and even more fundamental question. As Armstrong writes: "Conflicting readings can occur because interpreters with opposing presuppositions about language, literature, and life can generate irreconcilable hypotheses about the meaning of a text. The role of belief in understanding makes disagreement inevitable in interpretation" (ix). Differing presuppositions have much to do with the critical question of *why* interpreters choose the contextual foci they do from among the text's multiple contexts.

[15] These images are presented in a slightly different form in the conclusion to Malbon, 1991a.

neither as concrete nor as striking as the first, but it may prove more useful. It is the image of complication. To complicate, not to clarify, is the task of the historian or historian of religions, according to Jonathan Z. Smith.

> The philosopher has the possibility of exclaiming with Archimedes: "Give me a place to stand on and I will move the world." .... There is, for such a thinker, at least the possibility of beginning, even of achieving *the* Beginning, a standpoint from which all things flow, a standpoint from which he has clear vision. The historian or the historian of religions has no such possibility. There are no places on which he might stand apart from the messiness of the given world. There is for him no real beginning, but only the plunge which he takes at some arbitrary point to avoid the unhappy alternatives of infinite regress or silence. His standpoint is not discovered; rather it is erected with no claim beyond that of sheer survival. The historian's point of view cannot sustain clear vision.
> The historian's task is to complicate, not to clarify (129).

As an historian of the New Testament period, as well as an interpreter of New Testament texts, Kelber has certainly "complicated"—in this positive, if hyperbolic, sense—our picture of Mark's Gospel. No longer can we assume an unbroken linear connection between oral tradition and the written text; Kelber's foundational work has complicated our understanding of media and media shifts. But it seems that in the very act of *complicating* the overall picture in Smith's positive sense, Kelber does sometimes *clarify* Markan interpretation in Smith's negative sense. The aspect of the historical *context* that "complicates" existing understandings (because it compensates for a lack of serious attention in previous scholarship) becomes the key to "clarifying" the *text*. For Kelber, the oral/written media shift "complicates" early Christian history but "clarifies" the Markan text.[16] This relation between "complicating" history and "clarifying" text points to the central issue raised above: the contextual saturation of the meaning of the text.

The concept of "contextual saturation," borrowed from LaCapra, together with the typology of contextual foci developed here, helps me to identify where and why I have certain difficulties with the reading of Jesus and the disciples in Mark presented by Kelber. First, I tend to be focally aware of aspects of the text of which he is subsidiarily aware (and vice versa, of course). Second, I judge that sometimes his focal awareness of certain of the text's contexts over-informs ("saturates") his understanding of the text, that "information" from one context is used either to

---

[16] According to LaCapra (340): "The general problem facing the 'human sciences' is to arrive at a differential understanding of the relation between documentary and other than merely documentary components of various texts and types of text." Certainly that is a problem here.

answer or to deflect important questions that are more sharply raised in another context. Accordingly, as an interpreter with a contextual focus more on text and less on history than Kelber, I feel responsible, first, to be attentive to the more complicated view of Markan history he enables me to share and, second, to share alternative views of the Markan text that may serve to "complicate" his own. Kelber and others will, in turn, evaluate whether my "complication" fulfills the positive role Smith has in mind. All "complications" are not equally helpful, just as all interpretations are not equally compelling.

Still, *the* interpretation does not exist. "Complication" continues to renew the perhaps inevitable search for "clarity" (see Kermode, 1967). As James Kincaid puts it: "Readers proceed with the assumption that there must be a single dominant structuring principle and that it is absurd to imagine more than one such dominant principle" (783). But texts themselves resist such "clarity" (or "coherence," as he calls it): "most texts, at least, are, in fact, demonstrably incoherent, presenting us not only with multiple organizing patterns but with organizing patterns that are competing, logically inconsistent"—with "a structure of mutually competing coherences" (783). As he argues against the text's single determinant meaning, Kincaid is not arguing for the text's indeterminacy (789-90). These seem to him, and to me as well, false alternatives. We are not free to assume that the text can mean anything just because it can mean many things. The argument is, rather, that texts "complicate" readings of themselves. Thus interpreters of the text take up their task from the text itself: to "complicate" interpretation. Both of these images, advocacy and "complication," are consistent with Paul Armstrong's suggestion for how to deal with *Conflicting Readings*:

> Interpreters must be forceful in applying their beliefs and assumptions to the text even as they remember that their convictions about textual configurations are only hypotheses and are therefore provisional and open to change and refutation. As hypotheses, guesses about meaning must be held with conviction even as they must also be viewed tentatively and warily. The paradox that hermeneutic power requires limitation to be effective is a reflection of the doubleness of belief as an epistemological structure. A belief is a guess about what we do not know, and it must consequently be both embraced with faith and questioned with skeptical detachment (139).[17]

Such faithful yet skeptical interpreters, interpreters who seek to be advocates of the text in its multiple contexts and yet to "complicate" and thus enliven interpretation, might well be described by the words Smith applies to historians: their "manner of speech is often halting and provisional"; they approach their "data" with "tentativeness"; in their work

---

[17] *Conflicting Readings* is the title of Armstrong's book.

they detect "clues, symptoms, exemplars"; they provide us with "hints that remain too fragile to bear the burden of being solutions" (129-30). Or, in the words of LaCapra: "The point here is to do everything in one's power not to avoid argument but to make argument as informed, vital, and undogmatically open to counterargument as possible" (38), although "the process of gaining perspective on our own interpretations does not exclude the attempt to arrive at an interpretation we are willing to defend" (45).

LaCapra's words (argument, counterargument, defend) return us to the image of advocacy, which, despite its final limitations, is not without useful application. It would appear unlikely that an interpreter could become an advocate for many different contexts. For this reason we must all, as interpreters of texts, seek to meet two requirements: (1) to understand as many approaches and appreciate as many contexts as possible, and (2) to read, listen to, and argue with other interpreters—especially those who are also working at the first requirement. We must argue our positions with conviction—but in order to "complicate." We must share our interpretations with faith—and also with skepticism.

WORKS CONSULTED

Armstrong, Paul B.
    1990   *Conflicting Readings: Variety and Validity in Interpretation.* Chapel Hill and London: University of North Carolina Press.

Black, C. Clifton
    1989   *The Disciples according to Mark: Markan Redaction in Current Debate.* Sheffield, Eng.: Sheffield Academic.

Boomershine, Thomas E.
    1974   "Mark, the Storyteller: A Rhetorical-Critical Investigation of Mark's Passion and Resurrection Narrative." Ph.D. dissertation, Union Theological Seminary, New York.

Dewey, Joanna
    1982   "Point of View and the Disciples in Mark." Pp. 97-106 in *SBL Seminar Papers.* Ed. Kent Harold Richards. Chico, CA: Scholars.

Dowd, Sharyn Echols
    1988   *Prayer, Power, and the Problem of Suffering: Mark 11:22-25 in the Context of Markan Theology.* SBLDS 105. Atlanta: Society of Biblical Literature.

Forster, E. M.
    1927   *Aspects of the Novel.* New York: Harcourt, Brace, and World.

Georgi, Dieter
    1964   *Die Gegner des Paulus im 2. Korintherbrief.* WMANT 11. Neukirchen-Vluyn: Neukirchener Verlag.

Kelber, Werner H.
    1974   *The Kingdom in Mark: A New Place and A New Time.* Philadelphia: Fortress.
    1979a   "Mark and Oral Tradition." *Semeia* 16:7-55.
    1979b   *Mark's Story of Jesus.* Philadelphia: Fortress.
    1983   *The Oral and the Written Gospel: The Hermeneutics of Speaking and Writing in the Synoptic Tradition, Mark, Paul, and Q.* Philadelphia: Fortress.
    1985   "Apostolic Tradition and the Form of the Gospel." Pp. 24-46 in *Discipleship in the New Testament.* Ed. Fernando F. Segovia. Philadelphia: Fortress.
    1987   "Narrative as Interpretation and Interpretation of Narrative: Hermeneutical Reflections on the Gospels." *Semeia* 39:107-133.
    1988   "Narrative and Disclosure: Mechanisms of Concealing, Revealing, and Reveiling." *Semeia* 43:1-20.
    1991   "Scripture and Logos: The Hermeneutics of Communication." Paper presented to the Bible in Ancient and Modern Media Group, Society of Biblical Literature, Kansas City.

Kermode, Frank
    1967   *The Sense of an Ending: Studies in the Theory of Fiction.* Oxford: Oxford University Press.
    1979   *The Genesis of Secrecy: On the Interpretation of Narrative.* Cambridge: Harvard University Press.

Kincaid, James R.
    1977   "Coherent Readers, Incoherent Texts." *Critical Inquiry* 3:781-802.

Krieger, Murray
    1964   *A Window to Criticism: Shakespeare's Sonnets and Modern Poetics.* Princeton: Princeton University Press.

LaCapra, Dominick
    1983   *Rethinking Intellectual History: Texts, Contexts, Language.* Ithaca: Cornell University Press.

Malbon, Elizabeth Struthers
    1983   "Fallible Followers: Women and Men in the Gospel of Mark." *Semeia* 28:29-48.
    1986a   "Disciples, Crowds, Whoever: Markan Characters and Readers." *NovT* 28:104-130.
    1986b   "Mark: Myth and Parable." *BTB* 16:8-17.
    1986c   *Narrative Space and Mythic Meaning in Mark.* New Voices in Biblical Studies. San Francisco: Harper & Row. Reprint: The Biblical Seminar 13. Sheffield: Sheffield Academic, 1991.
    1989   "The Jewish Leaders in the Gospel of Mark: A Literary Study of Markan Characterization." *JBL* 108:259-81.
    1991a   "The Poor Widow in Mark and Her Poor Rich Readers." *CBQ* 53:589-604.
    1991b   "Review of C. Clifton Black, *The Disciples according to Mark.*" *Int* 45:82, 84.

Petersen, Norman R.
　1978　　*Literary Criticism for New Testament Critics*. Philadelphia: Fortress.

Poland, Lynn M.
　1985　　*Literary Criticism and Biblical Hermeneutics: A Critique of Formalist Approaches*. AAR Academy Series 48. Chico, CA: Scholars.

Rhoads, David and Michie, Donald
　1982　　*Mark as Story: An Introduction to the Narrative of a Gospel*. Philadelphia: Fortress.

Robbins, Vernon K.
　1984　　*Jesus the Teacher: A Socio-Rhetorical Interpretation of Mark*. Philadelphia: Fortress.

Smith, Jonathan Z.
　1978　　*Map Is Not Territory: Studies in the History of Religions*. Leiden: Brill.

Tannehill, Robert
　1977　　"The Disciples in Mark: The Function of a Narrative Role." *JR* 57:386-405.

Weeden, Theodore J., Sr.
　1968　　"The Heresy that Necessitated Mark's Gospel." *ZNW* 59:145-58.
　1971　　*Mark—Traditions in Conflict*. Philadelphia: Fortress.
　1979　　"Metaphysical Implications of Kelber's Approach to Orality and Textuality." Pp. 153-66 in *SBL Seminar Papers*, Vol. 2. Ed. Paul J. Achtemeier. Missoula: Scholars.

WIFE AND SISTER THROUGH THE AGES: TEXTUAL DETERMINACY AND THE HISTORY OF INTERPRETATION

Robert B. Robinson
Lutheran Theological Seminary
at Philadelphia

ABSTRACT

The history of interpretation poses questions for the notion both of a determinate text and of an indeterminate text. Interpretations vary, suggesting that the text is at best a weak force to direct its own interpretation. Yet there is often substantial agreement between interpretations, suggesting the influence of a determinate text. This essay uses the concept of interpretive conventions as a third factor between interpreter and text to aid in understanding both variation and stability in interpretation. The application of two particular conventions, realistic reading and allegory, are illustrated through the interpretation of the wife/sister story in Genesis 12 by Philo, Augustine, Luther, and E.A. Speiser. Particular attention is paid to the relationship between interpretive conventions and the interests and practices of interpretive communities, with the conclusion that the determinacy of text is appropriately rooted in the life of interpretive communities.

It may seem hard to make Abraham out less than a scoundrel. There is a certain low cunning to the ploy of claiming that Sarai is his sister, but craftiness ill befits the hero. His actions offend common decency, perhaps even a code of chivalry adopted for epic characters, to say nothing of the obligation a husband owes his wife. Further, Abram's sense of timing is impeccably off. The precipitating decision to travel to Egypt follows immediately God's sincere promise of land which identifies Abram's destiny with the territory of Canaan. Jeopardizing his wife follows at no great remove an earlier promise that Abram would father a great people, presumably through the wife now consigned with unseemly alacrity to Pharaoh's harem. And what of Abram's trust? The visitation that promised offspring also assured Abram of God's protection and blessing. Abram either forgot or spurned the promises so recently received.

Yet to fault Abram's character, which seems perfectly justified, given even just the outline of the story, certainly puts the interpreter in the minority among all those who have read the twelfth chapter of Genesis. And in unaccustomed company. The Manichean Faustus, for instance, shared the low opinion of Abram's actions, but interpreters as disparate as Philo of Alexandria, E.A. Speiser, St. Augustine, Martin Luther, Umberto Cassuto, and the author of the Genesis Apocryphon from Qumran Cave 1 found nothing reprehensible in Abram's deeds, even if they acknowledged some appearance of impropriety. The most common appraisal of Abram, even in regard to this single passage, makes him out a knight of faith.

Either defending or demeaning Abram's character at this remove may seem of little purpose, and the point here is not to encourage such a dispute. But if the issue before us is the determinacy of the text, then the fact that the same text has been read with precisely opposite appraisals of the character of the main actor is highly pertinent. Would we not expect that a fully determinate text could establish so fundamental a matter as Abram's character without ambiguity or, minimally, without the polarization evident in the history of interpretation? Yet if we take the opposite position, that the text is indeterminate, and variant and even polarized interpretations are therefore hardly surprising, then the substantial agreement found through much of the history of interpretation on Abram's character becomes itself surprising and in need of explanation. Does not agreement in interpretation demand the hypothesis of a determinate text?

We are immediately into contested terrain in critical theory, yet in a favorable position within that terrain. The Bible has received continuous commentary since the period of its own composition. The record of biblical commentary reflects each generation's understanding of what the biblical text means, a concrete record of biblical meaning. For few other books is there anything like such an extensive and protracted record of response to the text. That is our great good fortune. The rich and diverse record of interpretation allows us to raise questions of textual determinacy in a manner that is not abstract or reductionist by referring to the actual practice of competent readers. Determinacy becomes a concrete matter of appraising to what extent interpreters have been guided by features of the text and by what features and to what extent they are guided by factors outside the text and by what external factors. To those questions we now turn, examining a number of interpretations of Genesis 12:10-18.

PHILO'S LITERAL INTERPRETATION

Philo's reputation resides in his practice of allegorical interpretation or allegoresis. Yet Philo was quite capable of non-allegorical interpretation of a text or, as in the present case, of allegorical and non-allegorical interpretations of the same passage, a remarkable fact in itself for our considerations; a single text, a single interpreter, and two interpretations. Because it differs so broadly from his literal interpretation of Genesis 12, Philo's allegorical reading of the passage will be considered separately later.

Philo's literal reading of the story of Abram's sojourn in Egypt is uncomplicated. A failure of crops in Canaan caused by excessive rainfall followed by drought and storm drove Abram to seek relief in Egypt, where the Nile and fortunate climate assured bountiful crops. The beauty and goodness of soul of Abram's wife attracted the attention of certain Egyptian officials, who told the king. The king sent for her and, seeing her great beauty, was driven by his licentiousness to bring her to ruin. Sarai was at the mercy of this cruel-hearted despot, nor could Abram protect her, owing to the inequity in power between himself and the king. So Sarai and Abram turned in extremity to God, who in great mercy protected them by inflicting nearly unbearable torments on the king and his cronies, who had made no protest against his licentious plans and so were complicitous in them. "Thus the chastity of the woman was preserved, while the nobility and piety of the man was evidenced by God . . ." (Philo: 53).

Philo's retelling of the story follows the biblical narrative but with significant additions and omissions. Philo draws out the causes of the famine in Canaan and the contrasting luxuriance of Egypt, expands the description of Sarai's beauty by adding beauty of soul to her attractions, attributes explicit motives to the characters' actions—the king's licentiousness, the cronies' mendacity, God's kindliness and mercy—and says not a word about Abram's deluding claim that Sarai was his sister. Much is going on here; the interpretation lies more within subtle additions and omissions than explicit commentary. The leading convention governing the interpretation is that the biblical passage is to be understood realistically, as if it were a window onto a real event. The assumption that the narrative refers to an actual episode in the life of Abram and Sarai allows Philo to exegete the event. Details not mentioned in the narrated depiction of the event may be supplied, obscure corners illuminated. For instance, the biblical text provides meagre description of the famine that induced Abram to leave Canaan. Yet it must have been of major proportions to compel so significant a move by Abram. Philo raises the famine to its appropriate proportions, adding excessive rainfall to stormy weather and drought to reach a continual catastrophe. Philo further understood clearly why Abram had sought Egypt as a refuge from the famine, and made that sense plain by enlarging from his experience the favored circumstances of his own fortunate land.

Philo's interpretation leaves little doubt that the immediate text exercises some control over the shape of the interpretation devised through the artful retelling of the story. The text establishes the general sequence of events and constrains both additions and subtractions from that sequence. Either to add too much or remove too much is to tell a different story, describe a different event. The narrative further stipulates the characters and again places constraints on the depiction of their relationships. Further, it may lie within the power of the text to establish the illusion of reference to an actual event which provides the tacit warrant for Philo's supplementary additions to the bare biblical narrative. The specific contours of the narrative composition—its conformity to ordinary chronological sequence, the setting of events in identifiable locations, the familiar concatenation of normal causal relations, the verisimilitude of narrated actions—all comport with the depiction of an ordinary event. More precisely, this text, no less than the sacrifice of Isaac, is composed in such a way that it is "fraught with background," to invoke Erich Auerbach's seminal reflections on realistic narrative (Auerbach: 12). Foreground events are clearly seen and provide the broad shape of the episode, but much of what would most interest an actual observer of the event—the characters' motives, the relationship of present actions to events before this episode, the values to be placed on particular actions—are unexpressed, an invitation and textual warrant for the interpreter's intervention.

It is equally clear that the text's control is not complete. On the broadest plain it has already been mentioned that Philo offers a second, allegorical interpretation of the passage, indicating that the realistic contours of the narrative do not impose a realistic reading of the narrative. Giving weight to the realistic features of the text, and consequently reading the narrative as depiction of an actual event, represents a decision, though it would be wrong to think of the decision as self-conscious or as an arbitrary choice among options. Philo stands within an interpretive community in which it is conventional to read such realistic narratives in a literal (τῆς ῥητῆς), realistic manner. He follows that convention.

Following the realistic convention gives weight in the interpretation to certain aspects of the text, but, again, does not grant absolute control to the text. Philo attributes the king's taking Sarai to licentiousness, although the text does not explicitly say so. Sarai is praised for her beauty of soul, although the text does not include this among her virtues. The question becomes what governs the direction Philo takes when he goes beyond the text.

There is no single answer. Some of Philo's additions are extensions of the realistic elements presented by the text. The description of the famine fills out the text's relatively terse depiction. Philo's appreciation of Egypt's fertility colors his geographical description. These additions are guided in part by the text and in part by the realistic reading convention. Added details must be on the same naturalistic plane as their correspondents in the text.

But there is more. Redescription of the event is also guided by thematic concerns. In increasing the bitterness of the famine in Canaan, Philo also subtly rationalizes Abram's decision to leave the land so recently promised. The inhabitants of Canaan all fled. Abram and Sarai were the last, reluctant refugees. The extended depiction of Egypt's reliable productivity subtly commends Abram's good sense in knowing where best to find food.

The thematic concerns are frequently stated explicitly. Near the beginning of this treatise on Abraham, Philo explains Moses' purpose in writing about the ancestors of the Jews, in the process revealing Philo's construal of the function of the ancestral stories within the larger scope of scripture. The stories are about "such men as lived good and blameless lives, whose virtues stand permanently recorded in the most holy scriptures, not merely to sound their praises but for the instruction of the reader and as an inducement to him to aspire to the same; for in them we have laws endowed with life and reason" (Philo: 7). Stories of exemplary lives then served broader purposes for Moses. "First, he wished to shew that the enacted ordinances are not inconsistent with nature; and secondly that those who wish to live in accordance with the laws as they stand have no difficult task . . ." (Philo: 7). The stories of the ancestors stand as commentaries on the laws not yet given and serve an exemplary function in conjunction with the laws, providing encouragement to the morally serious by example and living demonstration that the demands of the law do not exceed human capacity or nature. Given this understanding of the purpose of these stories, attributed here to Moses but certainly directed to Philo's own community, it is little surprising that Philo completely suppresses the inconvenient account of Abram misleading the king, moving the identification of Sarai as his sister from the foreground of the biblical narrative into the very deep background. That little detail would not be particularly edifying.

Philo's conception of the import of the specific episode of Abram and Sarai's sojourn in Egypt is also given. Abram proved his great faithfulness by moving from his home in Haran to Canaan at the behest of God. "God, then, approving of the action just related, at once rewards the man of worth with a great gift; for when his marriage was threatened through the designs of a licentious potentate, God kept it safe and unharmed" (Philo: 49). God rewards the pious. Such a dramatic example of virtue rewarded demands a clear villain. The king's motives are therefore carefully illuminated, but with the worst possible light. The king is licentious and cruel, his cronies procurers. The text itself did not lay the charge of licentiousness, but how else to characterize a man so fascinated with beautiful women? The cronies pander to the king's desires, seeking reports of women available to satisfy his appetite. The king's character is rendered deplorable so as to increase the danger to Sarai's chastity, enhancing the magnitude of God's protection. Naturally,we hear not a whisper of Abram's deception of the king.

A final broad concern of Philo's retelling of the ancestral stories is to establish the preeminence of his own people, "one species of that [human] race, which species is called 'royal' and 'priesthood' and 'holy nation'" (Philo: 33). Sarai's perfections, which include not just the physical attractiveness which the biblical text affirms but also goodness of soul, makes her worthy mother of ". . . a whole nation, and that the nation dearest of all to God, which, as I hold, has received the gift of priesthood and prophecy on behalf of all mankind," (Philo: 53). The addition of Sarai's goodness of soul to her physical beauty, the feature that presumably attracted the licentious king, may be partly guided by a midrashic convention. The biblical text uses two different terms to describe Sarai's physical attractiveness, an inadmissible divine redundancy resolved in Philo's bilateral anthropology by understanding one term to refer to her physical appearance, the other to the character of her soul. If midrashic influence is to be seen here, then it works in full congruence with Philo's desire to build up the virtue of this ancestress of the chosen people, which in Philo's anthropology would certainly have been incomplete were her goodness limited to her physical nature. Philo's elaboration of the unendurable torments of the king, by which "all appetite for pleasure was eradicated" (Philo: 51) also protects the reputation of the ancestress by giving assurance that she was shielded from the king's advances, a point left much too obscure in the biblical account.

Textual and extra-textual elements interact in complex ways in Philo's retelling of the story of Abram and Sarai in Egypt. The text stands fixed yet open. Interpretation begins, it seems, outside the text, with adoption of the realistic reading conventions that regard the passage as descriptive of an actual interchange between Abram, Sarai, and the king. The adoption of the realistic convention is itself a very complex matter. In part it is controlled by the text itself. The text by its structure and composition must minimally be capable of accepting a realistic reading. Were all the characters in Genesis 22 angels, for instance, or were the setting subterranean, a realistic reading would be most difficult. The text exercises control. Yet the reading convention lies outside the text itself, even outside

Philo. Realistic reading is conventional in a community of readers who habitually read such narratives as if they were interconnected events in a coherent world that overlapped the readers' own experience. Details in that coherent world necessarily make sense in the same ways as similar details in the readers' world. Philo simply participates unreflectively in this convention as a condition of intelligibility for his interpretation. If he departed too radically from prevailing convention, no one would understand him.

At the same time adoption of the realistic convention is a conditioned choice. The text will accept other conventions. Philo himself also interprets Genesis 12 allegorically. The choice to read realistically is included in Philo's particular intent in presenting this interpretation to his audience. Philo's announced desire is to exhort his community to faithfulness and moral seriousness through observance of the law. Israel's ancestors represent concrete models of the moral life. But their examples are only cogent if the Jews' ancestors inhabit the same reality as the present community. The realistic convention assumes that the stories of the ancestors took place in the same dimension as contemporary experience; the narrative is a window on real events. Philo's Jewish community can emulate the rectitude of its forbears.

Still further, Philo's concern to establish the identity of his people as the "nation dearest to God" demands the clearest and most concrete relationship between the present community and the ancestors who bore the clear marks of God's favor. The realistic convention allows that relationship to be defined biologically, between a real couple, Abram and Sarai, and their lineal descendants, the Jewish community of Philo's acquaintance. Again, the purpose that lies behind retelling the story includes unproblematically the conventions by which it is read.

Reading within the realistic convention is a remarkably open process, so open that it is necessary to ask if there is any control on what may be discovered in the text's background. Are there any controls or may a text be realistically read to any effect? It seems to me that there are three types of control. The first is textual. Additions are keyed to a specific textual warrant. The characterization of the king's licentiousness is a tendentious expansion on the textual report that he summoned the beautiful Sarai to his harem. The textual notice provides an occasion for the expansion, which then unfolds in a direction set by his thematic interests and by his construal of the shape of the ancestral narratives within scripture. Likewise, the text apparently prohibits gross additions. Philo may not, it seems, manufacture new characters or additional events not mentioned in the biblical account, although it is interesting, and I think, understandable, that he can successfully ignore an event that is described, Abram's conversation with the king.

Philo is also guided by his understanding of the relationship of the present text (or the events it narrates) to the larger scope of texts of which it is a part. The Abraham narrative, with the other ancestral stories, are related to the legal material coming later as anticipation and exemplification, a relationship that precludes the negative depiction of Abram or Sarai in this episode.

The second form of control lies in the realistic conventions. Added details must have verisimilitude as possible elements of the event being described. God's deliverance of Sarai from the king's power is accomplished through "all manner of scarce curable plagues" (Philo: 51), rather than the *force majeur* of a host of angels, in part because of the realistic convention governing interpretation. The reader must be able to assimilate additional details on the level of everyday occurrences.

The third control resides in the interests of the interpretive community that received Philo's work. Philo addressed a particular community of Alexandrian Jews, a community with particular needs and interests, a need for moral exhortation and an interest in its own identity, to judge by Philo's statements. The interest of the community of which Philo was a part shaped his interpretation. Had he failed to incorporate their interests, his interpretation would have been irrelevant. As it is, Philo's interpretation takes its impetus and its seriousness from the life of his community.

This discussion does not exhaust by any means the range of forces that influence Philo's interpretation. Additional complexity is hinted at by the possibility of the interaction of midrashic conventions in Philo's realistic reading. Other factors doubtless enter in.

Augustine's Literal Interpretation

Augustine's interpretation of the story of Abram and Sarai in Egypt appears in a polemical interchange with the Manichaean Faustus. To a large extent Faustus sets the terms of the debate and, although we have only Augustine's representations of Faustus's positions, it is clear that Faustus cited the immoralities of Abram and the other ancestors of the Jews to discredit the Old Testament. Indeed, Faustus attempted to present Augustine a conundrum which would force him to abandon the authority of the Old Testament. Faustus was prepared to grant that the biblical authors had libelled Abraham. There were, he allowed, no distressing acts to explain, no sale of Sarai to Pharaoh or Abimelech for Abram's gain. The biblical stories were fabrications (Augustine, 1909: 272). If Augustine accepted this generous proposal, he would not be forced to defend the questionable honor of Israel's ancestors. But, of course, the price would be high. The Old Testament narratives would become a tissue of lies.

Faustus's carefully poisoned bait was intended to induce Augustine to abandon the prevailing realistic conventions of reading, according to which the biblical narratives were regarded as transparent windows on the events they described. In place of interpreting the events themselves, as reliably depicted in the narrative, Faustus suggested interpreting the authors' motives or intentions. However one characterized the authors' motives, as reliable or libelous, motives as an object of interpretation were less secure than transparent realistic narration. Faustus could hardly lose.

Augustine, however, declined the gambit. He refused to accept the imposition of the author between text and event as an intermediate object of interpretation. He implicitly affirmed the realistic convention of reading the text and, in the process, incurred the responsibility for defending the honor of Abram and Sarai. If their actions could not be defended, the authority of the Old Testament would be undermined.

In defending Sarai and Abram against Faustus's charges of immorality, especially Abram against the charge that he profited at the expense of his wife's chastity, Augustine was aided by the conventions of realistic reading, conventions shared by Faustus once his suggestion to interpose the author between narrative and event collapsed. That is, both Augustine and Faustus in following realistic reading practice tacitly agree to interpret the event to which the narrative refers. The possibility of meaningful discussion between Augustine and Faustus hangs on their sharing this convention and the difference between them turns on how the convention is to be applied. More precisely, it turns on how the obscure areas of the text are to be illuminated and, still more specifically, on the motives to be imputed to the characters. The text, we will remember, conveniently fails to make anyone's motives explicit.

Faustus is less reticent in ascribing motives. Abram acted "from avarice and greed . . . in sacrilegious profanation of his marriage" (Augustine, 1909: 273). Not once but on several occasions. The conclusion seems fully justified by the narrative if, as in common law, motive is to be deduced from the effect of actions. Abram emerges wealthy from both episodes.

Augustine's task is more difficult. Because of the polemical situation, Augustine cannot simply ignore interchanges in the biblical account, as Philo was able to do. Faustus would throw the omissions up to Augustine. Augustine must find plausible explanations for Abram's actions that do not impute fault to him. The argument is quite involved.

Faustus had charged that Abram acted from greed. Augustine counters this charge by downplaying the part of the biblical account which speaks of the gifts Abram took with him when he left Egypt. Instead, Augustine focuses on the threat to Abram's life. By taking that threat very seriously, Augustine begins to justify *in extremis* actions that would not be acceptable under ordinary circumstances. Then comes the tour de force. Abram's exposure of his wife is an act of faith. Abram trusted that God would protect her from harm; only so could he leave her unprotected. Far from being an act of cowardice, Abram's surrender of his wife was a supreme act of confidence in God's protection (Augustine, 1909: 286).

This suggestion may solve the immediate problem of providing honorable motives for Abram's actions, but it seems to invite a further, fatal riposte. If Abram trusted God to protect Sarai, why did he not equally trust God to deliver his own life? Again, Augustine proposed a profoundly pious explanation. Abram did not wish to put God to the test. Since Abram had at his disposal means to preserve his own life without God's assistance (the ploy with Sarai), not to avail himself of those means was to test God's faithfulness. This the pious Abram refused to do.

With the major charge of greed and avarice answered by presenting Abram's true motives, Augustine can discharge the minor allegations. Abram technically never lied to the Pharaoh. He never claimed Sarai was not his wife because he was not asked. Here Augustine reads very closely. And, as for the claim that Sarai was his sister, well, she was. Or perhaps Abram spoke metaphorically. Biblical examples of such usage are adduced. Cleared of all charges.

Several points merit reflection in this interchange between Augustine and Faustus. First, both Augustine and Faustus must operate with the same fundamental reading conventions in order for meaningful discussion to take place. Shared reading conventions are the grounds of common discussion of the text. An unusual feature of this polemical circumstance is that a preliminary negotiation takes place between Faustus and Augustine over what those conventions should be. Is the text to be read realistically, as window on event, or as authorial artifact, with emphasis on authorial intent? The choice has polemical implications, as we saw, but when Augustine declined to accept the author as the focus of discussion, both he and Faustus de facto accepted realistic convention as the common ground for discussion. Were one debater to convince the other, it would in this case be because he had presented a more credible realistic explanation of the characters' actions in this concrete situation.

Secondly, on those grounds of credibility it is necessary to concede the palm to Faustus. Greed and avarice are more plausible realistic explanations of Abram's actions than Augustine's convoluted invocation of Abram's piety. But somehow the inherent implausibility of the motives Augustine supplies does not seem to matter. Augustine is not really trying to convince Faustus or a candid world. Although his interpretation is framed by the debate with Faustus, the real control on Augustine's realistic reading resides within the practice of his own interpretive community, the body of Catholic Christians who requested that he reply to Faustus. Their ingrained practice of reading the Old Testament and the New as testifying to the actions of the same God is maintained by mounting an explication of Abram's motives sufficiently plausible to be advanced without embarrassment which will allow them to continue to venerate Israel's ancestors. Such an explication Augustine provides, clearly on an ad hoc basis within the interpretive space allowed by the realistic convention of interpreting the event. Augustine's interpretation is rooted in the deepest concerns of his interpretive community as he perceives them and grows out of those concerns. At the same time it finds its deepest validation not in abstract standards of plausibility but in the efficacy of the interpretation in continuing to shape the common life and practice of his interpretive community.

LUTHER

Commenting on verses 14 and 15 of chapter 12, Luther wondered how it was possible that the Egyptians found Sarah attractive (Luther: 303). Sarah was already a woman of at least seventy years by Luther's calculation when she entered Egypt. How was it imaginable that her beauty would be praised, let alone that the king would fall in love with her and take her to his house?

The question is natural enough if one is trying to imagine an actual event. And Luther, no less than Philo and Augustine, is indeed trying to imagine an actual event, is reading through the text to imagine the king's first laying eyes on Sarah and instantly desiring her. The matter of Sarah's age, which is not in the immediate text but involves a calculation from the preceding narrative of this same Sarah and Abraham, derails the imagination. That powerful men desire and demand attractive women requires no imagination at all. That powerful men desire and demand seventy year old women is nearly unimaginable. If Luther is to treat this story as an actual occurrence, then some plausible explanation of the unimaginable is necessary.

Luther was never one to give one explanation when four or five will do. Sarah's beauty may have been a miracle. But recourse to miraculous causality tends to undermine the realism of an account, so Luther buttresses the suggestion of miracle by giving it an immanent motivation in the event: God endowed Sarah with great beauty to capture the Egyptian's attention so they would pay heed to Abraham's preaching. Or, more likely, Luther's age had so deteriorated from the time of Abraham and Sarah that a seventy year old woman then looked like a thirty year old now. Then again, Sarah had not yet had a child, "she was not yet worn out by the pains and the travail of childbirth." (Luther: 304)

It is easy to smile at the forced nature of these explanations. In Luther's times they were undoubtedly more plausible—the interpreter's understanding of what is realistic changes through time. Yet they served a most important function in his exegesis: they preserved the realistic reading of the Genesis text. If no plausible explanation of such details as Sarah's desirability at advanced age could be found, then Genesis would have to be read as fantasy or myth fundamentally incongruent with Luther's realistic experience of the world. Luther's explanations acknowledge that there are some differences between the biblical world and his own. People age differently now. Humanity has deteriorated. But the differences are not so great that they cannot be harmonized by a plausible, mediating explanation, which Luther supplies. The mediating explanation preserves the fundamental identity of Abraham and Sarah's world with Luther's understanding of his own world.

Luther's exegesis then draws out the full possibilities of realistic reading, particularly the opportunity to explore the unexpressed motivations of the characters. Because the biblical narrative is so chary of attributing explicit motives to character, it is necessary to deduce their motives from their actions, with the sort of leeway in the deduction that we have previously seen. Luther's deductions of motivation in this episode begin with God, a character not even explicitly mentioned in the opening verses. The story opens with Abraham and Sarah driven from Canaan by a famine. In the biblical account the famine is described flatly; it simply happens. But in Luther's understanding of natural events, famines do not simply happen. Natural occurrences of moment are intentional acts. Famine is God's handicraft, other biblical passages make clear, and the means for manipulating human activities. But as an intentional act of God, the famine is incongruous. What could move God to drive Abraham and Sarah out of the land so recently promised to them?

Some speculations are excluded. God did not renege on the promise; the suggestion may only be raised to point the way to the true explanation. The famine was sent to test Abraham's faith, a seeming denial of the promise sent to probe Abraham's tenacity to God's word. "God is wont to act in this way . . . in order to test the faith of the saints" (Luther: 289). Unlike, for instance, Genesis 22, the sacrifice of Isaac, the biblical text does not explicitly identify this episode as a test, but Luther's seizes on the category of test to explain God's otherwise inexplicable reversal. The speculation about God's motives then casts the whole sojourn in Egypt as a continual testing of Abraham's faith in the face of adversity. Abraham's actions are consistently construed as responses to this test and interpretation enters the familiar ground of supplying motives for actions recorded in the text.

On the whole Luther finds Abraham's intentions honorable, even exemplary. When Abraham was driven out of Canaan (the godless Canaanites expel him for causing the famine by introducing a new religion [Luther: 290]) he did not doubt that he would return, but trusted God's word of promise and employed his reason to seek out Egypt, a fit place where he and Sarah might survive the famine. Moses, choosing words carefully, signaled Abraham's faithfulness by indicating that Abraham only intended to sojourn in Egypt (לָגוּר שָׁם), not to settle there permanently.

Still, Luther seems prepared to go further than many before him in conceding that Abraham sinned. In part the culprit was reason. When first speaking of Abraham's decision to enter Egypt, Luther found that Abraham was guided by reason and this was commendable. "In this instance Abraham is guided not entirely by the Word but by his reason as well . . . . In earthly dangers reason has its place; it has the capacity to concern itself with some things and to give advice" (Luther: 290). Faint praise but praise nonetheless. But, when considering the lie to Pharaoh, Luther says, "Thus when Abraham had let the Word get out of his sight and heart and, yielding to his reason, considered the dangers, he began to waver but was not altogether overwhelmed." (Luther: 293) Reason and faithfulness to the Word appear as conflicting motivations, a standing theme in Luther's anthropology, with Abraham succumbing to the lesser.

But then Luther pulls back. Another thought occurs to him, another motivation better meets the text's silence. Abraham did not weaken but, in full faithfulness, declined to put God to the test. Augustine's opinion is adopted.[1] If Abraham weakened at all, it was only in the face of pressing danger. More likely, he piously preserved God's freedom of action.

Luther's theological commitments acknowledge Abraham as both saint and sinner. The polemical situation did not compel him to defend Abraham or surrender the authority of scripture, as in Augustine's argument with Faustus. Consequently, the ascription of motives is more delicately poised, entertaining the reality of Abraham's sin, then pulling back at the last moment. In this instance the initial decision to treat the whole episode as a test of Abraham by God seems to have determined the valence of the motives ascribed to Abraham. The category of test , for Luther, casts Abraham in an exemplary role, his faithfulness in withstand-

---

[1] Luther follows Augustine but also the practice of much of late Medieval exegesis with regard to the faults of Israel's ancestors. See Bainton.

ing adversity modelling faithfulness for the Christian facing the Canaanite famine in reformation Germany. Abraham could have served as the model of the backslider by identifying him with Moses at Meribah or David in the matter of Bathsheba, both of whom Luther mentions (Luther: 293). Luther hesitates, then returns Abraham to the positive model of faith by explicitly connecting him to the test in Genesis 22 and the praise of Abraham's faithfulness in offering Isaac in the Letter to the Hebrews (Luther: 294). Interpretation here is in part guided by Luther's construal of how this particular passage fits into the shape of the whole biblical story.

Few other interpreters exploit the hortatory possibilities of realistic reading of scripture as powerfully as Luther. The assumed identity between the world of the event represented in the text and his own world sustains an easy mobility. The realistic convention unites two worlds, the world of the full biblical text and Luther's own, into a single common world, within which Luther and Sarah and Abraham and Luther's readers (and, most significantly, Christ) all move. Abraham and Sarah directly teach the Christian gospel, through their example. Abraham leaves Canaan's famine in full confidence that God's promise will be sustained. "Therefore he overcomes this trial by his patient hope for the future blessing." (Luther: 289) Immediately, Luther draws the moral.

> Let us do the same thing when we experience the same adversities. As I stated above, the masses are complaining now about various misfortunes like high prices, pestilence, wars, etc.; and it is true that these are more numerous and more frequent than they used to be. But in addition to the sins and the great ingratitude, which provoke God to inflict punishment, let the godly remember that this happens as a trial for those who believe. (Luther: 289-90)

The same adversities, the same thing. The needs of the interpretive community for encouragement and models in the face of adversity here reinforce the realistic convention and direct its application. Realistic reading conventionalizes the identity between the biblical world and sixteenth century Germany that allows fluid passage from the banks of the Nile to the Rhine. At the same time realistic reading provides enough openness in the matter of motives to allow Abraham's actions to be construed positively as a model of faith.

Speiser

E.A. Speiser's Genesis commentary in the Anchor Bible series is well known, available, and still well respected after nearly a third of a century. The distance between Speiser's interpretation and that of any of the pre-critical commentators examined is readily apparent. None had access to the wealth of historical information about ancient Israel whose use is the hallmark of Speiser's commentary. But for all the differences, Speiser still operates within the realistic convention. He is concerned to interpret the event itself visible through the text.

Speiser's apologetic interests are greatly attenuated when compared to the earlier interpreters', although his explanation of the event does tend to exonerate Abraham of the main charge of nonchalance about his wife's chastity. His effort is to understand the event itself on its own historical terms, and this, once again, involves filling in motives that are largely unspoken in the text. But Speiser is truly a modern historian. He cannot fill in the motives speculatively, from the store of his own experience of the contemporary world. He is too acutely aware of the historical gulf that exists between his own world and that of Abraham. The silences in the text, even on matters of motive, must be filled with information *a propos* the historical moment of the event itself. To illuminate the specific matter of Abram calling Sarai his sister, Speiser adduces a curious custom from ancient Hurrian society, "from whom the patriarchs branched out," living "in closest cultural symbiosis" with them (Speiser, 91). The force of Speiser's argument is summarized in a single line. "In Hurrian society the bonds of marriage were strongest and most solemn when the wife had simultaneously the juridical status of a sister, regardless of actual blood ties" (Speiser: 92). Sisterhood conveyed a status higher than marriage alone. Consequently, Abraham had presumably adopted Sarai as his sister in order to obtain for her the higher status. When Abraham apprised the Egyptians that she was his sister, therefore, he was not exposing her to greater danger, but in fact acting to protect her. Though the Egyptians might not respect her status as a married woman, still they would honor the double status of wife and sister. Unfortunately, the Egyptians were not Hurrians.

Although Speiser maintains the convention of realistic reading by interpreting the event behind the text, the matter of control of the interpretation has changed markedly. Pre-critical interpreters assumed the fundamental identity of the biblical world with their own and in this assumption found a tacit warrant for adding details to the text from their structured store of experience. Validation of those additions was largely informal. The audience for the interpretation shared the store of experience from which the interpreter drew and recognized the scene depicted by the interpreter on the basis of that shared experience. Speiser begins with the historian's assumption that the world of the event differs from the contemporary world. Amplifications of the text must lodge comfortably within that distant world of Hurrian symbiosis and the only defensible access to that ancient culture is through the disciplined canons of historical research. Validation of interpretation becomes far more formal, a matter of method and sufficient evidence, rather than self-evident correspondence between textual world and interpreter's world. To establish his interpretation Speiser must both demonstrate the Hurrian custom and link Israel's ancestors to it.

In this matter of validation, since the Enlightenment central to interpretation, the text plays a role. Not every Hurrian custom will illuminate the event obscurely behind the text, but only one that trades on the identity of wife and sister. Details of the text obviously direct Speiser's research and his selection of appropriate explanatory material, the realistic substance of his interpretation. Yet the text does not exercise complete control, by any means. The explicit statement of the text is that Abraham sought to mislead Pharaoh in order to protect himself, not that he attempted to protect Sarai. Speiser has an explanation: ". . . it can be shown on internal grounds that the narrators themselves were no longer aware of the full import of their subject matter" (Speiser: 91). Later authors forgot the Hurrian past.

A text that proves an unreliable guide to the event it reports demands a scholarly commentary better acquainted than the author with the event. That demand is the legacy of the long tradition of realistic reading and one branch of its modern conventional form. Reconstructing the event, illuminating its obscurities, constitutes interpretation, but current epistemology mandates that the event now be recovered through evidence external to the text itself. Neither the text nor the interpreter's own experience constitutes a reliable guide to the obscurities of Hurrian marital customs. The demand for a *via externa* marks one, perhaps decisive, break with the exercise of earlier realistic conventions.[2]

The nature of the difference between pre-critical realistic and modern realistic reading may help us understand why the text may seem indeterminate. In both forms of realistic reading the convention locates the meaning of the text in the event to which the text refers. Equating reference with the meaning of the text has the effect of locating meaning outside of the text itself, in a certain sense outside of the text's control. The text draws its meaning from the event it depicts. In pre-critical realistic reading the unproblematic assumption held that the text accurately correlates with the event described. The interpreter begins with the text, which is determinate so far as it goes in reflecting the underlying event, but because the assumption is that there is more to the event than the text depicts, the realistic convention grants the interpreter a warrant to add details in the manner we have seen. In modern realistic reading there is no

---

[2] See Hans Frei, *The Eclipse of Biblical Narrative*, for historical documentation of the epistemological shift involved. Frei sees modern departures from pre-critical realistic conventions as radical — and radically mistaken.

assumption that the text correlates fully with an underlying event. The event itself must be established insofar as possible on external grounds, through independent evidence, and that event then constitutes the meaning of the text, what the text is about, we would say. If the text does *not* correlate with the independently reconstructed event, then the authors who are no longer aware of the full import of their subject matter are to be corrected. The text gives ground to its reference.

The community that received Speiser's interpretation clearly has little interest in the biblical figures as models of either virtue or faith. Apology is beside the point and although the Hurrian custom tends to exculpate Abraham, that is just by the by, not the intent of the interpretation. Interest lies in the history of Israelite culture and religion and the biblical text, however unreliable, makes a significant contribution to the reconstruction of that culture and religion . Although it preserves the memory imperfectly, the biblical text recalls an event in which wife and sister were identified. Only Hurrian society features a similar identification, as Speiser emphasizes (Speiser: 92). The biblical account, properly interpreted, therefore leads Speiser to the origins of Israelite culture and to the original meaning of customs distorted through time. The interest of the community of scholars concerned to trace the actual development of Israelite culture are served.

Philo's Allegorical Interpretation

It is odd, perhaps, and somewhat troubling to return to Philo (and more briefly Augustine, later). Nothing has changed. It is the same text, the same interpreter,the same audience and, presumably, the same situation in which interpretation occurs. No variables, no variation. Yet Philo offers two widely differing interpretations of Genesis 12 within the same tract. Our concern may not reside in the multiplicity of interpretations—multiple interpretations are not startling, even though more than one interpretation by a single interpreter may be unusual. Disquiet may arise from the nature of the interpretation, from allegory. Since early in the Reformation allegorical interpretation has been viewed with increasing disfavor until today, there are no real practitioners except, of course, the liturgies of most churches. Uncontrollable, arbitrary, eisegesis—matters of validation and control dominate the attitude toward allegory, leading to the denial that allegorical interpretation is in any way a sense of the text.

For our purposes it is important not to foreclose the discussion of the relation of allegory to the text. In particular, I think it inappropriate to allow questions of control and validation to dominate and define the discussion, and, still more particularly, to allow one model of validation and control (correspondence to a determinate textual meaning) to exclude *a priori* allegory from consideration. We have been proceeding, at least in part, historically, and, historically, Philo and the other allegorists present their interpretation as the sense of the text. That claim at least warrants our consideration of their efforts.

A distinct break separates Philo's allegorical interpretation of Genesis 12 from his literal reading. Philo himself distinguishes the allegorical interpretation by attributing it to unnamed natural philosophers (φυσικῶν ἀνδρῶν) (Philo, 53). Edmund Stein argued that this particular formulation (φυσικοὶ ἄνδρες) always indicates theological allegorists in Philo's usage (Stein: 27), although it is not certain that the formula cites any particular figure. The use of the introductory formula does, however, announce the application of different conventions of interpretation and signals the reader to shift to the appropriate conventions for allegory.

The interpretation begins on a slender textual base. Abraham's name had earlier (Philo: 45) been etymologized as "elect father of sound" and this etymology interpreted to make Abraham stand for the Sage. Sarai's name now also receives an etymological interpretation as sovereign lady (ἄρχουσα) which is immediately interpreted as "Virtue," because "nothing is more sovereign or dominant than virtue." (Philo: 53). Philo's etymologies occasionally make no sense whatsoever (Stein: 23-4), but in both present instances the connection to the Hebrew is obvious. Since Philo apparently knew next to no Hebrew (Stein: 20-4), he must have depended on a source that was familiar with the Hebrew. The existence of such a source points to an established tradition of etymological interpretation related, Edmund Stein argued, to the Palestinian midrash and diverse Jewish-Hellenistic authors (Stein: 25), while John Dillon speaks more broadly of a combination of Stoic and Jewish practice (Dillon: 85). If the practice of etymology was well-established, reading Sarah as virtue may have been as unremarkable as recognizing the import of the name Christian in *The Pilgrim's Progress* is for us. The etymological significance of the name would be a textual feature that guided the allegorical interpretation.

The etymologies of the names Sarah and Abraham lead into a somewhat obscure discussion. Sarah represents virtue and Abraham as the sage represents thought. However, virtue (Sarah) is an active principle and therefore masculine in Philo's view, while thought (Abraham) is more passive and therefore female. The facts of the text fail him and Philo abandons them. "If anyone is willing to divest facts of the terms which obscure them and observe them in their nakedness in a clear light he will understand that virtue is male, since it causes movement and affects conditions and suggests noble conceptions of noble deeds and words, while thought is female . . . ." (Philo: 55) Philo's only attempt at resolving the inversion of genders is an uncertain argument contrasting marriage brought about by pleasure and involving bodies (σωμάτων) with true marriage made by wisdom . "Now the two kinds of marriage are directly opposed to each other." (Philo: 53). The opposition may account for the inversion, although the connection is not explicit. In any case, through the etymologies the text establishes the terms of the interpretation but the discussion of those terms follows its own logic, not that of the text.

The second stage of Philo's allegory follows the text far more closely. The king of Egypt is taken to represent the mind which loves the body (νοῦς φιλοσώματος), for obvious reasons. Such a mind fixed on the body shams fellowship with virtue "in his desire to earn a good repute with the multitude." (Philo: 55) God hates the sham and inflicts painful tortures. The instrument of these tortures is the incompatibility between baseness and virtue. Nothing pains falseness and dissimulation more than to be confronted with virtue. The influence of the text here is obvious. Once the identification of Sarah with virtue is granted on the basis of the etymology, the allegorical interpretation follows the movement of the biblical story. The clearest influence of the biblical text is the introduction of God, who is not strictly necessary for the allegory (the tortures do not need to be inflicted, the juxtaposition of baseness and virtue is sufficient) but whose inclusion follows the biblical text, which attributes the affliction of Pharaoh to God.

Although the allegory is related to the text and to some extent controlled by it, to our eyes that connection seems weak. The etymology must be granted before the allegory can begin and most modern readers are disinclined to accept etymology as a textual feature because current conventions of reading ascribe no role to the etymology of words in the text. The etymologies of proper names in particular are accorded no significance; their function is purely referential. Some biblical scholars still may use etymologies to define Hebrew terms, although even this practice is waning under the influence of synchronic linguistics. To make the point explicitly: what is regarded as "in" the text, controlling its interpretation, depends on conventions that ascribe significance to particular features. In Philo's time conventions of reading understood etymological meaning as "in" the text. Modern conventions do not.

Even adjusting our sensibilities to accommodate the conventions of an earlier time, it still appears that the allegorical meaning proposed is only marginally influenced by the text. Efforts to demonstrate a more organic if idealistic relation between the literal text and the allegorical meaning, such as Irmgard Christiansen's suggestion of Platonic diairesis as the intermediate lines of projection between text and allegorical interpretation, are interesting but have not been convincing (Christiansen: 99-133).[3] Far more obvious is the influence of the interests of the interpreter and the community on the specific form of the allegory. Conventions resident in the interpretive community allow allegorical interpretation, while the interpreter's specific interests direct the details. Philo's specific concerns are too extensive to review here. His general goals are admirably summarized by Peder Borgen in a recent survey of Philo's influence.

> It may be maintained that Philo attempts to make the allegorical method serve his aims as a Jewish exegete. ... He spells out abstract principles which he sees in the biblical text, and these in turn can be applied to individuals and the Jewish community, serving to interpret specific events. Philo also adapts allegorical interpretation to the Jewish notion of election, which he uses to claim for the Jews and their sacred writings elements from Greek philosophy, education, ethics, and religion. Conversely, to Philo allegorical interpretation is a way in which the wisdom of the laws of Moses and Jewish religious institutions can be disclosed to the world (Borgen: 262).

Allegorical interpretation allows biblical application to specific contemporary events, and mediates for the interpretive community the interaction between Jewish biblical tradition and religious institutions, on one side, and dominant elements of Hellenistic thought and culture on the other. In this mediation the matter of textual control absorbs relatively little attention. Opponents did not press individual allegories, which might have forced the question of textual control. Some opponents contested the propriety of allegorical interpretation, others went too far, in Philo's view, allegorizing the texts enjoining such fundamental Jewish customs as the Sabbath (Borgen: 260-1). Philo guarded against excessive allegorical interpretation by maintaining the literal interpretation concurrently and by restraint in applying allegory to sensitive texts. The argument supporting allegorical interpretation was simple: allegory was a recognized form of interpretation in the community and, the proof of the pudding, it reached a higher level of meaning in the text. Why would anyone be content with just the literal meaning? Specific allegories are not contested on either front, damping a pressure that might otherwise have required closer scrutiny of the relation between text and allegorical interpretation. The allegorical interpretation enjoys a great deal of freedom, as the situation requires. Validation of that interpretation depends on the strength of the allegorical convention, the acceptance of the method, including such features as the etymology of names. It depends equally on the depth of the community's need for the mediation between Jewish and Hellenistic cultures and Philo's exegetical success in providing that mediation.

---

[3] "a rather desperate suggestion" (Dillon: 77).

AUGUSTINE'S ALLEGORICAL INTERPRETATION

Augustine's allegorical practice may seem to belie the previous observation that Philo's allegory flourished in a non-polemical interpretive situation that afforded fluidity in relating interpretation to features of the text. Augustine also regularly employs allegory, not least in his intensely polemical tract against Faustus. Indeed, Augustine introduces allegory precisely at the most highly charged polemical moment, when the disputation turns on the contested interpretation of Old Testament texts. Having completed the literal interpretation of the Abraham and Sarah story, Augustine inquires into "the prophetic character of the action," knocking "at the door of the mystery," (Augustine, 1909: 287). Who is this wife who "while in a foreign land and among strangers, is not allowed to be stained or defiled, that she may be brought to her own husband without spot or wrinkle" (Augustine, 1909: 287). The question practically answers itself, although perhaps more for Augustine than for Faustus. The bride is the Church, at once spouse of Christ and sister, by which are symbolized two different aspects of the Church's relation to Christ. Faustus cannot have been expected readily to accept this interpretation. To accept it would involve an act of conversion.

Conversion is precisely the aim, so far as the allegory is directed at Faustus. Augustine had been a Manichaean himself. Allegorical sermons by Ambrose of Milan had contributed to his own conversion, by clearing some of his objections to scripture (Bonner: 72-3). Through allegory Augustine was able to read the whole Bible, both literal and allegorical senses, in a manner consistent with the emerging Catholic *regula fidei* and thus to become a Catholic. At least part of the point of injecting allegory into his argument with Faustus was to replicate the course of his own conversion, to recommend to Faustus a set of conventions for reading scripture which might also clear his objections and allow him to embrace the Catholic rule of faith. At stake between them were precisely the conventions of reading which were profoundly bound up with a manner of life, within the Catholic faith rather than outside it.

Although nominally directed to Faustus, Augustine's treatise was equally or more written for those already within the Catholic Church who needed a response to Faustus' challenges. For Catholic Christians Augustine's allegory reinforced, in this specific instance, the intimate and elect relationship between the Catholic Church and Christ. More broadly, allegory allowed Augustine and the Church to read all of scripture as directed toward its true end in the love of God and love of neighbor (Augustine, 1947: 56-7). Adoption of the conventions of allegory was rooted in the prior commitments of the Catholic Church to the rule of faith that regulated its common faith, life, and practice. Both specific allegorical interpretations of particular texts and the allegorical convention itself finally drew their validity from the power of the interpretation to support the life of faith.

Conclusion

This essay began as an effort to comprehend both the stability and variation evident in the history of interpretation of the Bible. Frequently the issue of stability and variation is discussed as a two term equation. The text represents the principle of stability and the individual interpreter represents the variable principle. Often the two principles are seen as locked in a struggle over who will get to decide on the meaning of the passage, the text itself or its interpreter. It will take no one by surprise that I do not share the two term model. It is not clear to me that we know what we mean by "the text" or, if we do, that we can reach agreement on what is determinative about it. Again, interpretation may involve a struggle, to quote again the Cheshire cat, over "who shall decide," but it does not invariably involve such a struggle. Nor does the text seem to me that stable nor the interpreter quite so variable. Often I would reverse the equation. And, obviously, add another term to it: interpretive conventions.

I have not defined conventions, preferring to this point to allow them to emerge from the examination of specific instances of interpretation. By conventions, however, I have understood structured sets of tacit rules and procedures which govern the process of interpretation of texts. Conventions are shared by communities of interpreters and are learned by participation in institutions in which textual interpretation is an integral part of the practice of the institution. As the interpretation has indicated, different distinguishable sets of conventions may exist within an institution or community simultaneously, serving different purposes or responding to different circumstances.

Conventions aid in addressing questions of stability and variation in interpretation. First, conventions can help us understand why a presumably determinate text does not guarantee a single determinate interpretation. A text is multifaceted, composed of many potentially meaningful elements, from unspoken gaps to the etymology of personal names and everything in between.[4] All of these elements are "in" the text and poten-

---

[4] Jonathan Culler described the multiplication of potentially meaningful elements in the text inherent in structuralism's powerful descriptive *organon* and offered interpretive conventions as a means of explaining which elements actually are meaningful and which are not (Culler: 113-160). My use of conventions draws heavily on his argument, but my reading of the history of interpretation indicates that interpretive conventions organize features of the text in excess of those described through structuralist analysis.

tially help determine meaning. The text is composed of such a multiplicity of such elements that the text is, ironically, a source of instability. The diversity of meaningful elements in the text is resolved by the various conventions of reading, which determine precisely which elements in the text will count in this particular interpretation. The conventions of allegory allow etymologies to count, as in Philo's allegorical interpretation, while the conventions of realistic reading ascribe no role in determining meaning to etymologies. The conventions of reading identify the meaning-bearing features of the text and, once given their place in the interpretation, those features do exert a determinative force on the interpretation. Conventions of reading make textual elements determinate. Read according to established conventions, the meaning of the biblical text was determinate and stable, certainly anything but a solecism. Conceiving conventions as rule-governed procedures for reading that exist independently of single interpreters guards against both charges of arbitrariness in interpretation and insipid appeals to subjectivity to justify weak reading.

Reading conventions also aid in understanding the stability of interpretation through time. Conventions may themselves be remarkably stable. Luther could appropriate Augustine's literal interpretation of the Abraham and Sarah story without friction because the conventions of realistic reading had changed little in the eleven hundred years separating them. Even when major changes in conventions do occur, as may be gauged in the differences between Luther and Speiser, major areas of continuity still appear. The basic convention of filling in gaps in the text with material at a realistic level is still in place, although the source of the material used to fill in background has changed.

At the same time reading conventions can explain variation in interpretation. Alternate conventions coexist, even within the same interpretive community. Philo's Alexandria and Augustine's Catholic Church were competent in both allegorical and realistic conventions. In addition different communities developed and maintained specific conventions of reading. I have not considered the rich haggadic conventions developed within Judaism, but this tradition might be fruitfully traced using Genesis 12 from the Genesis Apocryphon of Qumran Cave 1 to Umberto Cassuto's remarkable Genesis commentary.

Conventions also change through time, and as they change, interpretation changes. Speiser's commentary shows the effects of Enlightenment epistemology and the modern explosion of historical and philological knowledge on the conventions of realistic reading. Still more recently, both feminist and womanist criticism are again reshaping realistic conventions, so that elements previously overlooked are recognized "in" the text and the unilluminated background of the narrative receives a characteristic new illumination.

Conventions also decline. Luther, for instance, hastened the decline of allegorical interpretation. His opposition, never complete, was not on methodological grounds, or because of the looseness of connection between interpretation and text. His opposition was theological and practical. Allegory had been used to interpret scripture non-christologically, for instance, in support of the monastic form of life. Such interpretation led scripture away from its true spiritual sense which always concerned Christ and thus constituted a danger that Luther countered by restricting allegory (Bornkamm: 88-9). The conventions of allegorical reading were subsequently largely lost within Christian tradition.

Finally, the conventions of reading contribute to variability by the very freedom that they allow to interpretation. Realistic reading provides a powerful warrant for the interpreter to fill in what is not explicit in the text. The interpreter is to treat the narrative as if it depicted an actual event and the interpreter is therefore warranted to incorporate what the text does not say, but what the interpreter knows would have pertained to such an event. It is within that "what the interpreter knows" that much of the variation in interpretation arises. Modern conventions of realistic reading place greater control on what may be introduced into the depiction of the actual event. Yet anyone familiar with modern biblical criticism knows that such control is a very relative thing and interpretation continues to vary within the space afforded by the realistic conventions. For its part, allegorical interpretation had its own appropriate freedoms. In certain situations, particularly polemical situations where a precise and agreed meaning of the text was crucial to the discussion, the freedom of such conventions could be a drawback and more restrictive conventions were necessary. But in many other circumstances the freedom in interpreting the texts within common interpretive conventions was highly positive, allowing Philo to mediate Jewish and Hellenistic culture, for instance, or Luther to exhort faithfulness in the face of adversity.

I am conscious that it may seem that I have missed the heart of the question of textual determinacy by focusing on the history of interpretation and then interpretive conventions. Conventions represent competencies in the interpreter; they lie on the interpreter's side of the equation. Stressing the rule-governed nature of those competencies may make the interpreter look less arbitrary, but would we not still want to distinguish even conventionally governed readings from the meaning of the text? Even if we accept the importance of conventions, would we not want to define the meaning of the text as the original text read according to the original conventions of either the author or the original audience? Such a stipulation would exclude most of the factors influencing variability and would give a determinate object to stand over against later variation.

Such a stipulation is fully possible. It would, perhaps ironically, constitute a new set of conventions for reading. And it would privilege that set of conventions. Claims to privilege must be justified. What justifies such a claim? I do not see any foundational argument that substantiates such a claim to privilege. Pragmatic rationales, however, are easily conceived. Scholars would achieve a common and determinate object to describe. Study of the ancient text could easily correlate with other historical studies. Canons and standards of validation of proposed interpretations could develop. Such conventions could effectively fill the need of some interpretive communities for the fiction of a determinate text. Indeed, the conventions develop out of the need of particular interpretive communities for that fiction and, although this may seem mere whimsy, convert the fiction into a reality.

We are all inclined to think that the notion of a determinate text must be grounded in some foundational argument, on the ontological character of textual meaning or some fundamental correlation between the sign and the reality signified. When that foundational argument proves elusive or the fundamental correlation cannot be demonstrated, we may conclude that the text is indeterminate. Determinacy is a fiction. But a determinate text was not a fiction for Philo. Or for Augustine. Or Luther. The effect of the conventions that guided their exegesis was to create an appropriately determinate text, appropriate to the specific needs of the community of interpretation which developed the conventions of interpretation. The determinacy of the text rests in the concreteness of the life of the community that uses it to shape its faith and practice.

WORKS CITED

Auerbach, Erich
    1968   *Mimesis.* Trans. Willard R. Trask Princeton: Princeton University Press.

Augustine
    1909   *Reply to Faustus the Manichaean.* Trans. R. Stothert. New York: Scribners.
    1947   *On Christian Doctrine.* Trans. John Gavigan. Washington: Catholic University of America Press.

Bainton, Roland
    1930   "The Immoralities of the Patriarchs According to the Exegesis of the Late Middle Ages and of the Reformation." *HTR* 23: 39-49.

Bonner, Gerald
    1963   *St Augustine of Hippo.* Philadelphia: Westminster.

Borgen, Peder
    1984   "Philo of Alexandria." Pp. 233-82 in *Jewish Writings of the Second Temple Period.* Assen: Van Gorcum; Philadelphia: Fortress.

Bornkamm, Heinrich
    1969   *Luther and the Old Testament.* Trans. Eric and Ruth Gritsch. Philadelphia: Fortress.

Cassuto, Umberto
    1964   *A Commentary on the Book of Genesis.* Vol 2. Trans. Israel Abrahams. Jerusalem: Magnes.

Christiansen, Irmgard
    1969   *Die Technik der allegorischen Auslegungswissenschaft bei Philon von Alexandrien.* Tübingen: Mohr.

Culler, Jonathan
    1975   *Structuralist Poetics.* Ithaca: Cornell.

Dillon, John
    1983   "The Formal Structure of Philo's Allegorical Exegesis." Pp. 77-87 of *Two Treatises of Philo of Alexandria.* Chico: Scholars.

Fitzmyer, Joseph
    1971   *The Genesis Apocryphon of Qumran Cave 1.* 2d ed. Rome: Biblical Institute.

Frei, Hans
    1974   *The Eclipse of Biblical Narrative.* New Haven and London: Yale.

Luther, Martin
    1960   *Lectures on Genesis.* Vol. 2 of *Luther's Works.* St. Louis: Concordia.

Philo
    1950   "On Abraham." Vol. 6 of *Philo.* Cambridge: Harvard University Press.

Speiser, E. A.
    1964   *Genesis.* Garden City: Doubleday.

Stein, Edmund
    1929   *Die allegorische Exegese des Philo aus Alexandreia.* Giessen: Toepelmann.

READING TEXTS THROUGH WORLDS, WORLDS THROUGH TEXTS

Vincent L. Wimbush
Union Theological Seminary
New York City

ABSTRACT

The history of African Americans' interpretation of the Bible offers a fascinating case study in the cultivation of the reading of religious texts as the "reading" of "worlds." There are in such readings implications not only for general theory regarding the determinacy of interpretations of texts, but also in the understandings of "text" and "Book" themselves.

For ye are all children of God by faith in Christ Jesus. For as many of you as have been baptized into Christ have put on Christ. There is neither Jew nor Greek, there is neither bond nor free, there is neither male nor female: for ye are all one in Christ Jesus. (Gal 3:26-28 KJV)

Then Peter said unto them, "Repent, and be baptized every one of you in the name of Jesus Christ for the remission of sins, and ye shall receive the Holy Ghost. For the promise is unto you, and to your children, and to all that are afar off, even as many as the Lord our God shall call." (Acts 2:38-39 KJV)

Then Peter opened his mouth, and said, "Of a truth I perceive that God is no respecter of persons: But in every nation he that feareth him, and worketh righteousness, is accepted with him." (Acts 10:34-35 KJV)

I

Readings of texts, especially mythic, religious texts, are seldom cultivated by the lone individual; they are generally culturally determined and delimited. The cultural worlds of readers not only determine what texts are to be read—viz. what texts are deemed of value or are included within the canon—how canonical texts are read and what they mean, they also determine the meaning of "text" itself. Cultural readings are, like cultures themselves, rarely static; they are almost always dynamic and complex. They can, for example, represent at one time the struggle of a fledgling nation for self-definition and purpose, at another, the rhetorical arsenal for the reform and revitalization of a rather old nation. They can represent for a minority group the rhetorics and visions of resistance—against the new or the established nation state. Whatever the character of and motive behind particular readings of mythic and religious texts, such readings are defined, and receive their impetus from, socio-political contexts and circumstances, and in turn function as "readings" of those contexts and circumstances.

No more dramatic and poignant example of the nexus between "readings" of religious texts and the "readings" of world can be found in modernity than in the history of engagement of the Bible by African Americans. Their history of engagement of the Bible not only reflects a particular history of consciousness, but also a provocative hermeneutical challenge, especially regarding an understanding of and response to the "worlds" of the Bible, and the notion of "text" itself. About this more discussion below.

II

A comprehensive interpretive history of African Americans' "readings" of the Bible remains to be written. Such a history cannot be offered here. But a summary treatment that hints of important developments is in order.

African Americans' engagement of the Bible is a fascinating historical drama. It begins with the Africans' involuntary arrival in the New World that came to be known as the United States. That the drama of the engagement of the Bible among African Americans continues in the present time is a sign of the creativity and adaptability of the African world view, and of the evocative power of the Bible. From the beginning of their captive experience in what became the United States Africans were forced to respond to the missionizing efforts of whites. They were challenged to convert to the religions of the slavers. These religions or denominations, for the most part of the establishment or the landed gentry, did not have much appeal to the slaves. The formality and the literacy presupposed by the religious cultures of the slavers—in catechetical training and Bible study, for example—clearly undermined efforts to convert the Africans in significant numbers. Not only were the Africans, on the whole—given both custom and law—incapable of meeting the presupposed literacy requirements of those religions, they did not generally seem emotionally disposed toward the sensibilities and orientations of the devotees, their piety and spirituality (Cornelius: chap.4).

To be sure, the Bible did play a role in these initial missionary efforts. But that role was not primary: its impact was indirect. It was often imbedded within catechetical materials or within elaborate doctrinal statements and formal preaching styles.

The Africans' introduction to "the Bible," or "the Scriptures," by whatever agency in the New World, would have been problematic: cultures steeped in oral traditions generally find the concept of religion and religious power circumscribed by a book at first frightful and absurd, thereafter, certainly awesome and fascinating (Gill: 226f).

It was not until the late eighteenth century, with the growth of non-establishment, evangelical, camp meeting revivalistic movements in the North and South that African Americans began to encounter the Bible on a large and popular scale. Appealed to by the new evangelicals and revivalists in vivid biblical language and with earnest emotion and fervor, the Africans began to respond enthusiastically and in great numbers. They joined white evangelical camps and began throughout the South and North to establish their own churches and denominational groups. What did not go unnoticed among the Africans was the fact that the white world they experienced tended to explain its power and authority by appeal to the Bible. So they embraced the Bible, transforming it from the book of the religion of the whites—whether aristocratic slavers or lower class exhorters—into a source of (psychic-spiritual) power, a source of inspiration for learning and affirmation, and into a language world of strong hopes and veiled but stinging critique of slave-holding Christian culture. The narratives of the Old Testament, the stories of and about Jesus the persecuted but victorious one in the New Testament, captured the collective African imagination. This was the beginning of the African American historical encounter with the Bible, and it has functioned as phenomenological, socio-political and cultural foundation for the different historical "readings" of the Bible that have followed.

From the late eighteenth century through the late twentieth century African Americans have continued their "readings" of the Bible. These "readings" reflect major changes and nuances in the self-understandings and orientations of a major segment of African Americans. The founding of the independent churches and denominations beginning in the late eighteenth century historically postdates and logically presupposes the cultivation of certain identifiable African diaspora religious worldviews and orientations. The Bible has played a fundamental role in the cultivation and articulation of such worldviews and orientations. It was rediscovered as a language world full of drama and proclamation such that the slave or freedperson could be provided with certain rhetorics and visions.

The "reading" of the Bible that was most popular was developed in the nineteenth century and continued into the twentieth century. According to this "reading" the (Protestant, viz. mainstream or establishment) canon provided the more aggressive and overtly political rhetorics and visions of prophetic critique against slavery, and the blueprints for "racial uplift," social and political peace, equality and integration as ultimate goal in the era of Jim Crowism and beyond. In addition, steps toward personal salvation were a vital part of the "reading." It reflected the dominant socio-political views and orientations among African Americans in this period. This "reading"—of both the Bible and of American culture—expressed considerable ambivalence: it was both critical and accommodationist: on the one hand, its respect for the canon reflected its desire to accommodate and be included within the American (socio-economic-political and religious) mainstream; on the other hand, its interpretation of the Bible reflected a social and ideological location "from below," as demonstrated in the blistering critique of Bible-believing, slave-holding, racist America. Important personalities—from Frederick Douglass to Martin Luther King, Jr., are among the powerful articulators of this "reading." But the popular sources—the songs, conversion narratives, poetry, prayers, diaries, and the like—most anonymous, are a truer, more powerful reflection of history.

That this "reading" reflected considerable ambivalence about being in America on the part of a considerable segment of African Americans over a long period of history is indisputable. That it reflects class-specific (and to some extent, perhaps, depending upon the historical period, gender-specific) leanings within the African American population is also indisputable. Those who continued to "read" the Bible and America in this way continued to hope that some accommodation should and could be made. Those most ardent in this hope on the whole saw themselves as close enough to the mainstream to make accommodation (integration) always seem reasonable and feasible.

The historical interest in the dramatic narratives of the Old Testament notwithstanding, there was a certain cluster of passages from the New Testament, especially Galatians 3:26-28 and Acts 2; 10:34-36, that provided the evocative rhetorical and visionary prophetic critique and the hermeneutical foundation for this dominant "mainstream" African American "reading" of Bible—and American culture. These passages were important on account of their emphasis upon the hope for the realization of the universality of salvation. They were often quoted and paraphrased in efforts to relate them to the racial situation in the U.S. by generations of African Americans—from the famous to the unknown.

III

Attention to the evocation and engagement of the major theme of one or two of these passages in selected literature is in order. Such attention can not only provide greater clarity about the impetus behind one of the most powerful, if not dominant, "readings" of the Bible and of American culture among African Americans, it can also illuminate the relationship between social location, consciousness, and orientation and interpretive presuppositions and strategies. More specifically, it can help illuminate the complex relationship between the reading of texts and the reading of worlds.

David Walker's famous Article III of his 1829 "Appeal in Four Articles . . . to the Coloured Citizens of the World," deals with the problem of religion that frustrates, instead of cultivating, racial unity and harmony. His understanding of Christianity as mandating racial justice and harmony is made clear throughout the essay. Such understanding is the presupposition for both biting prophetic critique against contemporary white Christianity and further cultivation of a type of African American spirituality. The quotation of and allusions to the motifs of the biblical passages quoted at the beginning of this essay are obvious:

> Surely the Americans must believe that God is partial, notwithstanding his apostle Peter, declared before Cornelius and others that he has no respect to persons, but in every nation he that feareth God and worketh righteousness is accepted with him.—"The word," said he, "which God sent unto the children of Israel, preaching peace, by Jesus Christ,(he is the Lord of all.") [Acts 10:36]
>
> . . . .
>
> How can the preachers and people of America believe the Bible? Does it teach them any distinction on account of a man's color? Hearken, Americans! to the injunctions of our Lord and master . . . . Go ye, therefore, and teach all nations, baptizing them in the name of the Father, and of the Holy Ghost . . ." [Matt.28:19]
>
> I declare, that the very face of these injunctions appears to be of God and not of man. They do not show the slightest degree of distinction....Can the American preachers appeal unto God, the Maker and Searcher of hearts, and tell him, with the Bible in their hands, that they make no distinction on account of men's colour?   (Walker: 191-192, 194)

Frederick Douglass (1818-1915), abolitionist and writer, was a most articulate critic of the slaveholding Christianity of his day. His critique was based upon his acceptance of Christianity as a moral force that had particular authority in the debate about slavery, and in the construction of a society of racial equality. So Douglass embraced, as he called it the "Christianity of Christ," as opposed to morally bankrupt slave holding Christianity. The former was understood to be "good, pure, holy . . . peaceable . . . impartial" (104). There is little doubt that the reference to Christianity as "impartial" is most significant. An allusion to the theme that runs through the New Testament passages quoted at the beginning of this paper, this reference reflects Douglass' (and his world's) conceptualization of the key, defining element for "true" Christianity. Without the emphasis upon impartiality—especially as regards the races—Christianity could not be pure. His inclusion of a parody of slaveholding religion written by a Methodist minister makes clear his and many others' sentiments. The last lines of each stanza, in which the sarcastic reference to "union" occurs, was probably the reason for selection of the piece; it makes the point that Christianity is understood above all to represent the unity of the races, that it fails most miserably when this unity is undermined:

> Come, saints and sinners, hear me tell
> How pious priests whip Jack and Nell,
> And women buy and children sell,
> And preach all sinners down to hell,
> And sing of heavenly union.
>
> They'll bleat and baa, dona like goats,
> Gorge down black sheep, and strain at motes,
> Array their backs in fine black coats,
> Then seize their negroes by their throats,
> And choke, for heavenly union.
>
> They'll church you if you sip a dram,
> And damn you if you steal a lamb;
> Yet rob old Tony, Doll, and Sam,
> Of Human rights, and bread and ham;
> Kidnapper's heavenly union.
>
> They'll loudly talk of Christ's reward,
> And bind his image with a cord,
> And scold, and swing the lash abhorred,
> And sell their brother in the Lord
> To handcuffed heavenly union. (Douglass: 107)

....

Reverdy Ransom's address entitled "The Race Problem in a Christian State, 1906" may be one of the strongest examples of the African American reading of the Bible and culture under discussion. The address focuses upon the racial problem in the United States in the early twentieth century. The perspective is that of a Ohio born, relatively well-educated, activist African American cleric. His entire professional life was devoted to "racial uplift." This required, according to Ransom's thinking, levelling prophetic critique against the abuses and weaknesses and perfidy of both white and African American churches (especially including his own, the African Methodist Episcopal Church).

The address, delivered in a Boston church, is fascinating on a number of scores. First, it fits the genre of public address, functioning as a type of social prophetic critique, befitting an activist cleric. Third, as social critique the address employs a wide range of appropriate rhetorical strategies, including Enlightenment ideas, references to events in world history, theological argumentation, allusions to denominational doctrine, and loose quotations of and allusions to the Bible. Fourth, as public address it exhorts and critiques the immediate audience and the United States in general as "Christian State," with all that such an entity implies for the issues raised.

Racism is of course the primary theme of the address. But it should be noted that racism is defined and accounted for with the use of biblical language. In Ransom's opening statements the biblical notion of the kinship of humanity figures as the historical, theological foundation of Christianity, and is the hermeneutical key to the interpretation of all Scripture and of Christianity:

> There should be no race problem in the Christian State. When Christianity received its Pentecostal baptism and seal from heaven it is recorded that, "there were dwelling at Jerusalem Jews, devout men, out of every nation under heaven. Parthians, and Medes, and Elamites, and the dwellers in Mesopotamia, and in Judea, and Cappadocia, in Pontus and Asia, Phrygia, and Pamphylia in Egypt, and in parts of Libya about Cyrene; and strangers of Rome; Jews and Proselytes, Cretes and Arabians." [Acts 2:5-11a]
>
> St. Paul, standing in the Areopagus, declared to the Athenians that, "God hath made of one blood all nations of men for to dwell on all the face of the earth." [Acts 17:26]
>
> Jesus Christ founded Christianity in the midst of the most bitter and intense antagonisms of race and class. Yet he ignored them all, dealing alike with Jew, Samaritan, Syro-Phoenician, Greek and Roman . . . God, through the Jew, was educating the world, and laying a moral and spiritual foundation. That foundation was the establishment of the one God idea. Upon this foundation Jesus Christ built the superstructure of "the Fatherhood of God," and its corollary, "the Brotherhood of man."
>
> The crowning object at which Jesus Christ aimed was, "to break down the middle wall of partition," between man and man, and to take away all the Old Testament laws and ordinances that prevented Jew and Gentile from approaching God on an equal plane. And this He did, "that He might reconcile both unto God in one body by the cross, having slain the enmity thereby, so making peace." [Ephesians 2:14-15] (Ransom: 296-97)

All of the above was applied to the racial situation in the Christian State that was the United States in 1906, ". . . the first nation that was born with the Bible in its hands." (Ransom: 297) According to Ransom, the Christian State that does not seek to address concretely in the spirit of Jesus the challenge inherent in the ideal of the universal kinship of all humanity— an ideal accepted by the integrationist/accommodationist African

American culture, including "mainline" African American churches, even becoming the motto of Ransom's church, African Methodist Episcopal—is a state that has failed to live up to its creed and calling. That the United States has so failed was clear to Ransom.

> ... the history of our past is well known. The Race problem in this country is not only still with us an unsolved problem, but it constitutes perhaps the most serious problem in our country today. In Church and State, from the beginning, we have tried to settle it by compromise, but all compromises have ended in failure ... American Christianity will un-Christ itself if it refuses to strive on, until this Race Problem is not only settled, but, settled right; and until this is done, however much men may temporize and seek to compromise, and cry "peace! peace!" there will be no peace until this is done. (Ranom: 298)

The final point made by Ransom is that the Christian State has an obligation to translate its theological heritage and foundations into social and political realities. This should require correspondence between the transcendence of God above worldly matters and the Christian state's transcendence over human or worldly, especially racial, accidents. This is understood to be the special burden and calling of the United States, which in spite of its history of slaveholding and institutionalization of racial inequality, is seen by Ransom (very much a squaring with the political and popular notions—among whites and African Americans—of the day) as a special, divinely inspired experiment with a divine manifest destiny.

> As God is above man, so man is above race. There is nothing to fear by forever demolishing every wall, religious, political, industrial, social, that separates man from his brotherman. God has given us a splendid heritage here upon these shores; he has made us the pioneers of human liberty for all mankind. He has placed the Negro and white man here for centuries, to grow together side by side. The white man's heart will grow softer, as it goes out in helpfulness, to assist his black brother up to the heights whereon he stands, and the black man will take courage and confidence, as he finds himself progressing, by slow and difficult steps upward toward the realization of all the higher and better things of human attainment; thus will these two peoples one at last become the school masters of all the world, teaching by example the doctrines of the brotherhood of man. If the new Jerusalem tarries in its descent to earth, coming down from God out of heaven, then we, not like some foolish tower-builders upon the plains of Shinar, but taught from heaven in a better way, shall build upon the teachings of Jesus, with the doctrine of human brotherhood as taught by Him, until fraternity realized, shall raise us to the skies. (Ransom: 304)

Ransom's address is an interpretation of the world that he experienced in the early part of the twentieth century: post-slavery, post-war urban America sometimes in some places struggling with the racial problems, most times in too many places ignoring the racial problems altogether. As a part of the relatively privileged class among African Americans—with access to some educational opportunities, with some independence, on account of location within a relatively less oppressive urban environment—Ransom's reading of the world was class- and race-specific. The goal of full integration within American society made sense to those who defined themselves as those in the middle—close, but not close enough, to the acceptable type of American citizen.

The Bible was appealed to as one of the most important sources of authority in order to persuade different publics of the wisdom of the course of integration, the acceptance of all human beings as part of the American experiment. This type of use of the Bible was not unique in American history or for Ransom's times, especially in the context of discussions about racial matters. But clearly Ransom's position reflected a particular type of engagement of the Bible that assumed the key to its mysteries to be the truth of the inclusion of all human beings within God's economy.

So as Ransom used the Bible to read his world, to interpret and critique it, he also reflected a particular type of reading of the Bible. This readings in turn, reflected heightened consciousness of social location as determinant of engagement.

IV

The Bible may have been a most welcome and powerful ally of Ransom and others during the early part of the twentieth century. But what remains to be explained is how this could have happened, how the likes of Frederick Douglass, David Walker, Reverdy Ransom and many other women and men of color could come to embrace the Bible in the first place. This is now not the question about the mere historical events (Great Awakenings, founding of African American churches, etc) leading up to the works and careers of those discussed. The question is rather about how the phenomenon of African Americans' coming to engage the Bible at all developed. How can a people by tradition and sensibility steeped in oral tradition make the step toward psychic acceptance of a Book as source of authority and power and spirituality? How does a people enslaved by a people of a Book come to accept that Book as authoritative and legitimate? How can a people come to interpret their experiences in the world through a Book (with its narratives and codes) that has little to do with its origins and immediate historical experiences? Again, the question is not about the mere historical events or antecedents; it is about phenomenological and psychic changes.

The most defensible explanation lies in a meeting of "worlds"—similar ways of viewing the self in the world—between African Americans and the ("worlds" of the) Bible. With its arresting stories of underdogs surviving and conquering and of a Savior figure who is mistreated but who ultimately triumphs, it is little wonder that the Bible came to be embraced by African Americans. This was so not simply because of the proselytizing efforts and successes among whites or African Americans, but because of the identification of African Americans with the protagonists of the biblical dramas. Again and again the real situations of the heroes and heroines of the Bible appeared to be similar to those of the historical experiences of most African Americans. The oppressed of the New World heard themselves being described in the stories of the Bible. The Africans in the New World applied to themselves the inclusion of all humanity within the economy of God.

Only some such phenomenological event can be assumed and thus help explain how the likes of Douglass and others could engage the Bible. Only the Bible understood not as the road map to nation-building, but as a manifesto for the oppressed and the marginal could have been taken up by such persons. Only the assumption of a hermeneutic of and from the perspective of the racially oppressed can explain the history of African American engagement of the Bible. Only such a hermeneutic explains the particular version or gloss upon the historical engagements of African Americans by those figures discussed above. Their positions make sense only the extent to which they can be placed in the middle—between white (Protestant) mainline culture and sensibilities and African marginal culture and sensibilities.

The African American history of engagement of the Bible suggests the power and challenge of the nexus between social location and biblical interpretation, and of a consistent hermeneutic "from below." African Americans, by virtue of their dramatic history, challenge every reading of the Bible to be more honestly and explicitly (and provocatively) a reading of a world.

Even as the strength of the connection between social location and interpretation is established in African American religious history, it also becomes clear that the very notion of "text" undergoes a change: if the core or foundational hermeneutic among African Americans is—as I have suggested—primarily defined by commitment to defining the African presence in the New World, radical inclusiveness from below or from without emerging as the dominant principle argued and advocated by the majority of the African American religious, then there really is no separate "text"—"out there"—with assumed universal authority; there is primarily a language and image world, a world of stories that dramatize the dominant principle (and explanatory words) necessarily accepted on account of a life situation, the principle personified by characters within that language world and by which the Christian God, the Christian Savior figure, and Christian traditions generally are judged. Only on the basis of commitment to these principles can the African Americans' "conversion" to Christianity be understood, and their engagement of that part of the tradition that is Holy Book be understood. The latter was fundamentally changed from "text"—understood as static source of eternal truth that required a certain authority (intellectual or ecclesiastical or doctrinal) to be engaged—to a language world that could easily, freely, with much creative play, be engaged "from below," or from the margins. Taking the Holy Book off its repository-of-truth pedestal was a radical phenomenological event and challenge, given the status of African Americans and the respect accorded to reading in the American culture (Isaac: 230f; Gill: 224-28). To view the Holy Book as full of stories illustrating the truth about the radical inclusiveness of God's economy of salvation was to explode the notion of canon as it was understood. Not meanings of texts, but interpretations of world, of socio-political and cultural events, became primary; texts functioned to supply rhetorics and images, helping African Americans—in the way of a prism—to see themselves and the world in different colors. The Bible became important because it was received as "world" that could interpret "world." The contribution of African American religious traditions to hermeneutical theory is its modelling of a radical and consistent adherence to the primacy of interpretation (determination) of everything, including religious texts, through (a particular) "world."

Works Consulted

Cornelius, Janet D.
    1991   "When I Can Read My Title Clear": Literacy, Slavery, and Religion in the Antebellum South. Columbia: University of South Carolina Press.

Douglass, Frederick
    1845   "Slaveholding Religion and the Christianity of Christ." Pp. 100-109 in Afro-American Religious History: A Documentary Witness. Ed. Milton C. Sernett. Durham: Duke University Press, 1985.

Gill, Sam D.
    1985   "Nonliterate Traditions and Holy Books: Toward a New Model." Pp. 224-39 in Holy Books in Comparative Perspective. Ed. Frederick M. Denny and Rodney L. Taylor. Columbia: University of South Carolina Press.

Isaac, Rhys
    1983   "Books and Social Authority of Learning: The Case of Mid-Eighteenth Virginia." Pp. 228-49 in Printing and Society in America. Ed. William L. Joyce, David D. Hall and Richard D. Brown, et al. Worcester MA: American Antiquarian Society.

Ransom, Reverdy C.
    1906   "The Race Problem in a Christian State, 1906." Pp. 296-305 in Afro-American Religious History: A Documentary Witness. Ed. Milton C. Sernett. Durham: Duke University Press, 1985.

Walker, David
    1829   "Our Wretchedness in Consequence of Religion." Pp. 188-95 in Afro-American Religious History: A Documentary Witness. Ed. Milton C. Sernett. Durham: Duke University Press, 1985.

II
COMMENTS

THE ROLE OF THE TEXT IN THE READING PROCESS

Adele Berlin
University of Maryland at College Park

When reader response approaches first gained ascendancy in literary circles, it was as a corrective to the long-entrenched "objectivism" that sought the one true meaning of a text and determined how that one true meaning could be uncovered. By now there are few who would claim that a text has but one meaning and that anyone seeking it can be totally objective. Nevertheless, the other extreme—that a text has infinite meanings and that meaning resides solely in the reader—is beginning to be questioned, if only because the principle of textual indeterminacy threatens to undermine the ability of communities of readers or guilds of scholars to share common ground in their quest for textual meaning. This does not signal a return to the old days. It signals, rather, a compromise between the extremes; one that acknowledges that readers bring something to their reading of a text, but that, in addition, the text, for its part, influences how it is read. Exactly how the text exerts influence on the process of reading is the subject of the papers by Robert Culley and Elizabeth Struthers Malbon.

Malbon proposes a structure with four foci to account for the different contexts in which a text may be read. The grid contains "internal" and "external" contexts which intersect with "literary" and "historical" contexts. It is the set of "internal" contexts which interest me here, for it is these that have been traditionally invoked by biblical scholars, as opposed to literary scholars, who, of late, have emphasized the "external" contexts. Malbon's "internal-literary" context refers to the interrelations of the elements in the text; and her "internal-historical" context refers to the original location or audience of the text (as opposed to the way the text was perceived or used by later audiences). This is a rather neat way to divide up the territory; if only it were so easy in real life.

Most of 19th and 20th century biblical scholarship has been occupied with the "internal-historical" task—ascertaining the time and place of composition—with the kind of consensus that leaves much to be desired. (Was the Book of Ruth composed during the Davidic monarchy or in the time of Ezra? How many editions of the Deuteronomic History were there? Did P pre-date D?) Such agreement as exists seems more a product of which generation and school a scholar belongs to than of historical investigation by means of objective methodology. So once again, we see that the reader cannot keep himself or herself out of the process, although, I would argue, the attempt to do so is laudatory.

The "internal-historical" axis has been the butt of much attack from the literary-critical camp. The argument centers around the difficulty (readily acknowledged by historical-critical biblicists) in ascertaining the actual time and place of composition, and around the question (rarely addressed by historical critics) of whether a modern reader could actually understand a text as an ancient Israelite did.

On the other hand, more and more literary critics, weaned now from New Criticism and other exclusively synchronic approaches, are coming to appreciate the need for historical investigation into the original context from which a work emerged. (After all, if the context of the reader determines how he or she reads the text, then all contexts in which the text has been read take on significance in how the text has been understood.) Most scholars would admit that earlier contexts and meanings are no less important than current ones, and that the attempt to retrieve the "original" meaning, or at least the original context, is valid, despite the dangers of the hermeneutic circle.

It is, however, to the "internal-literary" context that I would like to turn, since of the four foci this holds out the greatest possibilities for future research. This is because, to a large extent, biblical scholarship has been so occupied with the "internal-historical" that it has overlooked the "internal-literary." True, it has been mindful of grammar and vocabulary, but the myriad of other literary features of the text have gone unnoticed until relatively recently. Structural analysis and narratology have begun to reveal many of these features, but too often the data about the structure of the text and its poetics were not brought to bear on how its meaning could be constructed. At the other end of the spectrum are a wealth of interpretations which appear free of deterministic constraints, but which actually derive from textual features. In other words, many reader-response practitioners have been calling on internal-literary criteria, and sometimes even internal-historical criteria, without fully acknowledging the degree to which features within the text have influenced their readings. In fact, it could be argued that just as no reading is free of input from the reader, so no reading is free of input from the text.

It is at precisely this juncture that I would locate Robert Culley's discussion of Psalm 102. Culley has given us a masterful analysis of the Psalm, but, more important to the theoretical discussion, he has become conscious of the ways in which his analysis led to his interpretation. Based on Culley's explanation and my own experience, I would describe the process as follows.

As we read, we notice certain textual features or phenomena, such as repeated words, patterns, unusual constructions, and so forth. This may be partially instinctive or intuitive, but in many cases we have been taught to look for certain things. What we find is not totally determined (not every reader finds the same things), but it can all be said to exist within the text. For example, the "key-word" *guard* in Psalm 121 may not be immediately obvious to a reader, or a reader may find a different "keyword" in this psalm, but those who perceive *guard* as a "key-word" can point to its presence in the psalm as proof. It is a feature of the text, regardless of the context of the reader. So the first step is to find textual features on which to base a reading.

The second step is to select those features which will become important in our interpretation. This step is even less determined than the first, and much less understood. To continue with the simplest case of keywords, why do we select one and not others? Why select *guard* in Psalm 121 and not *Lord*? Or should we select both? There is a certain amount of freedom (indeterminacy?) in the selection of textual features to serve as the basis for interpretation.[1] But whatever features are chosen, they can be said to reside in the text.

The third step is to decide what to do with the features we have selected. How do we make sense of them? How do we move from individual features to a well-formed interpretation of the whole discourse? Here hermeneutics plays a role, for the reader must adopt or create a hermeneutic system whereby the observed features are manipulated to form a complete picture. The rabbinic Hermeneutic Principles of Rabbi Ishmael do this very thing: they instruct the reader to compare certain textual phenomena and to read one against the other, for example, to argue from a minor premise to a major, to make certain inferences, etc.[2] In modern literary hermeneutics, too, repetitions and omissions become important because, as in the rabbinic view, they are assumed to be indicative of the text's underlying meaning, rather than just random occurrences. The hermeneutics is what allows us to gather the observed features and construct a scenario which takes them into account in a meaningful way.

A hermeneutic system does not fully determine the meaning; rather, it channels the process whereby meaning is found. Hermeneutics supplies the rules for making sense out of the observed phenomena. Modern

---

[1] How one selects features and what significance one assigns to them is a difficult issue. Roman Jakobson was criticized for just this aspect of his work on parallelism. See P. Werth and L. Waugh. For a continuation of the critique and defense of Jakobson see Z. Zevit and F. Landy.

[2] For an entree into rabbinic hermeneutics see *Encyclopedia Judaica* 8:366-72 and *Anchor Bible Dictionary* III:154-55.

literary critics of the Bible are being naive or disingenuous if they suppose that they do not operate within a hermeneutic system. Just because that system has not been acknowledged or described does not mean it does not exist. The urgent task before literary critics of the Bible is to describe the hermeneutic system or systems that have come into use: to chart the changes from historical-critical hermeneutics, to compare feminist hermeneutics with non-feminist hermeneutics, to describe African-American hermeneutics, and so forth. All of the papers in this volume are in some way engaged in this task.[3] Most important and most neglected is the description, of the type Culley offers, of the ground-level reading process which we take for granted, but which is the product—no less than, say, feminist readings—of a definable hermeneutic stance.[4] The multiplication of legitimate interpretations that we find before us is not due so much to textual indeterminacy as to proliferating hermeneutical systems.[5] And the very fact that we can make meaning at all, on whatever level, is due to our having learned a hermeneutics of reading which helps us to assign meaning to various textual structures and configurations.

---

[3] Other studies have appeared recently, often in the form of critiques of individuals. See, for example, B. Long, D. N. Fewell and D. Gunn, M. Sternberg, and also A. Berlin (1991).

[4] I have attempted a similar analysis, based on text-linguistic principles, in A. Berlin (1989).

[5] Unless one means by textual indeterminacy that the text permits any and all hermeneutic approaches, which of course it does—thereby rendering that definition meaningless.

Works Consulted

Berlin, A.
    1989   "Lexical Cohesian and Biblical Interpretation." *Hebrew Studies* 30: 29-40.
    1991   "Literary Exegesis of Biblical Narrative: Between Poetics and Hermeneutics." Pp. 120-28 in *"Not in Heaven." Coherence and Complexity in Biblical Narrative*. Ed. J. Rosenblatt and J. Sitterson, Jr., Bloomington: Indiana University Press.

Fewell, D.N. and D. Gunn
    1991   "Tipping the Balance: Sternberg's Reader and the Rape of Dinah." *JBL* 110:193-211.

Landy, F.
    1992   "In Defense of Jakobson." *JBL* 111:105-113.

Long, Burke O.
    1991   "The 'New' Biblical Poetics of Alter and Sternberg." *JSOT* 51:71-84.

Sternberg, M.
    1991   "Biblical Poetics and Sexual Politics: From Reading to Counter-Reading." *JBL* 111:463-88.

Waugh, L.
    1980   "The Poetic Function of the Nature of Language." *Poetics Today* 2/1a:57-82.

Werth, P.
    1976   "Roman Jakobson's Verbal Analysis of Poetry." *Journal of Linguistics* 12:21-73.

Zevit, Z.
    1990   "Roman Jakobson, Psycholinguistics, and Biblical Poetry." *JBL* 109:385-401.

THE CHALLENGE OF MULTICONTEXTUAL INTERPRETATION

John Dominic Crossan
DePaul University.

My response focuses on Elizabeth Struthers Malbon's essay, "Text and Contexts: Interpreting the Disciples in Mark," not just in itself but as opening up and offering a solution to the problem of the volume as a whole. I intend, therefore, to stay as much as possible on the level of theory and method rather than of case and instance and to resist, as much as I can, the temptation to debate particular details and specific interpretations. I want to stay, in other words, on the level of her title rather than of her subtitle, and that may prove difficult because I have opinions about the latter as well.

MONOCONTEXTUAL AND QUADROCONTEXTUAL INTERPRETATION

Malbon offers us a very helpful typology that invites, provokes, and even guarantees dialogue and debate, and she applies it, in illustration, to major works of Werner Kelber such as *The Kingdom in Mark* (1974), *Mark's Story of Jesus* (1979), and *The Oral and Written Gospel* (1983).

In the first major division of her article, she asserts as a basic principle that "one must refer to the contexts of a text, not its singular context," and she then proposes a fourfold typology of contextual foci based on the intersection of two axes: the internal/external and the literary/historical. That gives us these four possibilities:

A is internal-literary or
"the interrelations of the elements of the text"

B is external-literary or
"the interrelations of the text with other texts"

C is internal-historical or
"the immediate societal/cultural situation of the text (esp. its origin or preservation)"

D is external-historical or
"the broader societal/cultural situation of the text"

That is an extremely useful formulation and it focuses discussion in an equally useful way. That *quadrocontextual* map is, of course, but one investment of the fundamental *multicontextual* imperative, but it stands quite adequately over against any *monocontextual* situation.

Hierarchical and Interactive Quadrocontextuality

Already at this stage one could imagine certain degrees of hermeneutical rectitude, as follows:

(a) Monocontextual Interpretation

(b) Hierarchical (imbalanced) Multicontextual Interpretation

(c) Equal (balanced) Multicontextual Interpretation.

If one accepts, as I would, the preferential option for multicontextuality, then presumably a too hierarchically controlled multicontextuality is merely disguised monocontextuality. The hermeneutical ideal would have to be a truly interactive multicontextuality in which, no matter where one starts, all contexts would interplay evenly with one another by the end. Otherwise, one must defend clearly and not disguise cleverly any hierarchical controls over multicontexuality.

Malbon next applies that fourfold typology to Kelber's major studies and concludes that, while all four foci are present, there is a certain imbalance among them:

> Kelber ignores none of the contextual foci of the typology; but concerns for A and D seem to serve C, that is, the 'internal'/'literary' context and the 'external'/'historical' context seem primarily useful in clarifying the 'internal'/'historical' context. B also serves C, that is, the 'external'/'literary' context serves to clarify the 'internal'/'historical' context; but one gets the feeling at the close of *Oral and Written* that genre (B) is becoming as intriguing to Kelber (and as focal) as genesis (C) .... Basically Kelber studies the relation of text (A) and history (D) in Mark and comes to an understanding of, firstly, Mark's genesis (C) and, secondly, Mark's genre (B).

At this stage, Malbon is certainly not criticizing Kelber for monocontextuality. All components of her quadrocontextual field are clearly and admittedly present. The criticism, if I understand it correctly, is, in my terms, that he has used or allowed an unequal and hierarchical rather than an equal and interactive play between his four contextual foci.

The Retreat to Monocontextuality

At this stage, that is as Malbon moves from her first major division to the second and then on to the third one, something very strange happens in an article that has started out so promisingly and even provocatively. Instead of moving forward, especially on the level of theory and method, to show how an interactive quadrocontextuality would furnish a more satisfactory reading than Kelber's (alleged) hierarchical quadrocontextuality, Malbon retreats herself to an alternative monocontextuality.

That retreat is rendered even more striking by her use of Dominick LaCapra's critique, in his 1983 book *Rethinking Intellectual History*, of Allan Janik and Stephen Toulmin's 1973 study about *Wittgenstein's Vienna*. They had insisted that the point of the *Tractatus Logico-Philologicus* was ethical rather than logical, an attempt to show what logic could and could not do because what ethics could and could not do was much more important (Wittgenstein to Ficker: *"The book's point is an ethical one"*). I refrain, but with some difficulty, from any judgment on who has the best of that argument and note only LaCapra's warnings against focusing on a single context which then serves "to saturate the text with meaning." Saturation, in other words, occurs by monocontextual concentration, by acting as if there could be but one context, "*the* context." His alternative is termed "'intertextual' reading" which I presume means what is here termed quadrocontextuality as one example of the multicontextual ideal. Surely there is no possibility of meaning being saturated by multicontextuality?

With that warning against monocontextual saturation accepted on the level of theory and method, and with Kelber's work allegedly weakened not by monocontextuality but by an inadequately interactive quadrocontextuality, the next move would seem obvious. Malbon will show how a more balanced, even, equal, and perfectly interactive analysis will improve on Werner's. Or, within the limitations of space, she will sketch out such a process. But, as I see it, what happens, especially in her third division, is an alternative monocontextuality: "My questions about the disciples are raised from a different contextual focus from Kelber - from a focus on the interrelations of the elements of the text (A)." I reiterate, once again, that I am trying to work on the level of theory and method and I refrain, as much as I can, from making any judgments about whose A-level or internal-literary operations are the more satisfactory in themselves. To follow Malbon's analogy, a saturated sponge is useless for mopping up anything and it is no matter whether that saturation comes from water or from wine.

What I have termed a retreat to monocontextuality is most disappointing in that Malbon has herself shown superbly how to interweave ABCD (or more) together in her 1990 book *The Iconography of the Sarcophagus of Junius Bassus*, the Christian prefect of the city of Rome who died in 359. That work had actually a tricontextual focus of iconography, literature, and history, or, if you include that internal-external axis, a sixfold contextuality. I particularly admire that manifold contextuality because I attempted a similar sixfold contextuality with anthropology, history, and literature, each along an internal/external axis, in *The Historical Jesus: The Life of a Mediterranean Jewish Peasant*.

I conclude, therefore, that the more important challenge of Malbon's present article is not to Kelber on the disciples in Mark but to all of us on the multicontextuality of interpretation in texts (or images).

THE MARKAN DISCIPLES IN QUADROCONTEXTUAL FOCUS

This section attempts to sketch out what I think Malbon should have done, on her own principles, by pushing onwards towards a balanced quadrocontextuality concerning the disciples in Mark rather than retreating to a comparative monocontextuality. I am trying, still, not to do what I criticize her for doing and judge between those monocontextualities, let alone present a third such alternative.

First, I presume that there is (I am seeking a safe, neutral, and acceptable expression) *strong criticism* of the disciples in Mark. I find it positively unhelpful to speak of their "failure" and then to argue for or against that word. When somebody is criticized or opposed, as distinct from being unknown or ignored, they are doing something important to somebody. They are worthy of criticism rather than oblivion.

Second, "the disciples" could have one not of two but of at least three meanings: an *historical*, a *symbolical*, or a *structural* focus. Kelber reads them primarily in that first meaning, as denoting a specific group in Jerusalem who claimed their authority from the disciples of Jesus. Malbon reads them in the second meaning:

> The Markan Gospel discredits not the disciples, but the view of discipleship as either exclusive or easy.... Kelber hears the Markan Gospel as an attack on the disciples as the claimed authorities of an esoteric group ... I sense in it the pulling of the rug out from under any and all such groups, including the audience. Neither the disciples nor the hearers/readers can rest on their insider status; in this the two groups are alike, not different. Kelber's negative reading of the disciples and positive reading of the audience risks encouraging the readers' shared sense of superiority; I think Mark pulls the rug out from under us too.

Once again, I will not debate her reading but I will insist that, if one accepts it, the rug has also being *pulled out by Mark from under herself or himself as well*. If the disciples are to be taken symbolically, with no deliberate and specific historical focus, to mean those closest or who consider themselves closest to Jesus, then Mark is most disqualified of all. Nobody enjoys vertigo as much as myself, but I am not sure that Mark shared my taste for paradox. However, that is not my present point which is simply this: if we are involved in general rug-pulling, Mark must be the first to fall or at least must fall with all of us together (disciples, hearers, readers, interpreters). Finally, what about a structural reading? Could the "disciples" mean any external group or maybe any centralized group claiming right of authority and interpretation over the Markan group? Again, I do not choose here between those three options but simply insist that there are at least three and not just two options to choose from.

Finally, if we agree, at least for the present theoretical discussion, that A-level monocontextualities on the Markan disciples are at an impasse, what if one shifts focus to B-level study for a moment? I am not, of course, proposing an alternative B-monocontextuality instead of Malbon's or Kelber's competing A-level ones, but *beginning* the process of establishing an egalitarian quadrocontextuality by moving from A to B and onwards to C and D.

In the same year as *The Oral and Written Gospel*, Stevan Davies published *The Gospel of Thomas and Christian Wisdom*. He noted the following details concerning "the disciples" (the Coptic uses the Greek as a loan-word) and Jesus (82-83; my italics):

> Thomas contains a variety of logia which are in the form of questions and answers, questions by the disciples as a group and answers by Jesus. The questions predominantly are about the time of the end or about the nature of Jesus. *In both cases the disciples' questions seem to indicate their failure to understand.*
>
> Questions regarding the end:
>
>   18 "Tell us in which way our end will occur."
>   51 "When will be the rest of the dead and when will the new world come?"
> 113 "On what day will the Kingdom come?"
>
> In all three cases the response given by Jesus is that what they look for is already present, their error is in awaiting it rather than seeking to discover it.
>
> Questions regarding the nature of Jesus:
>
>   24 "Show us the place where you are, or it is necessary for us to seek it."
>   37 "On what day will you be revealed to us and on what day will we see you?"
>   43 "Who are you that you say these things to us?"
>   52 "'Twenty-four prophets spoke in Israel and all of them spoke about you."
>   91 "Tell us who you are so that we can believe in you."
>
> The responses to these questions (or statements requiring response) are similar to those re-grading the end time. The answers, Jesus seems to say, are present immediately to the questioner.

If that data from the *Gospel of Thomas*, from, that is, the external literary context, "the interrelations of the text with other texts" (B), was taken seriously, how might it change "the immediate [and] broader societal/cultural situation of the text" of Mark (C & D)? Notice, for example, that Malbon, in her first section, summarizes Kelber as presenting, by 1985, "Mark's Gospel as 'an anti-genre to the genre of a sayings tradition' ... the parabolic reversal of 'the revelation dialogue that has been embedded in 4:1-23' ... and is exemplified by the Gospel of Thomas." Are "the disciples" here just abstract questioners used to demonstrate misunderstanding or do they have, as in Mark, some sort of historical, symbolical, or structural referent? Are they connected with the "leaders" mocked in *Gos. Thom.* 3 where a transcendental future Kingdom is for the birds? What about *their question to Jesus* in *Gos. Thom.* 12 which results in praise of James the Just especially in comparison with *Jesus' question to them* in *Gos. Thom.* 13 which results in (even greater?) praise of Thomas? Is the criticism of "the disciples" any worse here than in Mark, granted the differences between a discursive and a narratival or biographical gospel? Even if the opponent of my opponent need not always be my friend, how does the disciples' basic misunderstanding of christology and eschatology in both Mark and Thomas relate, if it does relate, to any historical situation or situations? If both have the same *symbolical* reading of "the disciples," is pulling-the-rug-from-under-oneself even more widespread than we imagined in early Christianity? If both refer to some specific *historical* group, what group receives that joint opposition, and how does Mark then oppose Thomas? If both refer to the same *structural* experience, are different groups resisting external or centralized control from any group operating in the name or tradition of "the disciples"?

Conclusions

My first conclusion is to accept and emphasize Malbon's call for multicontextual interpretation as the ideal horizon of our activity.

My second conclusion is that in doing multicontextual interpretation, and, of course, that will require what Malbon citing LaCapra calls "cooperation ... in a noninvidious spirit," we should attempt not to privilege any one focus over the others we are using. Since we must start with one, or with sighting shots from one to another, we should attempt to build in feedback processes to check the inevitable privileging of wherever we start. We should be very careful about practically, let alone theoretically, declaring this or that focus to be more normative than the others. I think, however, that she moves away from her own challenge, not just practically by considering Mark only in A-focus analysis, but even theoretically: "when one claims to say what the text says, one must be willing to be guided not only by fruitful suggestions from multiple contexts but *especially* by the 'internal'/'literary' context, the interrelations of the elements of the text" (my italics). I have no problem with anyone deciding to do monocontextual analysis of one type or another and would be quite willing to debate among competing A-focus studies of the disciples in Mark. But to start there is not to finish there, and to start there should not be to privilege ultimately that initiation. For my third conclusion, I need a detour through another of Malbon's writings.

I return once more to her beautiful book on the Junius Bassus sarcophagus. Her A-focus analysis of the "the interrelations of the elements of the text [image]" is profoundly persuasive. If it is wrong, I certainly cannot see why or where or how. But she also uses B-focus comparisons with other more or less contemporary sarcophagi, and I note than where some of them had pictures of the deceased in central pride of place, Bassus' has Jesus enthroned above the world as law-giver and Jesus entering triumphantly into Jerusalem in, respectively, top and bottom central panels. Which brings up some C-focus conclusions: "a relationship is expressed and established between the deceased Junius Bassus and the eternal Jesus Christ " (50). Bassus' picture *is* there, in other words, as prefect of Rome entering his city, seated upon its judgment throne, and passing its laws. And behind that is some D-focus materials as *entrance, enthronement,* and *law-giving* all have imperial ceremonial connotations; "Both scenes are christological and may be understood as presupposing the Peace of the church by their visual application of the analogy: Christ is to heaven (or all heaven and earth - the cosmos) as the emperor is to the empire" (50). Let me admit an immediate bias. That was the most important page of Malbon's book for me. All the iconographic connections, all the compositional delicacies, all the artistic creativities, all the linear relationships fell suddenly very silent before that line between Christ, Constantine, and Bassus, or should it be, Constantine, Bassus, and Christ? I felt no fear that A-focus would take over priority but rather a certainty that D-focus already had. I propose, in other words, that we privilege as ideal horizon not only multicontextuality over monocontextuality but, within multicontextuality, the total progress from life or world through text or image to life or world again. Our ancient texts or images came from and went on into a living world and our modern interpretations should do the same. Texts or images, from Mark to Bassus, speak not only about internal creative structure but about external political power. So do interpreters.

Textual Determinacy: A Response

Burke O. Long
Bowdoin College

In what follows, I shall comment on issues of textual determinacy as they emerged for me when I read the essays collected together in this volume. I am greatly indebted to each of the authors for providing me and the readers of *Semeia* with such stimulating material on which to reflect. I hope I do not misstate their points, or treat their essays with anything less than the appreciation they deserve.

I

Meaning, wrote Mieke Bal, is a dynamic readerly product based on an elaboration of the possibilities of text, such that a "reader formulates an ordering and reworking of the collection of possible meanings offered by the text." (Bal, 1989:14 as quoted in Milne). This paradigm, attractively positioned between extremes, assigns a minimalist status to the "text-out-there," and allows for a process of text-making, as it were, in the hermeneutical activities of readers. The model empowers readers by highlighting their subject-position and thereby making more public one's responsibility and accountability for a particular reading. The paradigm also suggests that a "text" imposes certain restraints—presumably not all possibilities for meaning are allowable, or "offered"—and this in turn creates space for critical scholarship to be invoked in discussions of a reader's accountability.

Milne appears to use this bundle of notions in two ways: as a general paradigm of hermeneutics and as a device to, on the one hand, structure her survey of feminist interpretations of Judith (the readerly products), and on the other hand, examine genre as a constraining characteristic of text (the possible meanings offered by text). Since feminist criticism by her definition involves engaging the politics of social change, Milne holds both a reader of the Book of Judith and the text of Judith accountable—a reader for reinforcing attitudes of patriarchy, and the text, at least its genre, for the social inequalities and misogynist expectations it encourages. If I do not overread the rhetorical form of her essay, Milne seems to suggest a rather unproblematic notion of genre, or at least "genric elements," as though they were defining properties inherent in the Book of Judith. By measuring the book's formal features against folkloristic examples, the genre of Judith, that is, "epic struggle," emerges as a rather stable constraint on her reading, so stable that Milne concludes that the text offers no possibility of fostering the kind of social change she seeks. Translating this result in terms of the underlying hermeneutical model, it would seem that a text, or at least its generic features, imposes itself forcefully, if subtly, on a reader.

I wonder, however, if Milne reads too much of an objectivist character into what might be suggested by the phrase "possible meanings" offered by a text. Are these constraints on reading (the offered possibilities) so independent of the assumptions and concerns that shape a particular reading? Consider, for example, our common sense, naturalized notion that the spelling of a word constrains its possible meaning, even allowing for some oscillation in denotation and connotation. Yet, authors of early midrashic texts, holding readerly purposes that differ considerably from our modernist or postmodernist ones, did not always accept consonantal order, what we might think of as a most basic, natural limit to the possibilities of meaning, as a constraint on their multivalenced readings of the Bible as divine address. It may be that when *we* speak about the possibilities that a text offers, its constraints on allowable readings, that we mask in objectivist language our situational choices about what counts as constraint, or allowable possibility of meaning, in the first place. Perhaps the hermeneutical model, a text offering possibilities of meaning to a meaning-creating reader, is best seen as a formulaic reduction of a dynamic interactive process in which our sense of objectivity attached to a text is already embedded in a process of reading.

Although the specifics of his case are entirely different from Milne's, Robert Culley's study of Psalm 102 implies a similar model of hermeneutics. He asserts that one's notion of text in general, and of what specific kind of text one is reading at the moment, governs "how we read, what we look for, what we notice, and what we ignore." However, while he is open to readerly definition, not *any* notion of text will do, and to help make discriminating choices in this case, he invokes a tradition of historically oriented literary criticism. Thus he brings to his reading of Psalm 102 the notion of biblical text as "traditional-composite," which is, at least as a working hypothesis, commensurate with historically conditioned literary characteristics of the text in its cultural milieu. Psalm 102 contains a good deal of *conventional* Hebraic material (e.g., themes, motifs, oral-literary formulaic and genric elements), and yet it was *composed* in ways that invite reading as unified whole. The psalm's various clusters of imagery, "set bounds within which reflection can take place." Yet relationships among these elements are not precisely determined, and so a reader is invited to pursue various possibilities presented by the elements of the text.

Just as Milne has done, Culley has focused attention on the features of a text that constrain or shape our reading. But are the features that add up to "traditional-composite" *in* the text in some way that is independent of our historical and literary theories, or indeed, independent of our location within the changing notions of scholarly truth about the Bible? I do not believe that Culley suggests that they are. He offers an "hypothesis" after all. I think his study of Psalm 102 offers clear evidence that the "bounds" within which his reflection takes place are closely related to what he takes as historically reasonable, if not exactly assured, knowledge about the Bible. But it is well to remember that the "traditional-composite" character of the Bible, like any construction of the past, is located within history. One can see it as knowledge created under certain socio-ideological conditions (for example, the collapse of a romantic notion of author as poetic-spiritual genius), as knowledge existing for a while (under the sway of a theory about collective-individual dynamics at work in archaic society and its *cultus*), and as knowledge that will someday give way to new constructions.

Wimbush's essay, for me, dramatically illustrates the historicality of reading. He stresses that the social location of a reader is of decisive importance in defining the rhetorical form and substance of one's reading. I take it that he also conceives "text" to be embedded in the socio-political circumstances of reading, especially those readings that build worldviews and empowering ideologies. Although the matter is not entirely clear to me, Wimbush appears to have found an awareness of this same notion of text among certain African Americans. In speaking out against racism, these readers of the Bible participated in a "radical phenomenological event" in which a Bible that had been in the keeping of white, Anglo-European ecclesiastical and intellectual authorities, and assumed to be a "static source of eternal truth," was removed from its pedestal. African American preachers and essayists, and their communities, laid claim to this Bible not as some objective "canon," as a text "out there," but as a "language world" that could be engaged from the margins of an oppressive society.

Yet the authors Wimbush cited did not, on my reading, assume such a self-reflexive awareness. Both David Walker and Reverdy Ransom sought to lay hold of an immutable imperative taken to be deposited in the Bible, or to have been taught by Jesus, but which had long been obscured and falsified by ecclesiastical control. They analyzed their social condition and called for political change on the basis of a word thus uncovered and presumed, because of its reputed divine origin, to have universal moral authority. Far from engendering a radical reformulation of the status of the Bible as text, I wonder if we might see Walker and Ransom in the line of many other theologically oriented, biblically grounded social reformers? *Why* they turned to the Bible, a book that was not part of their African heritage, and used it in the manner of other prophetical preachers, remains, as Wimbush observes, a question that demands complicated answers. But their hermeneutical assumptions about the Bible seem rather clear, and fully in line with an attitude of mind and practice that Catherine Belsey (1980:8) named "expressive realism." According to this commonsense notion, a reader seeks to lay hold of the meaning of an author's or speaker's original communication, a word or thought that is prior, and primary to, writing. By tracing the history of this notion inside and outside the circles of professional literary criticism, Belsey seeks to alert us to the socio-political conditions, the ideologies of power and control, which the notion of "expressive realism" fosters, especially when it has the status of a natural truth, so commonsensical indeed as to be beyond dispute and the particulars of human history.

Is the near identity that Wimbush suggests between the theory of text that drives *his* perspective, (with which I am in general agreement!) and that which he attributes to his predecessor biblical readers, somewhat forced? If so, what socio-political and ideological circumstances might be hidden in his attempt in effect to ground his operative view of text in these figures in the history of African American biblical interpretation?

II

Once the controls and norms of text have been dethroned, and the reader-subject has been given power to make insubordinate meaning, then questions of evaluation naturally arise. How can one discriminate among scholarly readings, if all readings and all notions of textual objectivity are thought to be embedded in subject-positions, in hermeneutical theory and practice? Is there a particular value to, for example, "critical" readings, those promulgated among trained scholars, as opposed to those produced by readers untrained in the ways of scholars?

I thought of these questions as I read Elizabeth Struthers Malbon's essay and pondered her typology of "contextual foci" through which scholars have interpreted the Gospel of Mark. Malbon believes that a literary work takes on different shapes according to opposing hypotheses about how, and through what foci ("contexts"), one configures it. Yet, *readers* configure, and they do so out of contexts which are different from, but not entirely unrelated to, the contexts attributed to the text. Malbon holds onto a sense of dynamic interaction between text and reader—just what, by the way, Mieke Bal's model of hermeneutics allows. Such contextual configurations are Malbon's main concern, and she puts this concern as a problem of managing multiplicity: "how to interrelate the multiple readings of a single text"? However, I take it that Malbon is also very interested in *evaluating* multiplicity. Thus, toward the end, she writes that the typology developed in the essay helped her identify where and why she had certain difficulties with Werner Kelber's reading of Jesus and the disciples in Mark. It did not help her establish *the* interpretation of the text, but it gave her some insight as to why she would argue for her own contributions. In the end, having welcomed multiplicity of readers and contextual foci, she is left with two main imperatives: "Advocate and complicate!" Invoking an implicit egalitarian imperative, Malbon says that one should argue for one's own reading, not to deny others, but to complicate the readings of others. None may claim, I gather, to escape slippery hermeneutical ground.

This irenic and equanimical acceptance of hermeneutical instability may yet harbor a contrarian impulse. Does Malbon finally long for some general non-slip surface from which to adjudge one reading better or more adequate than another? Malbon begins her essay by affirming limited truth in the cliché, "one must read the text in context, not use the text for a pretext," as though there exists, however vaguely conceived, some feature *in* a text (or perhaps in the ideal structures of reason and truth) that stands guard against private excesses. She returns to this concern at the end of her essay and limits her own freedom: "Anachronism in interpretative strategies would be the chief problem [in over-determining textual meaning]—reading the text in ways common enough in twentieth-century literary criticism but contra-indicated or undocumented in the ancient world." I wonder if historically oriented analysis, even when focusing on "text as mirror," finally reigns unchallenged and unchallengeable in her work? And if so, can some notion of the privileged, *a*historical authority of author, or its many surrogates, be far behind? Why are such standards, whose roots lie in Enlightenment edifices of scientific objectivity, invoked as though they were natural truths? What lies hidden in this apparent urge, contrary to the spirit that informs Malbon's essay, to appeal, even in examining her own position, to authority beyond her subject position?

Perhaps part of an answer involves—I speak to myself as much as to Malbon here—habits of mind and heart deeply vested in a culture of discourse that effaces subject and glorifies object. Daniel Patte confronts some of these questions as he works toward a theoretical ground that takes seriously a dialectics of practice: ". . . a critical interpretation is both subjective and objective; both interested and critical; both a reflection of the readers' interests, concerns, and contexts, and a submission to textual constraints." This claim, which becomes an ethical imperative, allows Patte to address the ethical issues that arise in maintaining accountability toward the guild to which he belongs and toward those who are affected by his and his colleagues' work, as for example, oppressed people, whose oppression might be abetted by critical exegesis. He feels bound by his own theoretical principles to destroy the arrogant, invidious, and theoretically incoherent distinction between "critical" and "ordinary" readings of the Bible. One must affirm that ordinary readings (e.g., the fundamentalist readings his students bring to class) are both situated in the psycho-social circumstances of the interested reader and under the sway of diversified textual constraints that allow a range of "legitimate" interpretations.

Conceiving "textual constraints" in such a way that they can be felt as external force and realized apart from theory and reading, remains a fundamental question for me, as it does with several of the other essays. What is so refreshing is that Patte confronts ethical as well as theoretical questions of text, and forces us to think about social divisions, perhaps in some sense class divisions, that separate readers of the Bible from one another. He finally seems driven to assert the power of the learned teacher, however, when he extends his prerogatives as a member of a guild of "critical" scholars to deal with "ordinary" readings, too. Patte seems willing to "demonstrate the legitimacy of ordinary readings," not on the basis of a presumed standard set by one or several practices at home in the academy, but by "elucidating the kind of meaning-producing dimension which is the basis of each given ordinary reading," and by demanding that such readings be consistent with their own premises. In other words, they must be "critical" in some foundational way.

What teacher, or who among the readers and producers of *Semeia*, does not respond to the reasonableness of such a mission, urged upon us by the privileges of education and position? But there may be both an ethical and intellectual problem in conferring a type of legitimacy on "ordinary" readings by insisting that they submit to, in effect, the tyranny of the coherent and self-consistent. I quake at the implications of what I have just written, but I also wonder about the ethics of continuing to suggest that we deal with difference by overcoming it. Patte may be as ambivalent in these matters as I am, for at the end of his essay he appears to back away a bit. The task of critical exegesis is finally *not* to evaluate legitimacy (while presupposing that "ordinary" means *illegitimate*), he writes, but to "elucidate the textual dimension which has been the basis of a given ordinary reading (with the presupposition that it is *legitimate*)" (emphasis mine).

WORK CONSULTED

Belsey, Catherine
   1980   *Critical Practice*. London and New York: Routledge.

"MIRROR, MIRROR...":
LACANIAN REFLECTIONS ON MALBON'S MARK

Stephen D. Moore
Wichita State University

"When an interpreter focuses on the text's 'internal' context (text as mirror) he or she looks to 'the text itself'... for the text's meaning and significance." (Malbon)

"The *mirror stage* is a drama... which manufactures for the subject... the succession of phantasies that extends from a fragmented body-image to a form of its totality...." (Lacan, 1977a:4)

"Do we not need, at some point, to read the text with primary reference to its own 'internal' relations...?" asks Elizabeth Struthers Malbon in her article, "Text and Contexts: Interpreting the Disciples in Mark." The question is posed in the midst of a reading of the role of the disciples in Mark (more precisely, a reading of Werner Kelber's reading of their role) that is characteristically astute and elegant. Particularly well-argued, for instance, is her claim that Jesus' predictions of his disciples' future heroism in 13:9-11 functions as a safety net for Mark's tightrope ending. Although the details of her reading are of considerable interest to me, they are not what I intend to tackle here. Instead I will inquire about the source of the "need" expressed in my opening quotation, the need "to read the text with primary reference to its own 'internal' relations...." As is well known, more and more biblical scholars are succumbing to this need. Indeed, it has become a powerful determinant of biblical readings, especially in the area of gospel studies. Here I wish to take a psychoanalytic look at what might be determining that need in its turn. As will be readily apparent, it is not Malbon herself whom I am presuming to put on the couch so much as narrative criticism and reader-response criticism in general.

"THROUGH A GLASS DARKLY"

Norman N. Holland, a psychoanalytic literary critic best known as a pioneer of reader-response criticism, once proposed an intriguing homology: "*Unity* is to *text* as *identity* is to *self*" (123). While I am largely persuaded by Holland's homology, I find his understanding of identity less convincing. For Holland, identity is "an unchanging essence ... that permeates the millions of ego choices" that constitute each human self (ibid.). Of course, Holland was not the first to propose that there is an unchanging essence within each of us. Plato, for one, beat him to it,[1] although Plato called this essence the soul, as did Augustine and numerous other Neoplatonic theologians. All of which suggests that Holland's concept of identity is yet another theological notion that has gone underground only to reemerge in secular guise.

Nearer to hand, Holland's concept of identity is plucked from that branch of the Freudian tree generally known as *ego psychology*—a thoroughly pragmatic, highly successful, and distinctively American version of the talking cure. For the founders of ego psychology (Ernst Kris, Erik Erikson, Heinz Hartmann, and Rudolph Loewenstein),[2] psychoanalysis was first and foremost a therapeutic technique designed to help individuals adapt to society. For them, the ego was the principle of unity and identity in the human subject, the integrative force that binds everything together by maintaining a delicate balance between internal demands and external prohibitions. The ego mediates between the claims of the id, on the one hand, and those of external reality, on the other. A robust ego is therefore the goal of analysis.[3]

What other goal could psychoanalysis possibly have? This brings us to the French poststructuralist Freudian, Jacques Lacan, who, as it happens, was himself analyzed by Rudolph Loewenstein before the latter emigrated to the United States. Here is how Lacan's biographer, Elisabeth Roudinesco, contrasts the two:

> In Loewenstein's eyes, psychoanalysis was first of all a medical method for curing symptoms and understanding resistances, whereas for Lacan, it was above all an intellectual epic, a discovery of the mind, a theoretical journey. Thus the therapy of the young psychiatrist by the future founder of "ego psychology" [in 1932] already bore within it the seeds of the conflict that would break out twenty years later and would oppose, on the one hand, the defenders of a psychoanalysis tending to see itself as a therapeutic ... technique, and, on the other, the partisans of a philosophical adventure that might renew the great message from Vienna. (119)

To put it all too crudely, whereas the ego psychologists took their lead from an optimistic reading of Freud's *The Ego and the Id*, in particular its characterization of psychoanalysis as "an instrument to enable the ego to achieve a progressive conquest of the id" (Freud:56), Lacan took his lead

---

[1] Holland himself is not unaware of this; he appeals to Aristotle, for example, in arguing his case (121-22).
[2] In his essay, Holland draws on the work of another influential ego psychologist, Heinz Lichtenstein (120-21).
[3] Further on ego-psychology and Holland's relationship to it, see Wright:56-68.

from a pessimistic reading of Freud's earlier works, those in which he explored the subversive operations of the unconscious. Lacan holds Freud to his unsettling early vision of the human subject as "split" or profoundly disunified, even to the point of accusing the later Freud of backing away from his early insights. More especially, Lacan accuses the international psychoanalytic establishment in general, and American ego psychology in particular, not to mention popular psychotherapy, "of having rendered Freud's revolutionary discovery banal" (Ragland-Sullivan:119). For the essence of that discovery, as Lacan reads it, is not so much that the unconscious exists as that it "speaks" (indeed, it cannot be silenced), that its discourse is the locus of truth for the subject (for it harbors the subject's unconscious desires), and that all conscious discourse is but a refraction of unconscious truth, which reveals itself only obliquely through dreams, slips of the tongue or pen, lapses of memory, bungled actions, and so forth. "All I can do is tell the truth," says Lacan, immediately adding, "No, that isn't so—I have missed it. There is no truth that, in passing through awareness, does not lie. But one runs after it all the same" (1977b, vii; cf. 1990a:95; 1990b:3). In Saussurian terms (and Lacan was an avid reader of Saussure), what Freud discovered is that a fissure opens up between the signified (unconscious desire) and the signifier (the alienated expression of desire in everyday speech and action), and that every conception of a unified human subject necessarily slides into that fissure. For Lacan, ego psychology and its popular variant, psychotherapy, seek "to return psychoanalysis to a pre-Freudian state" (Gallop:98), one in which the ego, as a principle of unity, continuity, and identity, is the center that controls the psyche. "The radical heteronomy that Freud's discovery shows gaping within man," objects Lacan, "can never again be covered over without whatever is used to hide it being profoundly dishonest" (Lacan 1977a:172; cf. 165-66).

The first thing that conceals this heterogeneity or disunity is the mirror. Lacan locates the mirror stage between the ages of six and eighteen months. Still in a state of relative motor incoordination, the infant sees its image in a mirror (not an actual mirror, necessarily—it could simply be an image of itself reflected from its primary caregiver). Henceforth the infant will attempt to assume this image, to mimic it, to model itself upon it, because the image appears to possess the coherence that the infant itself lacks. (Prior to the mirror stage, the infant experiences itself as a "body in fragments," an amorphous mass of sensations and impressions, with no clearly conceived bodily boundaries.) The real import of the mirror stage, for Lacan, is that individual identity is founded upon a fiction, a misrecognition, a division, and that the introjection of the mirror image sets the stage for a life of alienation. For like the mirror-stage infant, the adult subject will only ever be able to experience itself *as* a self through images that come to it from outside, to see its self only as the Other sees it or not to see its self at all.[4]

BETWEEN MARK AND A VOID

"... the human subject is always split between a mark and a void." (Schneiderman, 7)

Biblical criticism is at present passing through a mirror stage. An intriguing "symptom" of this passage crops up in Malbon's article. Like other narrative critics before her (e.g., Culpepper:4; Petersen:19), Malbon appeals to Murray Krieger's well-known "images of the text as mirror and the text as window." What might it mean to view the text as a mirror? "When the interpreter focuses on the text's 'internal' context (text as mirror)," explains Malbon, "he or she looks to 'the text itself'—its words and sentences, its characters and settings, its rhetoric and imagery—for the text's meaning and significance." Of course, when the interpreter looks to the text as a mirror, she also necessarily sees herself. As such, the more unity and coherence she is able to find in the text, the more gratifying and reassuring will be the reflection she receives back from it.

Relative to other narrative critics, Malbon's claims for Markan unity are commendably modest. But it is not only in its preoccupation with narrative coherence that current literary criticism of the Gospels shows itself to be situated in a hall of mirrors. Reader-response criticism is also performed in front of a mirror. To read as a reader-response critic (cf. Malbon) is to attempt to assume the image of the reader envisioned by the author and projected by the text, to mimic the image, to model one's reading upon it, because the image possesses certain desirable qualities that the critical reader lacks, such as innocence of what comes next in the plot and hence an ability to be affected by it (Prior to the mirror stage, the biblical critic experienced the text as a fragmented entity, a heterogenous mass of materials possessing relatively little overall coherence, and as such projecting no single, unified role that the critic could imitate).[5]

---

[4] For Lacan's own (difficult) explanation of the mirror stage, see 1977a:1-7. For a useful unpacking of this explanation, see Bowie:21-26.

[5] Malbon cites Kelber's claim that "the relationship between Jesus and his disciples is constructed on the oral principle of *imitatio magistri*, or in Platonic terms on *mimesis*" (Kelber:197, quoted by Malbon)—an intriguing claim from a Lacanian perspective, especially since the rhetorical purpose of Mark, as Malbon and others construe it, is to put the reader through the cognitive paces of an ideal disciple.

As Jane Gallop rightly remarks, "Lacan's writings contain an implicit ethical imperative to break the mirror . . ." (59).[6] The imperative is also an epistemological one, for it is urged in the name of truth. And if I am personally disposed to submit to that "imperative," it is because I strongly suspect that in the last analysis, or after the last analysis, our texts are no more unified than we are.

As will by now be apparent, the family resemblance between Lacanian psychoanalysis and Derridean deconstruction is considerable. Central to each is a necessary inability, the inability to dominate a text (for Lacan, the psyche is a kind of "text"),[7] to unify and center it through a reading that would harmonize everything that is going on in it. Like deconstruction, moreover, and unlike psychotherapy, Lacanian analysis "does not provoke any triumph of self-awareness . . . . It uncovers, on the contrary, a process of decentering, in which the subject delves . . . into the loss of his mastery . . ." (Roudinesco:255).

I readily concede, however, that if the idea of a unified identity, corresponding to the idea of a unified text (recall Holland's homology), is a displaced theological idea descended from the ancient and medieval concept of the soul, the opposite idea of a split or fragmented subject, corresponding to a fragmented text, is an idea itself no less theological. "Lacan's major statement of ethical purpose and therapeutic goal," as Gallop observes, "is that one must accept one's castration" (20)[8] —even, or especially, if one is a man. For me, what is most striking about this statement is that it smacks so strongly of the doctrine of original sin. Indeed, Lacan himself was capable of such lapsarian pronouncements as: "forever, by dint of a central fault, desire is separated from fulfillment" (1990a:86); or again: "[psychoanalysis] is engaged in the central lack in which the subject experiences himself as desire . . ." (1977b:265). Is it my own strict Roman Catholic upbringing that renders these austere ideas so attractive to me?

---

[6] More enigmatically, "the charge is to look into the mirror and see not the image but the mirror itself" (Gallop: 62).

[7] More precisely, a kind of language, one with profound similarities to literary language.

[8] This is a statement that would be greeted with deep suspicion by many, especially women; the Freudian tradition has generally considered women to be "castrated." For Lacan, however, as Gallop points out, castration is primarily a linguistic affair: "we are inevitably bereft of any masterful understanding of language, and can only signify ourselves in a symbolic system that we do not command, that, rather, commands us. For women, Lacan's message that everyone, regardless of his or her organs, is 'castrated,' represents not a loss but a gain" (Gallop: 20).

Works Consulted

Bowie, Malcolm
    1991   *Lacan*. Cambridge: Harvard University Press.

Culpepper, R. Alan
    1983   *Anatomy of the Fourth Gospel: A Study in Literary Design*. Philadelphia: Fortress.

Freud, Sigmund
    1923   *The Ego and the Id*. Pp. 3-66 in *The Standard Edition of the Complete Psychological Works of Sigmund Freud*, vol. 19. Ed. and trans. James Strachey. London: Hogarth, 1953-1974.

Gallop, Jane
    1985   *Reading Lacan*. Ithaca, NY: Cornell University Press.

Holland, Norman N.
    1980   "UNITY IDENTITY TEXT SELF." Pp. 118-33 in *Reader- Response Criticism: From Formalism to Post- Structuralism*. Ed. Jane P. Tompkins. Baltimore: Johns Hopkins University Press.

Kelber, Werner H.
    1983   *The Oral and the Written Gospel: The Hermeneutics of Speaking and Writing in the Synoptic Tradition, Mark, Paul, and Q*. Philadelphia: Fortress.

Lacan, Jacques
    1977a   *Écrits: A Selection*. Trans. Alan Sheridan. New York: Norton.
    1977b   *The Four Fundamental Concepts of Psycho-Analysis*. Trans. Alan Sheridan. New York: Norton.
    1990a   "Introduction to the Names-of-the-Father Seminar." Ed. Jacques-Alain Miller. Trans. Jeffrey Mehlman. Pp. 81-95 in *Television/A Challenge to the Psychoanalytic Establishment*. Ed. Joan Copjec. New York: Norton.
    1990b   "Television." Ed. Jacques-Alain Miller. Trans. Denis Hollier et al. Pp. 1-46 in *Television/A Challenge to the Psychoanalytic Establishment*. Ed. Joan Copjec. New York: Norton.

Petersen, Norman R.
    1978   *Literary Criticism for New Testament Critics*. Philadelphia: Fortress.

Ragland-Sullivan, Ellie
    1986   *Jacques Lacan and the Philosophy of Psychoanalysis*. Urbana and Chicago: University of Illinois Press.

Roudinesco, Elisabeth
    1990   *Jacques Lacan & Co.: A History of Psychoanalysis in France, 1925-1985*. Trans. Jeffrey Mehlman. Chicago: University of Chicago Press.

Schneiderman, Stuart
    1983   *Jacques Lacan: The Death of an Intellectual Hero.* Cambridge: Harvard University Press.

Wright, Elizabeth
    1984   *Psychoanalytic Criticism: Theory in Practice.* New York: Methuen.

www.ingramcontent.com/pod-product-compliance
Lightning Source LLC
Chambersburg PA
CBHW032255150426
43195CB00008BA/470